Abraham Lincoln: Contemporary

An American Legacy

A collection of essays

edited by

Frank J. Williams and William D. Pederson

Savas Woodbury Publishers
1475 S. Bascom Ave., Suite 204, Campbell, CA 95008

Manufactured in the United States of America

Abraham Lincoln: Contemporary
An American Legacy

Frank J. Williams and William D. Pederson, editors

Copyright 1995 by Savas Woodbury Publishers
1475 S. Bascom Avenue, Suite 204,
Campbell, California 95008 (408) 879-9073

Includes bibliographic references and index

Printing Number
10 9 8 7 6 5 4 3 2 1

ISBN 1-882810-01-5
(First Hardcover Edition)

This book is printed on sixty-pound
Glatfelter acid-free paper

The paper in this book meets or exceeds the guidelines for permanence
and durability of the Committee on Production Guidelines for Book
Longevity of the Council on Library Resources

for
Virginia Elizabeth Williams
and Myra Miller

TABLE OF CONTENTS

A photograph by Alexander Gardner of Brady's Gallery in Washington on Sunday, February 24, 1861. This most resembles "that serious, far-away look" which was often described by one of Lincoln's secretaries, John G. Nicolay. (The Frank and Virginia Williams Collection of Lincolniana)

A deliberate attempt is made in these essays to enunciate Lincoln's effect on contemporary America while remaining cognizant that views of him may change with each generation. The student of Lincoln must be constantly aware that Lincoln is both used and abused by those attempting to promote their own particular points of view—which may not be Lincoln's.

Frank J. Williams

Attorney Frank Williams is a leader in the Lincoln historical community. He served as the President of the Lincoln Group of Boston for twelve years and as President of the Abraham Lincoln Association for nine years. A member of numerous Lincoln-related advisory boards and committees, he also writes an annual report on Lincolniana for the *Journal of the Abraham Lincoln Association.*

The author of the "Afterword" to *Lincoln on Democracy* (HarperCollins, 1990), and an article in the *Lincoln Herald* on John Hay and Robert Todd Lincoln, Mr. Williams is co-editor of *Abraham Lincoln: Sources and Style of Leadership* (Greenwood, 1994). His current projects include a two volume bibliography of every Lincoln work published since the last century, and a monograph with Harold Holzer on *Abraham Lincoln: Lawyer.* An avid collector, he has assembled one of the largest privately-held Lincoln libraries in the nation.

William D. Pederson

Professor William Pederson is a political scientist who received his doctorate from the University of Oregon in 1979. He teaches at Louisiana State University in Shreveport.

Works he has edited include *Abraham Lincoln: Sources and Style of Leadership* (Greenwood, 1994), *Great Justices of the U.S. Supreme Court* (Lang, 1993), *Morality and Conviction in American Politics* (Prentice Hall, 1990), *The Barberian Presidency* (Lang, 1989), *Grassroots Constitutionalism (*University Press of America, 1988) *and the Rating Game in American Politics* (Irvington, 1987).

Preface

By almost any standard Abraham Lincoln ranks as America's greatest president. Experts on American history and government consistently rate Lincoln as our best chief executive.[1] Though heavily criticized during his presidency, he has been posthumously honored, as reflected by the fact that more geographical locations and schools have been named after him than any other president, and that Hollywood films have depicted Lincoln more frequently than any other chief executive.[2] Today, far more organizations are devoted to perpetuating the memory of Lincoln than all the other presidents combined.[3] Moreover, he is the only president with two academic journals devoted to him (*The Lincoln Herald* and the *Journal of the Abraham Lincoln Association*). President George Bush chose Lincoln to launch a White House lecture series on

---

[1] David L. Porter, "American Historians Rate Our Presidents," in William D. Pederson and Ann M. McLaurin, eds., *The Rating Game in American Politics* (New York, 1987), pp. 1337.

[2] *Shreveport Journal,* February 17, 1986, p. 1; *U.S. News and World Report,* July 10, 1989, p. 62.

[3] Gary R. Planck, "Lincoln Related Organizations, Publications, Collections," *Lincoln Group of Florida Newsletter* (July, 1991).

former presidents, and presidential candidate Bill Clinton was seen reading about Lincoln during the fall 1992 campaign.[4] Lincoln has transcended time to remain a contemporary figure in American life.

Though Lincoln was a traditional Whig politician before assuming
the presidency, he understood the necessity of John Locke's executive
model during times of crisis. In sharp contrast to his predecessor James
Buchanan's inability to act in crisis, Lincoln provided decisive leadership. Subsequent "Lincoln-type" presidents have likewise followed the
prescription of Alexander Hamilton in *Federalist Paper Number 70:*
"Energy in the executive is a leading character in the definition of good
government."

George Washington and Thomas Jefferson were Abraham Lincoln's
heroes. It's appropriate that two of the greatest presidents after Lincoln,
Theodore Roosevelt and Franklin Roosevelt, revered him as their presidential hero.[5] Theodore Roosevelt's "stewardship theory" of presidential
power was rooted in the example of Lincoln's willingness to act in a
crisis. The successful activist presidents also emulate the Lincoln model
by tempering their behavior with prudence and classical magnanimity.[6]

Not only did he provide decisive leadership during the Civil War,
but Lincoln also displayed consummate democratic political skills in
holding his administration together. Rather than surround himself with
secondary figures, he sought advice and help from the major influential
politicians of his time. Many of these politicians were convinced initially that they possessed greater skills than Lincoln, but over time
Lincoln demonstrated his superior wisdom.

He delegated power wisely to competent members of his cabinet
and he allowed Congress considerable latitude in domestic legislation.

---

[4] Donnie Radcliffe, "Bush and Company, Learning of Lincoln," *Washington Post* (January 9,
1990), p. D4; and Eleanor Clift, "Testing Ground," *Time* (March 30, 1992), p. 35.

[5] William F. Hanna, "Theodore Roosevelt and the Lincoln Image," *Lincoln Herald,* Vol. 94,
No. 1 (Spring, 1992), pp. 29; and Ronald D. Rietveld, "Lincoln's View of the Founding Fathers"
(Redlands, Lincoln Memorial Shrine).

[6] Larry Arnhart, "Statesmanship as Magnanimity: Classical, Christian and Modern," *Polity,*
Vol. 16, No. 2 (Winter, 1983), pp. 263-283.

He treated other politicians as professional equals. Capable of being a masterful Machiavellian in dealing with other politicians, Lincoln, however, went beyond a common brokerage leadership style and promoted democratic values.

Although his relationships with his cabinet and Congress, each composed of powerful individuals, have been recognized and praised, his jurisprudence has been questioned, at least by today's standards. If Lincoln took enormous liberty with the Constitution, he always sought and won retroactive congressional backing for his extra-Constitutional actions. More clearly than the Roger Taney court, Lincoln understood the political environment in which America's institutions, including the law, exist.

The ultimate triumph of Lincoln's presidency resides in its elevation of America's democratic values. In a time of civil war, Lincoln reformulated those values in context of the nation's founding documents and then communicated the renewed vision to the public. Rather than fixate on a narrow interpretation of the Constitution, Lincoln expanded the Constitutional vision to embrace the spirit of the Declaration of Independence as well as Western political tradition. His promotion of equality and the individual dignity of human beings was the essential democratic notion that defined Lincoln. He exemplified these values in his personal and public life. The public intuitively understood and eventually subscribed to his leadership style. These same political and personal values personify the contemporary Lincoln, and are the foundation for his relevance today.

The essays contained in this volume derive from the first in a series of academic conferences on America's greatest presidents. The series began in 1992, the bicentennial of the White House, with a program on Abraham Lincoln, the first national conference on our sixteenth president ever held in the Deep South. On September 17-18, the International Lincoln Association (ILA) hosted the conference at Louisiana State University in Shreveport. Founded in 1987 by James Neal Hastings, Richard W. Elliott, Sr. and Wallace H. Best, the ILA focuses on the importance of Abraham Lincoln as a universal role model for students in schools at all levels.

Co-sponsoring the conference with ILA was the Abraham Lincoln Association (ALA). The ALA is headquartered in Springfield, Illinois, Abraham Lincoln's hometown. First known as the Lincoln Centennial Association, the ALA was organized in 1908 to prepare for the national celebration of the 100th anniversary of Lincoln's birth the following February 12. Early in its history, the Association discovered and made accessible previously unknown facts about Lincoln's life. Its greatest contribution was gathering and publishing *The Collected Works of Abraham Lincoln* in the early 1950s. Since 1940, with the publication of *The Abraham Lincoln Quarterly,* and later the *Journal of the Abraham Lincoln Association,* emphasis has shifted to interpretation of already accumulated facts while at the same time focusing on critical aspects of Lincoln's presidency. The Association's charter mandates the ALA to promote the study of Lincoln. ALA sponsorship of the LSU in Shreveport conference and this resulting volume are representative of the diverse means that the ALA employs to achieve its mission of making new information about Lincoln available beyond the boundaries of Springfield.

As evidenced by this volume, the work of the Association continues. A deliberate attempt is made in these essays to enunciate Lincoln's effect on contemporary America while remaining cognizant that views of him may change with each generation. The student of Lincoln must be constantly aware that Lincoln is both used and abused by those attempting to promote their own particular points of view which may not be Lincoln's. Historian David Donald has called this "Getting Right With Lincoln." According to Professor Donald, Lincoln's ambiguity satisfied every conceivable national and political need, even for those who held diametrically opposed views. One can say that Lincoln also satisfies every international need: Lincoln the nationalist (for the early Italians), Lincoln the democrat (for the early French), and Lincoln the libertarian (for his few English admirers at the time of his presidency). We do not think that Lincoln is ambiguous. Rather we think he was adaptable. We know so much about him, yet so little, that people of divergent views find common strands within his philosophy to link them to Lincoln. He offers compatibility to almost everyone: laborers and businessmen, racists and anti-racists, and other groups in opposition. It is confirmation of Lincoln's strength, not a condemnation of weakness.

This book helps to answer some of the persistent questions and problems that arise in the study of Abraham Lincoln: Why does everyone want to get right with Lincoln? How do they use him? What does this Lincoln phenomenon tell us about American culture and politics? What do the uses that contemporaries make of Lincoln tell us about his career, words, image and myths?

This compendium of papers deals with Lincoln's continuing impact on America's institutional (governmental, spiritual, and educational) life. Opening essays treat the effect of Lincoln's legacy on subsequent presidents. Next are two monographs that explore Lincoln's impact on Congress and the cabinet. Lincoln's most controversial governmental views concerning the role of the Supreme Court are examined in two following articles. His effort to deal with the political crisis during the mid-nineteenth century are covered in the three subsequent essays, while the collection's final paper deals with Lincoln's place in today's classroom. Unfortunately, the illuminating legacy of our greatest president is dimmed in today's schools. We offer this volume as a reminder that Lincoln continues to have relevance for America's institutions and individuals.

*   *   *

We wish to extend our thanks to Louisiana State University in Shreveport, the Abraham Lincoln Association, and the International Lincoln Association. We are indebted for the secretarial skills of Donna J. Saffel, the editing assistance of Elaine King, and the technical services of LaserKing (Hal King). Our deepest thanks go to the participants at the first Lincoln Conference in the Deep South. The essays of the contributors draw attention to the continuing influence and legacy of Abraham Lincoln, as well as to the need to assure that his legacy is passed undimmed to successive generations. Finally, this volume is dedicated to Myra Miller and Virginia Williams, two retired public school teachers, mother and daughter, who each devoted twenty-seven years to opening young minds to the wonders of learning, and who have demonstrated unusual patience with a Lincoln collector's hobby.

Τhis observer is confident that Lincoln will not be forgotten. Despite the best efforts of revisionist historians and politically correct educators, this man will never be cast aside. The principles he stood for and the service he performed will stand apart from any and all other national leaders. Those qualities are enduring and eternal.

David E. Long

David Long holds a B.A. from Ohio State University, a J.D. from Ohio State University College of Law, and a M.A. and Ph.D. from Florida State University. He has contributed articles to the *Lincoln Herald*, the *Lincoln Newsletter*, *Abraham Lincoln: Sources and Style of Leadership* (Greenwood, 1994), and is the author of *The Jewel of Liberty: Abraham Lincoln's Reelection and the End of Slavery* (Stackpole Books, 1994). He serves on the Board of Directors of the American Blue and Gray Association, and is the Founder and President of the Manasota Civil War Round Table. Professor Long, who formerly taught at Manatee Community College in Bradenton, Florida, has recently accepted a teaching position at East Carolina University.

Introduction

It was the western world of the nineteenth century, an era of liberalism and nationalism, of romanticism and humanism, of discovery and progress, of colonialism and empires. It was the age of great national leaders and nation builders, of Napoleon Bonaparte and Otto von Bismarck, Victoria and Franz Joseph, Garibaldi and Alexander II. It was a period of revolution and upheaval, of Karl Marx and Charles Darwin. It was a time of literary and artistic achievement, of Dostoevsky and Keats, Monet and Beethoven. Across its panoply passed a parade of historic giants who shaped and reshaped the landscape of human experience and potential.

And yet the individual who stands like a colossus astride the nineteenth century was not a European; he was not a child of royalty or privilege, nor the product of a classical education, and did not receive specialized instruction at a military academy or religious monastery. He was an American, his roots the humblest imaginable, his formal education almost non-existent. Yet he rose to become the champion of democratic government and the common person at a time when the rest of the world had rejected such notions in favor of monarchs and despots and a system of class and caste. His name was Abraham Lincoln and he is at the center of American history.

There are many qualities of Lincoln's character and life which make him attractive. He has been adopted by political, religious, and special interest groups of virtually every hue and stripe. In American history he is the universal symbol, epitomizing whatever cause the adopting group is promoting. He has been used as a symbol by racial egalitarians and white supremacists, by supporters of big government and opponents, by Democrats, Republicans, and third party splinter groups. This would lead to the impression of Lincoln as a man who did not possess strong beliefs or lasting commitments. Such an impression could not be more erroneous. Despite twentieth century revisionist historians who seek to portray Lincoln as a racial bigot or a political conservative, he was a visionary and a remarkably effective statesman. Comparing his attitudes about black Americans with those of radical Abolitionists is an exercise in absurdity: Wendell Phillips could not have been elected to political office even in a local New England constituency, much less in a national referendum. Abraham Lincoln's genius was that he was able to build political coalitions which brought about change that was both permanent and meaningful.

What was at stake during the presidency of Abraham Lincoln? The continuation of the United States as one nation indivisible; the survival intact of the democratic government established by the founders of the American experiment less than a century earlier; the efficacy of a perpet-ual union of states defined by a written constitution as opposed to a voluntary association of independent states for purposes of commercial advantage and national defense; the exercise of the right to vote as the most fundamental and important right of the citizens of a democratic government; the emancipation of four million slaves; and the permanent abolition of slavery in the United States as a matter of constitutional law. Those who argue that Lincoln was not the greatest president or that he was lacking in qualities of ability or character compared with other American statesmen simply refuse to acknowledge the truth of what confronted the sixteenth president and the remarkable success he achieved in carrying out his program of change. Abraham Lincoln rede-fined the landscape of American politics. He did so while occupying the moral high ground, even in 1864 when that stance jeopardized his re-election and the prospective success of the government's war effort. He was unrelenting in his defense of the two overarching themes of his presidency: the preservation of democratic government under the constitution and the emancipation of the slaves.

How he was able to achieve these has been a source of inspiration for every generation of Americans since the Civil War. Professor William D. Pederson of Louisiana State University in Shreveport, one of the editors of this collection of essays, often writes and talks about Lincoln's leadership, especially during the final year of the war.[1]

The course of his life before coming to the White House was essentially a process of political maturation, of growth as a leader and statesman. But it went beyond that. It was his virtue, his loyalty and honesty, his adherence to principle even when doing so threatened some other goal. In 1863, while Union military fortunes were at a low ebb, Maj. Gen. Ambrose Burnside unwisely arrested Copperhead Clement Vallandigham, thereby inciting a political tempest that distracted the nation's gaze from the battlefield and threatened the war effort. Lincoln could simply have released Vallandigham and blamed the oafish Burnside for making an unwarranted arrest. Had he done so it would have spared his administration much of the abuse that followed. But whatever else he was, Burnside was a patriot and Lincoln would not scuttle the general merely to save face. He changed the terms of Vallandigham's sentence to banishment to the Confederacy, and then mounted a powerful defense of the arrest and conviction even though he preferred that they had not occurred.

When Congress sought to castigate Secretary of War Simon Cameron for malfeasance in awarding war contracts in 1861, Lincoln intervened. Even though the secretary already had an unsavory reputation based on his antebellum political activities, the president accepted the responsibility himself and defended Cameron's actions based on the exigencies of the government's need for men and materiel in the early months after Fort Sumter. It is difficult to imagine many other presidents who would have acted accordingly in the same situation.

---

[1] William D. Pederson and Kenneth G. Kuriger, Jr., "A Comparative Test of Jimmy Carter's Character," in *The Presidency and Domestic Policies of Jimmy Carter,* ed., Herbert D. Rosenbaum and Alexej Ugrinsky (Westport, 1994), pp. 243-257.

x David E. Long

In 1864, when peace negotiations with Confederate commissioners in Canada broke down, prominent newspaper editor Horace Greeley blamed Lincoln for misleading him. The president had commissioned Greeley to represent him in the negotiations, and it had been the editor, not Lincoln, who had engaged in deception about the course of events which ensued. Nevertheless, when the mercurial Greeley blamed Lincoln for "the failure of the negotiations for peace and the subsequent prolongation of the war," the president refused to become vindictive.[2] The accusation caused Lincoln to lose some of the public confidence, and he could have regained some of what had been lost simply by publicly upbraiding and exposing Greeley for his hypocrisy and petulance. But he chose instead to bear the blame unjustly directed at him for the breakdown of the negotiations.[3]

Harold Holzer, in his Introduction to *Lincoln on Democracy*, explains the enduring quality of Lincoln's character that continues to inspire Americans in the late twentieth century:

> To many, Lincoln is still Honest Abe, Father Abraham, the Great Emancipator, the Martyr of Liberty. His rise from log cabin to White House, from prairie lawyer to master statesman, justifiably remains the most famous and inspiring of all the validations of American opportunity. His face alone, homely yet intrinsically noble—"so awful ugly it becomes beautiful," in Whitman's words—remains indelibly inscribed on the national consciousness, whether one pictures it gazing down from the lofty heights of Mount Rushmore or staring out from the ubiquitous copper penny. In an increasingly diverse culture, it is a palpable emblem of our common aspirations, itself an icon of democracy.[4]

[2] Henry R. Raymond, *The Life and Public Services of Abraham Lincoln* (New York, 1865), pp. 195-196.

[3] David E. Long, *A New Birth of Freedom: Abraham Lincoln's Re-Election and the End of Slavery* (Ph.D. dissertation, Florida State University, 1993), p. 290.

[4] Mario M. Cuomo and Harold Holzer, eds., *Lincoln on Democracy* (New York, 1990), pp. xxix-xxx.

Just as most of Lincoln's contemporaries were able to see through the smokescreen of untruth fanned by unscrupulous editors and vindictive politicians, most twentieth-century Americans have cast aside the efforts of revisionist historians to rewrite the record of this man's life. It was this quality of the sixteenth president, the ability to communicate with and appeal to the common citizen, everyday people who have no political or personal agenda to pursue, that sets him apart from other American statesmen. Lincoln's character—and the trust people had in him—made it possible to mandate revolutionary change in the social and political history of the United States, despite the fact that emancipation was not a high priority for most nineteenth century Americans.

Though most white people in the North had strong negative feelings about Americans of African descent, Lincoln:

> recognized in them the same quality that was a part of himself—the capacity to rise above his own prejudices by trusting those instincts for fair play and decency which co-existed with those prejudices. If whites were not prepared to accept blacks as their equals in 1863, perhaps that negative attitude could be improved upon by adopting a different perspective. In 1858 Lincoln had countered Douglas' appeals to racism with the simple question, "Is the black man not equally entitled to enjoy the benefits earned by the sweat of his own brow?" By changing the question, he increased the common ground that he shared with those willing to continue fighting the war knowing that human slavery would be one of the victims of that war. His intelligence and sensitivity had elevated the war effort to a higher ground. In so doing he had reduced his detractors in the eyes of many who would make the important choices between war and peace at the ballot box in 1863 and after.[5]

The qualities personified by Lincoln were timeless. They are as attractive and have as much meaning today as they did to his contemporaries. His influence is pervasive, as demonstrated by this collection of essays, ably edited by Frank J. Williams and William D. Pederson.

---

[5] Ibid.

Every president since Lincoln has had the unenviable task of attempting to conduct his administration against the measuring stick left
by the sixteenth chief executive. It is a daunting task. Evidence of his
continuing impact is illustrated by the wide range of essays which com-
prise *Abraham Lincoln: Contemporary*. In Part I: The Presidency, the
first three papers of this collection either contrast the Lincoln presidency
with that of a successor or show how later presidents appropriated him
to support some theme or scheme they wanted to promote publicly.
Roger D. Bridges inaugurates this volume with "Abraham Lincoln's
Impact on Rutherford B. Hayes," an insightful essay about a contemporary of Lincoln who was impressed in 1860 by his "policy of kindness"
while remaining firmly opposed to any compromise that would "extend
the power and the deadly influence of the slave system." Bridges ana-
lyzes the similarities and differences between the two men, and the
positive impact that the sixteenth chief executive had on Hayes.

Franklin D. Roosevelt occupied the White House more than seventy
years after Lincoln, yet the influence of the latter pervaded the New
Deal, particularly beginning with the campaign for re-election in 1940.
In "Prudent Archery: Franklin D. Roosevelt's Lincoln," Philip Abbott
employs the Machiavellian instruction that "a prudent man should always follow in the path trodden by great men and imitate those who are
excellent" to explain Roosevelt's increasingly Lincolnesque tone in the
late stages of his second term. FDR would act as the "prudent archer,"
aiming well above his distant target so that he might have a fair chance
of reaching that object.

Gerald Ford, perhaps more influenced by the sixteenth president
than any other occupant of the White House, entered the executive
branch of government stating, "I am a Ford, not a Lincoln." And eight
months later, in his first address to Congress as president, he told his
former colleagues "I am still a Ford, but I am not a Model T." Edward L.
and Frederick H. Schapsmeier describe the powerful influence Lincoln
had on Ford's abbreviated presidency in "Gerald R. Ford and the Lincoln Legacy: A Time to Heal." Ford spoke of that influence at the
dedication of the Lincoln home site in 1976—"It is a comforting presence gently reminding his successors that no matter how worrisome,

none of their problems can be worse than he faced, none of their critics more cruel, none of their decisions more difficult."

In Part II: Congress and Cabinet, the papers focus not on Lincoln's influence on subsequent presidents, but on his own management of that office in his relations with Congress and his cabinet. Samuel Hoff describes the contrasting views of the sixteenth president's relations with Congress in "Legislative Messages of the Lincoln Administration." Lincoln as a wartime leader exercised "presidential powers in heretofore undreamed-of-ways," taking actions that "far exceeded his constitutional powers."[6] And yet as president-elect in 1861 he had said, "My political education strongly inclines against a very free use of any of these means, by the Executive, to control the legislation of the country." Hoff concludes that the remarkably activist presidency of Abraham Lincoln, in spite of his Whiggish principles, was made possible in large measure by his very effective use of the legislative message.

In "From Poltroons and Apes to Diamonds in their Setting: Lincoln's Practice of Cabinet Alchemy," the writing tandem of Arthur R. Williams and Amanda Noble presents an incisive argument for the effectiveness of Lincoln's presidency based on the strength of the members and diversity of opinion within his cabinet. "The fundamental thesis of this paper is that Lincoln did practice 'alchemy' by transforming a cabinet of contentious rivals into one of diamonds in their setting."

The essays in Part III: Constitutional Impact, address the constitutional influence of the Lincoln presidency. The years from 1861 to 1868 completely reshaped the constitutional relationship between the federal and state governments, in addition to altering forever the way Americans viewed their national government. That kind of change can only occur in the midst of turbulence and widespread social dislocation. No aspect of Lincoln's tenure as chief executive was so fraught with controversy as his relations with the Supreme Court, and particularly Chief Justice Roger Taney. In his insightful essay on "Lincoln and Judicial Review,"

---

[6] Stephen B. Oates, *Abraham Lincoln: The Man Behind the Myth* (New York, 1985), p. 122; Robert I. DeClerico, *The American Presidency* (Englewood Cliffs, 1990), p. 64.

William Bader takes the traditional view of the strict constructionist. Bader argues that Lincoln's assumption of extraordinary powers, and particularly his refusal to be bound by Taney's order to release Roger Merryman, was a usurpation of power that threatened the system of checks and balances inherent in the American constitution.

Mark Rozell takes the opposite view in his paper "Executive Prerogative and American Constitutionalism," arguing that Lincoln's exercise of extra-constitutional—if not unconstitutional—power, was necessary to preserve the Union. "Lincoln acted properly because he acted out of necessity." It was in his defense of such extraordinary means that Lincoln was at his most eloquent, such as when he asked, "Must I shoot a simple-minded soldier boy who deserts, while I must not touch a hair of a wiley agitator who induces him to desert?" Or when he asked the special session of Congress in July 1861, "Must a government, of necessity, be too strong for the liberties of its own people, or too weak to maintain its own existence?"

One aspect of Lincoln's personality that seemed out of character with the pragmatic politician, the peerless literary stylist, the eloquent champion of democracy, was the lonely and depressed man who was haunted by dreams, visions, and premonitions. In Part IV: Spiritual Impact, John Stuart Erwin explores how the spirit world, the world he entered during moments of fitful sleep or unbearable stress, affected Lincoln's perception of the apocalyptic events of the Civil War and influenced his decisions as president. Erwin's essay, "Abraham Lincoln's Visions, Dreams, and Premonitions," reveals a side of Lincoln's character that perhaps helps to explain his enormous reliance on God and scripture—despite the fact that this president never joined a church or aligned himself with a particular denomination.

Stephen K. Shaw concludes Part IV by writing about the religious dimension of the political history of the United States during the Civil War in "Abraham Lincoln and Civil Religion: The President and the Prophetic Stance." This public religion, or "public religious dimension is expressed in a set of beliefs, symbols, and rituals" that has been termed "the American civil religion."[7] It has been defined as "that religious dimension, found. . .in the life of every people, through which it interprets its historical experience in the light of transcendent reality."[8] According to one writer:

> No American President has achieved greater clarity in laying down the underlying political and moral principles on which his policies and actions were based. We look back to his political rhetoric and policy statements for the model of the leader speaking in his time and for the ages. . .He stands alone among American Presidents who thought clearly about political ethics.[9]

Lincoln adopted the prophetic (as opposed to the priestly) version of civil religion, which was out of the ordinary for an American president. He chose the path less traveled, "countering idolatrous religious nationalism and calling the nation to repent of its corporate political sins."[10]

Charles B. Strozier's intriguing "Abraham Lincoln and the Apocalyptic at Mid-Century," expands upon both the Erwin and Shaw themes, describing the "apocalyptic anxieties" of nineteenth century Americans, and the frequent use of apocalyptic rhetoric by Lincoln: "The apocalyptic, in fact, was everywhere in Lincoln's rhetoric: in military strategy. . . in his transmutation of individual soldiers' mortality for the nation's immortality in the Gettysburg Address, and in his characterization of the war as a 'fiery trial' through which we must pass." By so doing, Lincoln kept in front of the people the omnipresent theme that this war and its outcome was of surpassing importance, not just to them but to their children and their children's children. And though Lincoln, by his words and actions, trumpeted this message in terms which were both elegant

---

[7] Robert N. Bellah, "Civil Religion in America," *Daedalus*, vol., 96 (Winter, 1967), p. 4.

[8] Robert N. Bellah, *The Broken Covenant: American Civil Religion in Time of Trial* (New York, 1975), p. 3.

[9] Kenneth W. Thompson, ed., *Essays on Lincoln's Faith and Politics* (Lanham, 1983), p. ix.

[10] Richard V. Pierard and Robert D. Linder, *Civil Religion and the Presidency* (Grand Rapids, 1988), p. 24.

and inspiring, even he was not always able to control the apocalyptic tenor of the events during this turbulent period. In performing his part in the war's last act of apocalyptic violence, the one played out at Ford's Theater, Lincoln had not written the script and could not shape or influence the outcome. He became one of those whom he soberingly referred to in his second inaugural as the human sacrifice exacted by a vengeful God for the sin of slavery.

In the final essay of this collection—and the only monograph in Part V: Educational Impact—Sherry L. Field presents a somewhat disturbing examination of Abraham Lincoln in modern elementary academics in "The Legacy of Abraham Lincoln in the Elementary Classroom":

> A glimpse into the elementary school social studies classes has shown that Abraham Lincoln is remembered, for the most part, neither wisely nor well. Only two elementary teachers mentioned that they introduced the Gettysburg Address in teaching about Lincoln, and none made a connection in their teaching about Civil Rights or Dr. Martin Luther King, Jr. with the Emancipation Proclamation. No teaching about Lincoln's character traits, such as humor, tenacity, or equanimity appeared to make its way into the classrooms.

Field concludes her paper with a cogent, if understated, comment when she writes, "an awareness of the current status of teaching about Abraham Lincoln in elementary schools reveals a need to shore up, protect, and nurture the tenets of history instruction. Abraham Lincoln—the events surrounding his life and the contributions he made—should not be forgotten." She raises an issue that is relevant to us in the late twentieth century. As Lincoln and the era of the Civil War are increasingly extirpated from the basic educational curriculum of our children, should we deem this an acceptable expedient in order to accommodate the ever-increasing demands of social historians and multiculturalism? It is a question that we as Americans must address in some meaningful way. If we do not, we risk the loss of something so valuable that only in retrospect will the damage be realized. The late nineteenth and twentieth century Americans who allowed many of the hallowed grounds of the Civil War to fall victim to urbanization and commercial development were no less patriotic or virtuous than the present generation. However they were not vigilant to what events in their time would mean to a future generation. They had other things to do than stand guard over the sanctified fields where Americans fought and died. The march of time knows nothing of history and is oblivious to historic significance. It will not alter its course because Cemetery Ridge has value other than that which can be measured in dollars and cents. If those generations of Americans that allowed battlefields at Atlanta and Nashville and hundreds of other places to be turned into parking lots, shopping malls and housing subdivisions were alive today they would undoubtedly utter collectively, "I wish I had it to do over." They don't have that opportunity. They lost it. As any military commander will attest, it is much more difficult to recover ground once lost than it is to hold that same ground in the first place.

Will the present generation, at some future time when a generation yet unborn struggles to restore truth and balance to the teaching of American history—struggles to undo the trashing of our nation's history, an event that occurred during somebody else's watch—will this generation have to look back in shame and plaintively mutter, "I wish I had it to do over."

This observer is confident that Lincoln will not be forgotten. Despite the best efforts of revisionist historians and politically correct educators, this man will never be cast aside. The principles he stood for and the service he performed will stand apart from any and all other national leaders. Those qualities are enduring and eternal. They represent the best we have produced as a nation and the hope every generation of Americans has had for a better life. Because he lived the nation was saved, democratic government was given "a new birth of freedom," and slavery was finally and permanently ended in the United States. Common sense would seem to dictate that we should look more closely at this man's life, and teach our children about him in our schools.

To the end of his life, however, Hayes continued to look to Lincoln for inspiration and as the yardstick by which all other presidents and statesmen were to be measured. Even Hayes could not aspire to reach the lofty heights achieved by Lincoln.

Roger D. Bridges

Roger Bridges earned a B.A. and M.A. from the University of Northern Iowa and a Ph.D. in American History from the University of Illinois at Urbana-Champaign in 1970. He has taught at Bradley University, the University of South Dakota, Illinois State University, Sangamon State University, and currently is adjunct professor of history at Bowling Green State University. While a National Historic Preservation and Conservation fellow with the Ulysses S. Grant Association, he was assistant editor for volume 4 of the *Papers of Ulysses S. Grant* (Carbondale, 1972). He worked for the Illinois State Historical Library and the Illinois Historic Preservation Agency, where he was director before becoming director of the *Lincoln Papers* project. The author of several articles dealing with nineteenth century and Illinois political and black history, he edited (with Rodney O. Davis) *Illinois: Its History and Legacy* (St. Louis, 1984). Since 1988, he has been the director of the Rutherford B. Hayes Presidential Center.

Abraham Lincoln's
Impact on Rutherford B. Hayes

A generation ago, David Donald wrote that "Every four years Republican hopefuls sought—and presumably secured—Lincoln's endorsement."[1] Hayes was no exception to Donald's truism. While no one (to my knowledge) ever claimed Hayes was a second Lincoln, there were similarities between the two men. Like Lincoln, Hayes had a difficult childhood and lost a parent early in life. Both men became prominent lawyers in states of the Old Northwest, and both were Whigs long before the Republican party claimed their loyalties. Moreover, both men were politically ambitious, and succeeded in achieving their elective goals. Similarly, they were both antislavery men in the years before the Civil War, although Hayes was more outspoken than Lincoln had been.

In many ways, these two men were as different as they could be. Although Lincoln's mother died when he was nine, Rutherford B. Hayes never met his father, Rutherford Hayes, who died two months before his son entered the world. Moreover, unlike Thomas Lincoln, who married within less than two years of his first wife's death, Sophia Birchard Hayes never remarried. Although Lincoln was relatively impoverished as a youth, Hayes never wanted for material comforts. While Lincoln early on learned about the rough frontier life with its many discomforts

---

[1] David Donald, *Lincoln Reconsidered* (New York, 1961), p. 9.

and worked hard in the fields and forests, Hayes led a sheltered existence. Rarely even allowed out of his mother's sight (because of the death
of his father and the drowning of his older brother), Hayes spent much
of his youth in the company of relatively cultured women. Lincoln, on
the other hand, according to Charles Strozier, grew up and matured in a
male dominated social world and was always more comfortable in the
company of men.[2]

There were also significant differences in their educational backgrounds. Whereas Lincoln's formal education was at best sporadic and
limited, Hayes was among the best educated men any where in the
nation. Lincoln had somewhat condescendingly written "that the aggre-
gate of all his schooling did not amount to one year. He was never in a
college or Academy as a student; and never inside of a college or academy [sic] building till since he had a law-license. What he has in the way
of education he has picked up."[3] Hayes, on the other hand, after attending school briefly in Delaware, attended the Norwalk, Ohio, Methodist
Academy for a year and then Mr. Webb's school at Middletown, Connecticut. He then enrolled at Kenyon College in Gambier, Ohio, rather
than Yale, which he had wanted to attend. Only sixteen when he entered
Kenyon in the fall of 1838, he quickly developed a reputation as a
scholar. He graduated as valedictorian of his class.

Already better educated than Lincoln had been at this stage in life,
Hayes moved to Ohio's capital city and began to read law in the office of
Thomas Sparrow. Hayes soon tired of that and headed for Harvard Law
School where he studied with Joseph Story and Simon Greenleaf, among
others. Upon the completion of law school, he returned to Lower San-
dusky, Ohio, before moving to Cincinnati, where he took an active role
in the social, political, and legal life of the city. Like Lincoln, he married
a daughter of Kentucky, but with little of the drama connected with the
courtship of Lincoln for Mary Todd. Lucy Webb was nine years younger
than Hayes and well-educated. While Hayes was by nature conservative,

---

[2] Charles B. Strozier, *Lincoln's Quest for Union: Public and Private Meanings* (New York, 1982), pp. 40-43.

[3] "Autobiography Written for Campaign," in Don E. Fehrenbacher, ed., *Abraham Lincoln: Speeches and Writing,* 2 vols. (New York, 1989), vol. 2, pp. 161-162.

college-educated Lucy encouraged Hayes' reform positions. He soon took on some of the most notorious cases in Cincinnati, including the defense of runaway slaves and other unpopular causes. In this regard, Hayes was probably much more purposeful than Lincoln.[4]

Hayes joined the Republican Party reluctantly, clinging like Lincoln to the Whig Party so long as it existed. As late as 1856, Hayes told his old Kenyon classmate, Texan Guy Bryan, "he felt like 'a waif on the political sea.'"[5] Nevertheless, later that same year, he attended the organizing meeting of the local Republican party and enthusiastically supported John C. Fremont for President. In 1858, he became Cincinnati City Solicitor and withdrew from the most partisan aspects of politics while remaining a committed Republican. Hayes was not an early supporter of Lincoln; indeed, prior to the conventions he appears to have been indifferent about the election of 1860. In a note to his uncle Sardis Birchard, Hayes wrote: "Our delegates have left for Chicago. After Chase, they will prefer Wade, Frémont, or some such candidate—anyone named before Seward."[6]

Hayes' initial reaction to Lincoln was equally detached. He wrote Sardis late in the campaign: "I have made a few little speeches in the country townships, and shall make a few more. I cannot get up much interest in the contest. A wholesome contempt for Douglas, on account of his recent demagoguery, is the chief feeling I have. I am not so confident that Lincoln will get votes enough as many of our friends."[7] Although his early visits with Lincoln increased his admiration for him, Hayes still was not enthusiastic. In all probability, however, the opportunity Hayes had to meet Lincoln changed the former's willingness to let the six states that seceded depart in peace.[8] He and Lucy went to Indianapolis to join the presidential party on its way to Cincinnati. Hayes noted

---

[4] For more on Hayes' education and legal work, see Harry Barnard, *Rutherford B. Hayes and His America* (Indianapolis, 1954), pp. 130-191.

[5] Hayes to Bryan, April 16, 1856, cited in Barnard, *Hayes*, p. 193.

[6] Hayes to S. Birchard, May 23, 1860, in Charles Richard Williams, ed., *The Life of Rutherford Birchard Hayes*, 7 vols. (Columbia, 1928), p. 555.

[7] Ibid., September 30, 1860, p. 564, and the preceeding comments, pp. 556-557.

[8] Hayes Diary, January 27, 1861, ibid., vol. 2, p. 4.

with some admiration that Lincoln had ridden in "an open carriage, standing erect with head uncovered, and bowing his acknowledgments to greetings showered upon him. . . .the simplicity, the homely character of all was in keeping with the nobility of this typical American." Hayes continued in his letter to Sardis:

> You will read the speeches in the papers, and search in vain for anything to find fault with. Mr. Lincoln was wary at all times, wisely so I think, and yet I hear no complaint. . . .In private conversation he was discreet but frank. He believes in a policy of kindness, of delay to give time for passions to cool, but not in a compromise to extend the power and the deadly influence of the slave system. This gave me great satisfaction. The impression he made was good. He undoubtedly is shrewd, able and possesses strength in reserve.[9]

When the Civil War began, Hayes resigned his position and enlisted in the army, eventually rising through the ranks from major to general. His support of Lincoln through the war can best be described as tepid. In the autumn of 1861, he wrote Lucy that "Lincoln is, perhaps, not all that we could wish, but he is honest, patriotic, cool-headed, and safe. I don't know any man that the Nation could say is under all the circumstances to be preferred in his place."[10] Hayes' support of emancipation was less enthusiastic than one would expect of a man who had defended slaves in court and those who assisted slaves in the pre-war period. He told his uncle Sardis Birchard: "You will like the President's Proclamation. I am not sure about it, but am content." In the midst of the presidential election of 1864, while expressing support of Lincoln, Hayes allowed himself to speculate about the possible election of General George B. McClellan. He wrote Lucy that "I think he [McClellan] will make the best President of any Democrat. If on a sound platform, I could support him. Do not be alarmed. I do not think he will be elected."[11] Although

---

[9] Hayes to S. Birchard, February 15, 1861, ibid., vol. 2, pp. 5-6.

[10] Hayes to Mrs. Hayes, October 19, 1861, ibid., 2, p. 120.

[11] Hayes to S. Birchard, Middletown, MD., October 1, 1862, ibid., 3, p. 361; Hayes to Mrs. Hayes, Camp at Summit Point, VA., September 9, 1865, ibid., p. 505.

he reported with relish the support the 9th and 23rd Ohio had given Lincoln in the presidential election, he continued to have good things to say about McClellan.[12]

Hayes' attitude, like that of many Americans, began to change with Lincoln's assassination. While expressing his shock at Lincoln's death, he noted that it might have been worse. His shift from grief to hope is obvious. He told his uncle Sardis that "gradually, consolatory topics suggest themselves. How fortunate that it occurred no sooner! Now the march of events will neither be stopped nor changed. . . . Lincoln's fame is safe. He is the Darling of History evermore. His life and achievements give him titles to regard second to those of no other man in ancient or modern times. To these, this tragedy now adds the crown of martyrdom."[13] Hayes was more frank when he wrote to Lucy the same day. It was to his mind, Hayes wrote,

> a calamity so extensive that in no direction could be found any, the slightest glimmer of consolation. The Nation's great joy turned suddenly to a still greater sorrow! A ruler tested and proved in every way, and in every way found equal to the occasion, to be exchanged for a new man whose ill-omened beginning made the Nation hang its head. Lincoln for Johnson!

"But slowly," he continued,

> as in all cases of great affliction, one comes to feel that it is not all darkness. . . .Now the march of events can't be stayed, probably can't be much changed. It is possible that a greater degree of severity in dealing with the Rebellion may be ordered, and *that* may be for the best." Hayes closed by prophesying that "His success in his great office, his hold upon the confidence and affections of his countrymen, we shall all *say* are only second to Washington's; we shall probably *feel* and think that they are not *second* even to his.[14]

---

[12] See his letters to S. Birchard, September 12, 1864, and Mrs. Hayes, September 13, 1864, ibid., pp. 506-507.

[13] Hayes to S. Birchard, New Creek, W. VA., April 16, 1865, ibid., 2, pp. 575-576.

[14] Hayes to Mrs. Hayes, New Creek, W. VA., April 16, 1865, ibid., pp. 576-577.

One year after Lincoln's death, following a visit to Mount Vernon, Hayes wrote to Sardis Birchard: "The truth is, if it were not sacrilege, I should say Lincoln is overshadowing Washington. Washington is formal, statue-like, a figure for exhibition; but both were necessary to complete our history." The same day he told Lucy: "I feel more than ever that, taking him [Lincoln] all in all, he was the highest character. But it is like sacrilege to make these comparisons. It is probably true that neither could have done the other's work, and without the work of both we should have had a different history."[15]

It was not Lincoln's influence, however, but Hayes' own political views that kept him in the Radical Reconstruction camp and an ardent supporter of the Reconstruction Amendments and black suffrage throughout his years as a congressman, governor of Ohio, and president. He did believe, however, as suggested by Lincoln to Louisiana, that blacks (at least literate blacks) should have the right to vote. He confided to his diary: "My decided preference: Suffrage for *all* in the South, colored and white, to depend on education; sooner or later in the North also—say, all *new* voters to be able to write and read. [emphasis added]"[16]

By the time Hayes returned from Congress to run for Governor of Ohio, he was regularly quoting Lincoln. In his campaign for governor he carried and used a published compilation of Lincoln's views. The little book, *The President's Words*, was the only book he carried everywhere with him during his successful campaign.[17] After his second term as Governor, Hayes decided to return to Fremont, Ohio, where he managed his ailing uncle's affairs and raised his family amid the rustic woods at his uncle's estate, Spiegel Grove. His interest in politics remained high, although he seemed to take a detached view. His principal concerns, as they had been while Governor, revolved around education and civil and

---

[15] Hayes to S. Birchard, Washington, D.C., April 15, 1866, ibid., 3, pp. 23-24; Hayes to Mrs. Hayes, Washington, D.C., April 15, 1866, ibid., p. 24.

[16] Hayes Diary, May 15, 1866, ibid., p. 25.

[17] *The President's Words: A Selection of Passages from the Speeches, Addresses and Letters of Abraham Lincoln* (Boston, 1865), p. 186.

political rights, issues intensified in importance by the results of "Mr. Lincoln's War."

Hayes, as Lincoln before him, believed education and political rights were essential ingredients for obtaining civil rights, the great goal of America as set forth in the Declaration of Independence. He explained the relationship in a letter to his old Texas friend Guy Bryan in 1875. Education, he told Bryan, is "the most important thing." He continued, "I, of course, don't believe in forcing whites and blacks together. But both classes should be provided for. I recognize fully the evil of rule by ignorance. I see enough of it under my own eyes. . . .But the remedy is not. . .to be found in abandonment of the American principle that all must share in government. The whites of the South must do as we do, *forget to drive and learn to lead* the ignorant masses around."[18]

Hayes' retirement did not last long. Badly divided and threatened with defeat by the Democrats, Ohio Republicans begged Hayes to run for governor. They promised that a successful campaign would make him the leading candidate for the Republican presidential nomination. Hayes scoffed at the idea. "How wild! What a queer lot we are becoming! Nobody is out of reach of that mania."[19] Surprised by his success, Hayes accepted his election as a third-term governor without elation. He noted in his diary, however, that "papers from all the country counties [are] urging me for the Presidential nomination."[20]

Like Lincoln, Hayes became a compromise candidate for president. He succeeded over better known rivals that included Roscoe P. Conkling of New York, James G. Blaine of Maine, and John F. Hartranft of Pennsylvania. Also, like Lincoln, he was the most available candidate with the fewest objections from other candidates. Moreover, he had an exemplary public record as a Radical Republican.[21]

---

[18] Hayes to Guy Bryan, Fremont, OH., January 2, 1875, Williams, *Hayes,* 3, pp. 262-263.

[19] Hayes Diary, April 14, 1875, Williams, vol. 3, p. 269.

[20] Ibid., October 17, 1875, Williams, vol. 3, p. 295.

[21] Ari Hoogenboom, *The Presidency of Rutherford B. Hayes* (Lawrence, 1988), pp. 13-16.

Hayes remained in Columbus, or Fremont, and let others speak for him, as was the custom. He did, of course, issue the standard letter of acceptance in which he outlined his political views. Unlike Lincoln, however, he maintained a lively correspondence related to the contest, all for private consumption and the ideas not to be attributed as coming from his pen in public. Hayes' views centered on his desire for resumption, civil service reform, and a related matter, a one-term presidency. As he prepared his acceptance letter, however, he gave considerable thought to the failure of southern Reconstruction. He told confidant Carl Schurz that "Local self-government has nullified the Fifteenth Amendment in several States, and is a fair way to nullify the Fourteenth and Thirteenth. But I do favor a policy of reconciliation, based on the observance of all parts of the Constitution—the *new* as well as the old. . . ."[22]

Paralleling the Lincoln election a quarter of a century earlier, the contest was bitterly divisive. There was not, however, a clear winner as there had been in 1860. It took an extra-legal body to finally determine the winner.[23] What Abraham Lincoln began in 1861 ended in failure with the inauguration of Rutherford B. Hayes. At least that has been the conclusion of many historians and political scientists over the past 115 years. At the turn of the century Woodrow Wilson wrote: "With the coming of Mr. Hayes the whole air of politics seemed to change. . . . Almost at once affairs wore a normal aspect again. The process of reconstruction, at least, had reached its unedifying end, and the hands of political leaders were free to take up the history of the country where it had been broken off in 1861."[24] James M. McPherson concluded that when Hayes withdrew troops from the last of the southern states, effective efforts at reconstruction ended.[25]

[22] Hayes to Carl Schurz, Columbus, OH., June 27, 1876, ibid., p. 329.

[23] There is not space to review the literature on the disputed election of 1876 and the so-called compromise of 1877. For a listing of the most authoritative work, see Brooks D. Simpson, "Ulysses S. Grant and the Electoral Crisis of 1876-77," *Hayes Historical Journal*, vol. 11 (Winter 1992), pp. 20-21, note 1.

[24] Woodrow Wilson, *A History of the American People*, 5 vols. (New York, 1906), vol. 1, pp. 115-116.

[25] James M. McPherson, *Abraham Lincoln and the Second American Revolution* (New York, 1990), pp. 149-152.

Hayes believed, however, that if the process of reconstruction were to end, that it must complete the work begun by the Civil War under Lincoln's leadership. When the Electoral Commission decided the Oregon question, Hayes wrote in his diary that he must give great attention to the pressing problem of the "Southern question." "The great body of the people of this country," he wrote, "earnestly desire a wise and just settlement of that question. They want peace, they long for repose." He concluded:

> What is required is: First, that for the protection and welfare of the colored people, the Thirteenth, Fourteenth, and Fifteenth Amendments shall be sacredly observed and faithfully enforced according to their true intent and meaning.
>
> Second, We all see that the tremendous revolution which has passed over the Southern people has left them impoverished and prostrate, and we all are deeply solicitous to do what may constitutionally be done to make them again prosperous and happy. They need economy, honesty, and intelligence in their local governments. They need to have such a policy adopted as will cause sectionalism to disappear, and that will tend to wipe out the color line. They need to have encouraged immigration, education, and every description of legitimate business and industry. We do not want a united North nor a united South.[26]

As he prepared to leave Columbus for the White House, Hayes recalled Lincoln's leave-taking from Springfield, Illinois, another midwestern state capital:

> And to-day, if I am called to the work to which Abraham Lincoln was called sixteen years ago, it is under brighter skies and more favorable auspices. [Applause.] I do hope, I do fervently believe that by the aid of Divine Providence we may do something in the day of peace, by works of peace, toward re-establishing in the hearts of our countrymen a real, a hearty attachment to the Constitution as it is, and to the Union as it is. [27]

---

[26] Hayes Diary, February 25, 1877, Williams, 3, p. 421.

[27] Speech File, February 28, 1877, Columbus, OH., Rutherford B. Hayes Papers, Rutherford B. Hayes Presidential Center, Fremont, OH.

As president, Hayes continued to work toward completing the work Lincoln had begun. That work, according to James M. McPherson, was summed up in Lincoln's letter to Horace Greeley in August 1862: "My paramount object in this struggle *is* to save the Union."[28] But as the war ground to its conclusion, that object had come to include extending the liberty, freedoms, and privileges enumerated in the Declaration of Independence, to all Americans. The compassionate Hayes wanted the same things. That he believed they could be achieved by peaceful means is, perhaps, the most tragic aspect of his administration. As he prepared his second message to Congress, he reminded himself to:

> examine the messages of all of my predecessors—especially of Jefferson, Madison, J. Q. Adams, Van Buren, and Lincoln on all the topics of which I shall speak. I must make a clear, firm, and accurate statement of the facts as to southern outrages, and reiterate the sound opinions I have long held on the subject. What good people demand is exact justice, equality before the law, perfect freedom of political speech and action, and no denial of rights to any citizen on account of color or race—the same to colored as to whites."[29]

Hayes believed that could be achieved by eliminating the color line in the South by getting Southern whites to divide along political lines. In other words, the solution was to develop a viable two-party system in the South among whites.[30] He was disappointed that his efforts to complete Lincoln's work were unsuccessful. Still, he persisted. In a letter to Frank Hatton of Burlington, Iowa, Hayes noted that "The perpetuity of the Union is established." He admitted, however, "that there is still in our country a dangerous practical denial of the equal rights with respect to voting secured to colored citizens by the fifteenth Amendment to the Constitution. One of the cogent arguments in favor of extending the right of suffrage to freedmen was that it would furnish them with all the

---

[28] McPherson, *Lincoln*, p. 41.

[29] Hayes Diary, October 26, 1878, Williams, 4, p. 505.

[30] See his report of a discussion with South Carolina black Congressman J. H. Rainey. Hayes Diary, ibid., p. 501.

means of self-protection." To be effective, he noted, the vote must be an intelligent vote, demanding improved education for blacks and whites.[31]

Hayes never considered himself another Lincoln, despite the similarity of the tasks he believed they confronted. Hayes recognized that they had come from vastly different social and educational backgrounds, and that their personalities differed. In that regard, he believed the Republican nominee as his successor more nearly resembled Lincoln. Indeed, Hayes insisted that "no man ever started so low that accomplished so much in all our history [as Garfield]. Not Franklin or Lincoln even."[32]

Despite his differences from Lincoln and Garfield, Hayes believed his administration a success. He observed,

> The general public, content with the peace and extraordinary prosperity which signalized its close, are apt to forget the circumstances of unusual difficulty, violence, and danger with which it began. It encountered at the threshold a more serious situation than has confronted any Administration of recent times except Lincoln's. Notice these: The Southern question; the money question; the hard times and riots; the Indian question; the Chinese question; the reform of the civil service; the partisan bitterness growing out of a disputed election; a hostile Congress; and a party long in power on the verge of defeat. Is there any one of these which was not left in better condition than it was found. I have often said that, leaving out of the question Lincoln's Administration, it would be difficult to find one which began with so rough a situation, and few which closed with so smooth a sea.[33]

To the end of his life, however, Hayes continued to look to Lincoln for inspiration and as the yardstick by which all other presidents and statesmen were to be measured. Even Hayes could not aspire to reach the lofty heights achieved by Lincoln. He offered the following sentiments on commemoration of the twentieth anniversary of Lincoln's death:

---

[31] Hayes to Hatton, Washington, August 24, 1880, Williams, 4, p. 623.

[32] Hayes Diary, June 11, 1880, vol. 3, p. 601.

[33] Hayes to Alexander Johnson, Fremont, OH., June 6, 1882, ibid., 4, p. 80.

Abraham Lincoln was the martyr of a stainless cause. It was the cause of America—"the cradle of the future." It was more. It was indeed the cause of all mankind. The triumph of this cause, so good and so great, was due, under Providence, more largely to Lincoln than to any other man. He was the embodiment of its spirit, its principles, and its purposes. He was the truest representative and the highest type of the plain people whose courage, patience, and faith, in the army and at home, won the victory.

With each passing year, the unmeasured greatness and the price-less value of the work of which he was the leader becomes more clear. The twentieth anniversary of the appalling event which closed that momentous struggle, the great American Conflict, finds the world able to see Lincoln and his deeds with a larger and wiser appreciation than ever before. Every anniversary, to the end of time, of the event you now commemorate, will surely bring to Lincoln, to his character and to the results of his life, the increased esteem, admiration, and gratitude of all civilized men.[34]

---

[34] Hayes to My Dear Sir, Fremont, OH., April 11, 1885, ibid., pp. 204-205.

(The Frank and Virginia Williams Collection of Lincolniana)

To the extent to which Franklin D. Roosevelt followed Machiavelli's advice about the prudent archer in 1939-1941, his speeches illustrate both the assets and liabilities of Lincoln as an exemplary figure in American political culture and presidential policy making.

Philip Abbott

Philip Abbott, who received his Ph.D. in political science from Rutgers University in 1971, is Distinguished Graduate Professor at Wayne State University, where he teaches courses in American political theory and culture. His most recent books include *The Exemplary Presidency: FDR and the American Political Tradition* (University of Massachusetts Press, 1990) and *Political Thought in America* (Peacock Press, 1991). His articles have appeared in *Political Theory, Polity, Journal of Politics, Presidential Studies Quarterly, Soundings* and *Review of Politics*. He has been awarded grants and fellowships from the National Endowment for the Humanities, American Philosophical Society, Earhart Foundation, and Ford Foundation.

Not being always able to follow others exactly nor to attain to the excellence of those he imitates, a prudent man should always follow in the path trodden by great men and imitate those who are excellent, so that if he does not attain their greatness, at any rate he will get some tinge of it. He will do as prudent archers, who when the place they wish to hit is too far off, knowing how far their bow will carry, aim at a spot much higher than the one they wish to hit, not in order to reach this height with their arrow, but by help of this high aim to hit the spot they wish to.

—Machiavelli, *The Prince*

Prudent Archery: FDR's Lincoln

In *The Prince*, Machiavelli prefaces his discussion of the "exalted instances" in which men found new dominions by noting that "men walk almost always in the paths trodden by others, proceeding in their actions by imitation." If copy he must, "a prudent man should always follow in the path trodden by great men and imitate those who are excellent, so that if he does not attain their greatness, at any rate he will get some tinge of it." This essay examines how this Machiavellian advice was followed by one American president at one point in time by analyzing Franklin D. Roosevelt's imitation of Abraham Lincoln. I hope to show how complex this exemplary activity can be. For the "prudent archer" of which Machiavelli speaks, even by aiming high, selects a model that always contains its own liabilities, both in terms of the ambitions of the imitator and in terms of the consequences it can produce for the polity of which he is a member. To the extent to which the American presidency is an institution most suited to receiving Machiavelli's advice, I try throughout to evaluate the legacy of Lincoln as a presidential exemplar.

Just after the Supreme Court fight, the *New Republic* observed that "the New Deal is cracking up pretty fast."[1] After the 1938 elections, and the failure to purge the Democratic party of "reactionary" elements, there was speculation that the president could not win a third term even if he wished. At this point in the Roosevelt presidency the symbols of Jefferson and Jackson had been the primary edifices for FDR's policies. As early as 1925 Roosevelt had recommended to party leaders that "the difference between the Jeffersonian and Hamiltonian ideals for a method of government" be the focus of upcoming campaigns. Beginning with his "concert of interests" speech in 1932, he imaginatively outlined an approach for a "national Jefferson" and labeled Hoover and the Republicans as "modern day Hamiltons." In 1936 he compared his campaign to the challenge facing Jackson, who was "rugged and fearless" in his fights for the people.[2] As exemplars for new initiatives, Jackson and Jefferson appeared to be exhausted by 1938. One commentator had even asserted later that since the ghost of Monticello and Old Hickory had made their appearances at the FDR White House the only specter left to raise was the Great Emancipator.[3] In fact, the Lincoln model had been available to Roosevelt in 1932-33 and he had used the war analogy sporadically during the campaign and with great effect in his first inaugural. Now events in Europe and the Pacific made Lincoln as an exemplar again a possibility. This time FDR seized the opportunity.

Three Lincolns

But imitating Lincoln was no simple task, for there were many Lincolns to draw from and some to avoid. One aspect of the Lincoln exemplar was developed immediately after his death. This was the "Black Easter" Lincoln, the man who, through his vision of America as an indissoluble union, suffered and died for the cause that many did not

---

[1] *New Republic*, August 18, 1937.

[2] I have examined FDR's use of these and other exemplars in my *The Exemplary Presidency: FDR and the American Political Tradition* (Amherst, 1990). Portions of this chapter have been adapted from this book with the permission of the University of Massachusetts Press.

[3] Dixon Wecter, *The Hero in America* (New York, 1941), p. 461.

understand as fully as he. Lincoln was the savior of America as Washington had been its founder. The Biblical rhetoric that the Civil War president employed to justify the conflict was used to describe the fallen leader. One Northern minister, noting that the assassination had taken place on Good Friday, concluded that "it is no blasphemy against the Son of God that we declare the fitness of the slaying of the second Father of our Republic on the anniversary of the day on which he was slain. Jesus Christ died for the world, Abraham Lincoln died for his country."[4]

There was also another use of the Lincoln exemplar, one which emphasizes Lincoln's modest origins. Here was a Lincoln as a child of the frontier, prairie lawyer and peoples' politician. This interpretation has at least two major readings. One had been developed during Lincoln's career. Lincoln was portrayed as a man who was self-made in the new Whig tradition of Harrison and Tyler. "Honest Abe, the Rail Splitter" was essentially an anti-political politician who stood for the Whig principles of individual advancement and the tariff.

Another version of the frontier leader also focused on the president's origins, but rather than emphasizing the distance Lincoln had traveled spoke of the advantages of his beginnings as a man of the people. Here is the Lincoln of democratic folk, a model that fits far better the Jacksonian democracy that Lincoln had actually rejected. William H. Herndon's biography of Lincoln, published in 1899, still remains the best representative of this view. The President's law partner claimed that he wrote the biography to take the memory of Lincoln away from the "nice sweet smelling gentlemen." Herndon's Lincoln was born in a "stagnant, putrid pool," the son of white trash and the illegitimate daughter of a Virginia planter. Herndon even raised doubts about Lincoln's own paternity. The young Abraham is foremost a man's man, regaling his cronies with exploits of strength and carousing and dirty

---

[4] David Donald, *Lincoln Reconsidered* (New York, 1959), p. 153. The "Black Easter" tradition is also discussed in Stephen B. Oates, *Abraham Lincoln: The Man Behind the Myths* (New York, 1984), pp. 3-17; Lloyd Lewis, *Myths After Lincoln* (New York, 1929); Roy P. Basler, *The Lincoln Legend* (Boston, 1935); Richard N. Current, *The Lincoln Nobody Knows* (New York, 1958), pp. 282-287; Waldo W. Braden, *Building the Myth: Selected Speeches Memorializing Lincoln* (Urbana, 1990), pp. 1-24.

jokes. He is an avid reader but, according to Herndon, his studies were limited to a few books. "Lincoln himself never bought many books" although he did discuss issues with his partner. But it was Lincoln who warned Herndon: "Billy, don't shoot too high—aim lower and the common people will understand you. They are the ones you ought to reach—at least they are the ones you ought to reach."[5]

Although there are tensions among these interpretations, each seems to have supplemented rather than eroded the Black Easter Lincoln. Lincoln's modest origins fit both with the Horatio Alger myth and with the mystery surrounding the biological origins of all mythological heroes.[6] None of these Lincolns, however—Black Easter, Whig or the prairie lawyer—historically prevented a critical Lincoln literature. During the Civil War the president was alternately portrayed as a buffoon and as a diabolical Napoleonic usurper. Writing in 1904, Elizabeth Mary Meriweather made use of the Herndon Lincoln in her assessment of Lincoln as the frontier bully, the very opposite of the Black Easter Lincoln:

> Is it insanity or pure mendacity to liken a man of this nature to the gentle and loving Nazarene? Who for an instant can imagine Jesus swinging a bottle of whisky around his head, swearing to the rowdy crowd that he was the "big buck of the lick?" Or with whip in hand, lashing a faithful old slave at every round of her labor? Who can imagine Jesus sewing up hog's eyes? What act of Lincoln's life betrays tender-heartedness? Was he tender-hearted when he made medicine contraband of war? When he punished women caught with a bottle of quinine going South?[7]

---

[5] David Freeman Hawke, ed., *Herndon's Lincoln* (Indianapolis, 1970), pp. 3-7, 112, 122. For a recent interpretation of Lincoln as a "man's man" whose ideology was formed by the "fraternal democracy" of the midwestern frontier, see Robert H. Wiebe, *Lincoln's Fraternal Democracy* in John L. Thomas, ed., *Abraham Lincoln and the American Political Tradition* (Amherst, 1986), pp. 11-30.

[6] Thus, for example, Woodrow Wilson eclectically employed each version in his speech at Lincoln's birthplace in 1916. "This little hut," said Wilson, "is a place. . .of mystery" and an "altar of the vestal fire of democracy." The cabin assumed the significance of a manger as Wilson spoke of Lincoln's capacity to "comprehend all mankind." "The Sacred Mystery of Democracy," in Braden, ed., *Building the Myth*, pp. 178-179.

[7] Michael Davis, *The Image of Lincoln in the South* (Knoxville, 1971), p. 119.

Albert Bledsoe, the editor of the *Southern Review*, borrowed upon Lamon's biography of Lincoln to reach an assessment remarkably similar to contemporary psychological studies of the Great Emancipator: Lincoln's success "has been the wonder of all nations. . . .perhaps the wonder of all ages," but it was the outcome of a "ruling passion" not based upon a love of freedom or hatred of oppression but rather a thirst for personal distinction. Without a faith in God, "the one thought. . . which haunted and tormented his soul, was the reflection that he had done nothing, and might die without doing anything, to link his name and memory forever with the events of his time."[8]

The existence of these two traditions with their many variations was complicated by the re-evaluation that both Lincoln and the Civil War were undergoing in the Depression years. It is difficult to define a "Depression Lincoln" before FDR successfully appropriated his own version late in the decade. Yet most of the various reinterpretations which FDR confronted made his task an extremely difficult one.

Herbert Hoover attempted to close off any attempt to fashion a connection between the crisis of the Civil War and the Depression when in a radio broadcast on Lincoln's birthday he warned Americans who would use Lincoln as a justification for the creation of a "centralized government." "If Lincoln were living" he would seek solutions which provided "opportunity" for every person "to rise to that highest achievement of which he is capable" and oppose any policies which would lead to a "superstate where every man becomes the servant of the State and real liberty is lost."[9]

Hoover's Whig Lincoln, whose rise from humble beginnings epitomized policies of self reliance, was given a different interpretation by both the progressive and Marxist scholarship which dominated the thirties. To men like Charles Beard, the Civil War was indeed a "second American revolution," but both its origins and result involved an "arrangement of the classes, and the accumulation and distribution of wealth." The war provided the avenue for the rise to power of "northern

---

[8] Ibid., p. 125.

[9] William Starr Meyers, ed., *The State Papers and Other Public Writings of Herbert Hoover,* 2 vols. (Garden City, 1934), vol. 1, pp. 500, 504.

capitalists and free farmers."[10] Thus from the "realist" perspective of the progressive, Lincoln was an agent of the domination of capital. Marxists, too, tended to conceptualize the Civil War as an American instance of primitive accumulation, but searched for revolutionary lessons. For Louis Hacker the Civil War became a kind of American version of the Russian experience in 1905 with Southerners as "counter revolutionists." Hacker credited the North for its determination to engage in what Lincoln had called a "people's war." The pattern of post-bellum economic growth had also produced "the growth and discipline" of a working class which now stood poised to take power in the present "revolutionary situation." Both progressives and Marxists formally assigned little weight to individual acts in history, but some began to explore the policies and personalities of those to the "left" of Lincoln, like Wendell Phillips, who connected chattel to wage slavery.[11]

Southern commentators kept the anti-Lincoln tradition alive during the Depression. Edgar Lee Master's furiously negative biography of Lincoln attempted to dispel the Horatio Alger motif by suggesting that Lincoln's origins were so disgusting that they produced the model demagogue.[12] Masters compared Lincoln to Robespierre. Both men acted solely from cruelty, ambition and ruthlessness. "Armed with the theology of a rural Methodist" which he took from "the superstition of Pigeon Creek," Lincoln "crushed the principles of free government" through the use of "a dramatized Jehovah as a celebrant of horrible doctrines of sin and atonement." Other Southerners reiterated Masters' themes. Frank L. Owsley's essay in the manifesto, "I'll Take My Stand," described the legacy of the Civil War in terms of a Northern impulse to consciously destroy Southern culture and defiantly refused to accept the "self righteous Northern legend," asserted by Lincoln in his second inaugural, "which makes the South the war criminal."[13]

---

[10] Charles A. Beard and Mary R. Beard, *The Rise of American Civilization*, 2 vols. (New York, 1927), vol. 2, pp. 51-53.

[11] Louis Hacker, "Revolutionary America," *Harper's Magazine* (March, 1935), p. 444; V. F. Calverton, "The American Revolutionary Tradition," *Scribner's Magazine* (May 1934), p. 354.

[12] Edgar Lee Masters, *Lincoln: The Man* (New York, 1931).

[13] Frank L. Owsley, "The Irrepressible Conflict," in *I'll Take My Stand* (New York, 1930), p. 68.

The rebuttals of the Southerners might have been seen in what historian Don Fehrenbacher has called the "lonely splendor" of the anti-Lincoln tradition had not so many prominent historians begun to undertake a skeptical assessment of the inevitability of the civil war and Lincoln's missed opportunities as peace-maker.[14] Albert Beveridge's influential biography of Lincoln, published in 1928, argued that the war was not inevitable. Emanuel Hertz argued in his 1931 biography that the lesson of Lincoln actually rested with his anti-war message: "If Lincoln were alive today and in a position of power, he would prevent the contamination of the United States by union with people who thrive on war, who pray for war, and whose business is war." James G. Randall, writing on the eve of American participation in a war in Europe urged Americans to re-examine the civil war by ignoring the "splendor of battle flags" and focusing on war as "organized murder." Gilbert H. Barnes and Avery Craven portrayed abolitionist leaders as irresponsible and suggested that war guilt rested with their radical moralism. George Fort Milton's 1934 biography of Stephen Douglas attempted to rehabilitate Lincoln's famous opponent by contending that Lincoln had adopted a "sectional" perspective while Douglas offered a "national" one.[15] Milton was careful not to directly attack Lincoln, but if Douglas were genuinely committed to avoiding war through reason and compromise, the reader was left to ask what role Lincoln had played.

Presidents, of course, do not imitate leadership exemplars on the basis of current historiography. But the Depression biographies and histories of Lincoln and the Civil War represented a continuation of a generational re-examination of Lincoln in American political culture. Radical Depression scholarship and the antecedent progressive assessments reflected and crystallized doubts about the viability of Lincoln as a model. Did he represent the triumph of capital under whose rule

---

[14] Don E. Fehrenbacher, *Lincoln in Text and Context* (Stanford, 1987), p. 212.

[15] Albert J. Beveridge, *Abraham Lincoln, 1809-1858* (New York, 1928); Emanuel Hertz, *Abraham Lincoln: A New Portrait* (New York, 1931), p. 409 (Hertz used a quote by Lincoln against the Mexican war to support his assertion); Gilbert Hobbs Barnes, *The Antislavery Impulse, 1830-1844* (New York, 1933); Avery Craven, *The Repressible Conflict* (Baton Rouge, 1939); James G. Randall, "The Blundering Generation," *Mississippi Valley Historical Review,* vol. 27 (June 1940), p. 27; George Fort Milton, "The Eve of Conflict" (1934) (New York, 1963).

Americans were now suffering? Or was he, as Hoover argued, a beacon against those who would create a new tyranny through governmental regimentation? Was indeed Lincoln largely irrelevant compared to the enormous economic forces which determined the fate of nations? Did Lincoln work hard enough to avoid war? If FDR reached back to reconstruct a Lincoln to imitate could he convince the American people that he deserved to be compared to the Black Easter Lincoln? How could the Civil War Lincoln be portrayed in the face of anti-war sentiment? Would an adoption of the populist Lincoln center questions about race that had been submerged by the New Deal coalition?

"Roosevelt is Grim/Quotes Lincoln. . ."

The liabilities of the Lincoln exemplar were as clear in 1938-1939 as they had been in 1932-33. It was not just that Lincoln had been a Republican or that FDR was from Dutchess County, New York, not New Salem, Illinois, nor that Hyde Park was a whole world away from Pigeon Creek. Roosevelt could manage these differences as he cleared new ground for new policies. He had done as much in his employment of the Andrew Jackson metaphor. The towering liability was that Lincoln—any biographer's Lincoln—had become a *sui generis* in American culture. There was, of course, only one Jefferson as well. But since most Americans naturally spoke in Jeffersonian dialect, the exemplar was the national language. Admittedly, Jackson was a rarer ideological persona, but copies of populist protest had already appeared sporadically before FDR appropriated the exemplar in 1936.

Lincoln was different. The Black Easter Lincoln had created an image of a leader unlike any accorded by Americans. No event in American history even approached the tragedy of the Civil War. Generational memories were still orally transmitted as FDR himself illustrated in 1938 when scores of veterans from both armies arrived in Gettysburg to participate in the dedication of a Federal memorial. Lincoln had provoked and justified that war, and his speeches, memorized by school children, outlined the principles of the regime under the threat of disintegration. To draw upon Lincoln as an exemplar required not only a crisis as extreme as civil war (and save revolution or invasion, no more cataclysmic event exists for a nation state), but also required the exploration of symbols of redemption and unity rarely employed with such force in American political culture. Failure to convince Americans of the symmetry with a current crisis and a Lincolnian resolution could raise questions of usurpation, questions that are submerged in the Black Easter interpretation although they were a central theme of the critical tradition regarding Lincoln and formed a subtext in the Depression analyses. Roosevelt, particularly after the Supreme Court battle and the purges, was especially vulnerable on this point.

During the president's Jacksonian turn, Lincoln had been used as a supplement to the populism of the general. In his 1935 press conference on the Court, Roosevelt mentioned the Dred Scott decision and Lincoln's opposition to it. In 1936 he had noted that Lincoln could not have come from "any class that did not know, through daily struggle, the grim realities of life. . ." Part of his 1938 Jackson Day address was devoted to Lincoln as a man "scorned for his uncouthness, his simplicity, his homely stories and his solicitude for the little man." Lincoln's enemies were similar to Jackson's—and Roosevelt's "gold speculators in Wall Street," "a minority unwilling to support their people and their government unless the government would leave them free to pursue their private gains."[16]

During the 1938 primaries FDR made direct comparisons to Lincoln *post factum*. In 1787 there was a "grave danger that the states would never become a nation." "In the time of Lincoln. . . a tragic division threatened to become lasting." In 1933 another "test" had come.[17] This imitation of Lincoln actually represented something of a different kind of "test" on Roosevelt's part. FDR seems to have been engaged more in testing the imitation of the Black Easter Lincoln since the invocation of crises past avoided direct comparison with current conduct. Roosevelt in 1933 had acted like Lincoln did in 1860. In his 1938 Jackson Day speech, FDR was careful to disassociate himself (and Lincoln) from the aftermath of the Civil War. "Lincoln, too, fought for democracy," FDR told

---

[16] Franklin D. Roosevelt, *Public Papers and Addresses of Franklin D. Roosevelt* (New York, Octogon, 1938-1950), p. 222 (1936), pp. 40-41 (1938).

[17] *Public Papers* (1938), p. 520.

his audience, "and had he lived the South would have been allowed to rehabilitate itself on the basis of morals instead of being 'reconstructed' by martial law and carpetbaggers." He also suggested that there might not have been the "uninspired commercial era" after the war had Lincoln's moral leadership been followed.[18] Thus FDR skirted the bulk of the Nashville critique of Lincoln and the war and seemed to implicitly accept the progressive conclusion of the conflict as a victory by capital.

In 1940, however, a new use of Lincoln emerged. At the Jackson Day dinner Roosevelt announced that he planned to talk to his audience not only about Jackson but about Lincoln as well. The purpose of examining past leaders was not to advance the cause of party. "Yes, the devil can quote past statesmen as readily as he can quote Scriptures. . ." FDR's purpose was to examine "the motives behind leaders of the past" to see how they completed "the big job that their times demanded to be done."

The president cited three personal heroes in addition to Jackson. Jefferson, of course, made the list, but there was uncharacteristic criticism of the Sage of Monticello from the president. Jefferson was "a hero to me despite the fact that the theories of the French revolutionists at times overexcited his practical judgement." If Jefferson's radicalism was to be noted and condemned, Hamilton, the negative exemplar of the New Deal, was now added to the ranks of FDR's heroes: "he is a hero because he did the job which then had to be done—to bring stability out of chaos of currency and banking difficulties." Lincoln was the next hero. He had preserved the union and possibly the "united country that we all live in today."[19]

This Jackson Day speech represented something of an anomaly in FDR's traditional use of the event. It is a transitional address in Roosevelt's move toward the Lincoln exemplar. Jackson had been a perfect theme for these speeches. He was very much a partisan symbol and from 1936 on FDR had been able to employ Jacksonian populism to create the unique class base of the second New Deal. But these same

---

[18] Ibid., p. 41.

[19] Ibid., (1940), pp. 26, 29-30.

assets had become clear liabilities by 1940. In fact, after 1941 the Jackson Day address itself was abandoned entirely. The Rooseveltian addendum on Jackson, middle class apprehensiveness as the basis for a new social contract, had eroded on all sides. Rexford Tugwell's comment about farmers in 1938 (they "had a treaty with the New Deal, but it was a very limited one. . .") held for the political situation in general.[20] The "new faces" of the Seventy-Sixth Congress, men like Robert Taft and John Bricker, had moved offensively and were attempting to use that same apprehensiveness for their cause.

As significant, moreover, was the growing threat from abroad. By January of 1940, FDR could no longer concentrate on domestic concerns, using the international situation as a metaphor to attack corporate elites as he had done in 1936. A European war had begun; just months later Norway, Denmark, Holland, Belgium and France were to fall to the Nazis. The Jacksonian exemplar, with its class appeals, thrived on division. What FDR needed was unity, hence the selection of heroes that contributed to unity, men who "did the job which then had to be done." Jefferson's radicalism was presented in 1936 as a figment of aristocratic imagination.

In 1940, FDR carefully separated himself from this failure of Jefferson's "practical judgement." Jackson is praised for saving "the economic democracy of the Union for its westward expansion." And Hamilton, while he may always have had a bureaucratic presence in the Jefferson-Jackson New Deal, had never been positively acknowledged. But Hamilton was a nationalist and in 1940 the president, despite his comments about the devil's quoting, looked where he could for support. In fact, in September, Roosevelt returned once more to the Jefferson–Hamilton debate and acknowledged the "high motives and disinterestedness of Hamilton and his school." He would not openly betray Jefferson but he admitted this time that only "if government could be guaranteed to be kept always on the high level of unselfish service suggested by Hamilton there would be nothing to fear." The argument is the same as that in 1932 and 1936 but there is a sympathy now for Hamilton's effort to

---

[20] Rexford Tugwell, *The Democratic Roosevelt* (Baltimore, 1957), p. 403.

create a tradition of national service. Lincoln was the remaining hero discussed. FDR dismissed partisan affiliation: "I do not know which party Lincoln would belong to if he were alive in 1940. . .a new party had to be created before he could be elected President." In any case, Lincoln was "the legitimate property of all parties—of every man and woman and child in every part of our land."

The addition of Lincoln to the list of New Deal heroes (FDR's introduction to the 1938 volume of official addresses, written in 1941, cites a "liberal party" throughout American history that begins with Jefferson and included Jackson, Lincoln, Theodore Roosevelt, and Wilson) represented only one aspect of an ideological change that began in 1940. The Lincoln exemplar was used far more thoroughly than as a general legitimating device. The cultural openings that Lincoln had personally created were consciously studied and copied. The shift from "Doctor New Deal" to "Doctor Win the War," as contained in the slogan the president recommended to the popular press, reflected a series of options carefully selected, at least as far as events permitted.

In 1939-1940, FDR was willing to directly imitate the Black Easter Lincoln. Carl Sandburg's second volume of his Lincoln biography, *The War Years*, was published in 1939. The work in many ways reflected a shift from the radical perspective in America. Shortly after its publication Archibald MacLeish castigated the irresponsibility of a generation of intellectuals for focusing their energies on "revolt" rather than "acceptance and belief."[21]

Sandburg's wartime Lincoln epitomized this change of focus. Lincoln represented the "triumph of democratic will and the incredible burden of its translation into concerted action by a president: "To think incessantly of blood and steel, steel and blood. . .of a mystic cause carried aloft and sung on dripping and crimson bayonet points—to think so and thus across nights and months folding up into years, was a wear-

---

[21] Archibald MacLeish, "The Irresponsibles," *Nation* (May 18, 1940), pp. 619-623. Also see Lewis Mumford's "Faith for Living" (New York, 1940). Both MacLeish and Mumford had expressed militant anti-war positions a few years earlier. "When America Goes to War: A Symposium," *Modern Monthly* (June-July, 1935). See Philip Abbott, *"Leftward Ho!": V. F. Calverton and American Radicalism* (Westport, 1993) for an account of the rapid switch on the part of the American intelligensia on the war question.

ing and grinding that brought questions. What was this teaching and who learns from it and where does it lead?"[22] When a group of students arrived for a meeting at the White House in the spring of 1940 to complain about the guns and butter problem, the president halted the barrage of criticism by asking one questioner, "Young man, I think you are very sincere. Have you read Carl Sandburg's *Lincoln?*" When the man answered negatively, Roosevelt responded thusly:

> I think the impression was that Lincoln was a pretty sad man because he could not do all he wanted to do at one time, and I think you will find examples where Lincoln had to compromise to gain a little something. He had to compromise to make a few gains. Lincoln was one of the unfortunate people called a 'politician' but he was a politician who was practical enough to get a great many things for his country. He was sad because he could not get it all at once. And nobody can.

Privately FDR had referred to college pacifists as "shrimps"; publicly he took on the role as the suffering leader.[23]

Robert Sherwood, the author of the popular Broadway play, "Abe Lincoln of Illinois," was hired as a speech writer for FDR late in 1940. Viewing the film version of Sherwood's play, FDR had requested copies of two of Lincoln's speeches from the debates with Douglas. On election eve, as part of a nation-wide radio program, Carl Sandburg offered an emotional eulogy to Lincoln and closed with his support for Roosevelt. Sandburg implied that this election was much like the one in 1864, Lincoln was much like the prophet Samuel, and FDR was much like Lincoln. The Lincoln biographer spoke as an independent who belonged to "no political party, no faction, no political group open or secret," who recognized Franklin Roosevelt as earlier generations recognized Lincoln, as "not a perfect man and yet more precious than gold." On election day Stephen Vincent Benet published a poem in the *New York Post* which spoke of leaders who knew "the tides and ways of the people/As

[22] Carl Sandburg, *Abraham Lincoln: The War Years* (New York, 1939), vol. 2, p. 333.

[23] James MacGregor Burns, *Roosevelt: The Lion and the Fox* (New York, 1956), pp. 422-423.

Abe Lincoln knew the wind on the prairies." One was "A country squire from Hyde Park with a Harvard accent/Who never once failed the people/And whom the people won't fail."[24]

There were doubters. Raymond Moley, now a political enemy of the president, complained that college youth were being bombarded with what he characterized as "new cliches": capitalism has failed, a dollar spent is a dollar earned, Congress is terrible and Roosevelt is greater than Abraham Lincoln. Herbert Hoover noted that it was no coincidence that both Earl Browder and FDR claimed Lincoln as "a founder of their faiths." Both attempts were unfounded: "The spirit of Abraham Lincoln has not joined the New Deal." Willkie, during an election campaign visit to Springfield, denied that either he or the president deserved comparison to Lincoln. But the press as a whole had begun to explore the analogy on their own. Max Lerner, in the *Nation*, asked "How much Lincoln does Roosevelt have in him?" Proof of the success of the attempted parallel could be found in *Time's* tribute to Roosevelt as "Man of the Year" in 1942, in which the comparison to Lincoln was accepted.[25]

How correct was the Lincoln–FDR leadership analogy? The parallels in themselves were only broadly suggestive without further ideological support. The U.S. was not in the midst of a civil war. While the debate about intervention was widespread it carried none of the intensity of that of 1864 or even 1860. FDR spoke of the "troubled times" in the past when Lincoln "year after war-torn year. . .sheltered in his great heart the truest aspirations of a country rent in twain."[26] Such was not the case with the president 80 years later. The inevitability of war seemed a common assumption, but still most Americans hoped to avoid it. Both Willkie and FDR were the peace candidates in 1940, with Willkie charging first that FDR was an appeaser and then that he was

---

[24] Sandburg's speech is reprinted in "Home Front Memo" (New York, 1943), pp. 29-30. For FDR's relationships with Sherwood and Sandburg, see: Alfred Haworth Jones, *Roosevelt's Image Makers* (Port Washington, 1974).

[25] *Newsweek* (June 19, 1938), p. 56; *New York Times*, February 14, 1939, p. 14; Ibid., October 19, 1940, p. 8; "Lerner, How Much of Lincoln Does Roosevelt Have in Him?," *Nation* (June 22, 1940), pp. 753-754; *Time* (January 5, 1942).

[26] *Public Papers* (1940), p. 99.

secretly leading America to war. When FDR said in Boston at the end of October that "your boys are not going to be sent in any foreign war" he may have said so reluctantly and under electoral pressures. Nevertheless, the statement hardly showed Lincolnian leadership—at least as understood by the mythic readings—even though Lincoln himself had been infuriatingly vague about his reaction to secession as president-elect, a point, perhaps, that led later to the kind of charges that would suggest that Pearl Harbor was Roosevelt's version of Fort Sumter. In more general terms, Roosevelt's leadership in foreign policy did not seem to support the slightest claim to the kind of action required by the Lincoln exemplar. It is true that he campaigned for the League in 1920, but his reaction to Hearst's demands in 1932 did not parallel Lincoln's to Andrew Greeley in 1864. The rationale of the Good Neighbor policy was vaguely isolationist and FDR made no principled stand against the Neutrality Acts until 1939. When his 1937 quarantine speech received negative reaction he abandoned the statement; his reactions to the crisis in Munich could fairly be termed as appeasement.[27] Perhaps the most successful foreign policy address FDR had delivered was his 1936 Chautauqua speech, an emotional anti-war statement. Lincoln's career wasn't without inconsistencies, but from his early addresses to the senate debates, one can establish a conception of his developing vision on the slavery question and the Union. It is difficult to do so with Roosevelt.

Robert E. Sherwood did his best to defend the 1860 parallel. He noted Lincoln's opposition to war in 1848 as a Whig and his early indifference to slavery. Not until "Lincoln saw that the spirit of slavery was spreading—from Missouri to Kansas and Nebraska" did he turn from an "appeaser into a fighter." In this respect "Lincoln's attitude in the years before the Civil War paralleled the development of the attitude of the whole American people in the years before 1940."[28]

---

[27] For discussion of this point, see: Robert A. Divine, *Roosevelt and World War II* (New York, 1952), pp. 21-23; Burns, *Roosevelt: The Lion and the Fox*, pp. 386-387.

[28] Robert E. Sherwood, *There Shall Be No Night* (New York, 1940), pp. xxii-xxiv. Sherwood's statement was itself something of a confessional. He too had been an isolationist and an "appeaser" until 1939. "Idiot's Delight," written in 1935, was an anti-war play. If FDR had been an isolationist as well, he still kept good company with Lincoln.

Roosevelt's new speech writer had a point—especially if stated somewhat differently. The parallel to Lincoln was literally awkward and even fictitious. But the attempt to create the parallel itself indicated a change in the president's leadership. The adoption of Lincoln certainly had immediate partisan objectives but it also suggested a burden that FDR had implied he would undertake. "Judge me by the standards of Lincoln" involved a risk and a certain element of moral responsibility. Moreover, it now rested with Roosevelt to make a case for action as Lincoln had done.

As we indicated, FDR had not pursued the full consequences of the Lincolnian exemplar in 1933 despite his stirring evocation in the inaugural. Now in returning to this crisis exemplar he turned to the grey days of 1933. Instructing Samuel Rosenman about the tone of the fireside chat that became known as the "arsenal of democracy" speech he said, "I tried to convey to the great mass of American people what the banking crisis meant to them in their daily lives. Tonight, I want to do the same thing, with the same people, in this new crisis that faces America."[29]

Here was FDR's own "crisis" in 1940. The problem that Lincoln and FDR both faced was in a broad sense a heritage of the Jeffersonian mind: both slavery and Nazi conquest challenged American beliefs in pluralism. There was a widespread conviction in antebellum America that slavery was wrong. The belief that fascism was an evil was even less uncontested. The question in both cases was how in terms of national policy could the evil be resisted. Lincoln forcefully attacked what he called "declared indifference" to slavery in his Peoria speech in 1854 and made it a recurrent theme in the great senate debates with Douglas. Roughly, he used three lines of argument. He appealed to the self interest of white citizens. He reminded his audience at Peoria that the opportunities in the territories would be diminished with the spread of slavery. "Slave States are places for poor white people to remove from, not remove to. New free States are the places for poor people to go to, and better their condition."[30]

---

[29] Samuel I. Rosenman, *Working with Roosevelt* (New York, 1952), p. 259.

[30] Roy P. Basler, et. al., *The Collected Works of Abraham Lincoln*, 8 vols. (New Brunswick, 1953-1955), vol. 2, p. 268.

He insisted that if slavery were a moral wrong, indifference was not a suitable policy. Douglas "could not say people have a right to do wrong." And finally, he argued that the major reason for the evil of slavery rested with the fact that it directly contradicted the moral base of the American regime. Lincoln found this base to rest with the Declaration of Independence. If slavery was accorded any status higher than necessity, the "first precept of our ancient faith" was repudiated. In his famous Springfield address Lincoln concluded that conflict would not cease "until a crisis shall have been reached and passed." America could not "endure permanently half slave and half free."[31]

FDR employed not only Lincoln vocabulary but Lincolnian arguments in his third term acceptance speech in Chicago. It was to a certain extent the ideological equivalent of Lincoln's Peoria address. FDR did not mention forgotten men or economic royalists in 1940. New Deal legislation was described simply as the result of a "growing sense of human decency." This sense was "confined to no groups or class"; it was an "urge of humanity" that could "by no means be labelled a war of class against class." Rather it was a "war in which all classes are joining in the interest of a sound and enduring democracy."[32]

FDR claimed that much still needed to be done in terms of human decency, but now the task was entrusted to "poor and rich alike." There were still enemies. "Appeasers and fifth columnists" charged the president with "hysteria and war-mongering." But these were men and women who were unwilling to extend the principles of human decency to the democracies of the world. In the height of the Jacksonian period of the New Deal, Roosevelt had declared that economic royalists were "aliens to the spirit of democracy." "Let them emigrate," he told crowds at Madison Square Garden in 1936. In 1940 he spoke of "selfish and greedy people" whose desires for money led them to "compromise with those who seek to destroy all democracies everywhere, including here."[33]

---

[31] Ibid., p. 461.

[32] *Public Papers* (1940), pp. 298-300.

[33] Ibid., pp. 301-302.

In 1861 Lincoln had asserted that the Civil War was a "people's contest." FDR did not in 1940 call for armed conflict, although he did speak of military readiness and he did claim Lincoln as the authority for the truth that democracy can thrive only when it enlists the devotion of the common people. More generally, all the basic principles of the Lincoln exemplar were in place. If human decency was a principle of America's national identity, "our credo—unshakable to the end," then indifference to "free peoples resisting. . .aggression" was not possible. People do not have a right to do wrong. The ethical choice was "moral decency versus the firing squad."[34]

In September, the president repeated Lincoln themes. To a Teamsters Union Convention he reiterated his pledge of no foreign wars except in cases of attack, but he reminded labor leaders that it was in their self interest to "loyally cooperate" in the task of munitions making. "In country after country in other lands, labor unions have disappeared as the iron hand of the dictator has taken command. Only in free lands have free labor unions survived."[35] On registration day for selective service he announced that "we cannot remain indifferent to the philosophy of force now rampant in the world." To the Jeffersonian–Jacksonian principles of "equal rights, equal privileges, equal opportunities," Roosevelt added "equal service." "Universal service will not only bring greater preparedness. . .but a wider distribution of tolerance and understanding." It would "bring an appreciation of each other's dignity as American citizens."

In October, drawing the first numbers for the draft, the president referred to "our democratic army." At the University of Pennsylvania he reminded scholars of the fate of books under dictatorships as he also did at a dedication of three new schools in New York. In a letter read to the World's Fair on the 75th anniversary of the ratification of the thirteenth amendment, he noted the irony that in just three quarters of a century there were now forces who would "return the human family to that state

[34] Ibid., p. 302.

[35] Ibid., p. 408.

of slavery" from which emancipation came through the Thirteenth Amendment.[36]

"In his hands, our traditions are not safe"

Self interest, a people's war, the immortality of indifference—these arguments were repeated throughout the campaign of 1940. Opinion polls did suggest a sympathy for FDR's new Lincolnism. People were concerned about the fate of the world's peoples; they were concerned about the military security of the U.S. They seemed to have appreciated national as well as individual self-interest in a free Europe and they were willing to provide aid to meet these concerns. They were not yet convinced however of the necessity of war itself. Perhaps neither was FDR himself. But his immediate political situation required a delicacy that made the complete presentation of Lincoln as exemplar difficult.

The president confided to many that Willkie was the strongest candidate that he faced in a presidential election. Not that the Republican candidate did not have his problems. His August acceptance speech theme of unleashing the bourgeoisie ("Only the strong can be free and only the productive can be strong") was outstripped by world events. His early attacks on Roosevelt as an appeaser had been effectively rebutted by the president, so much so in fact that Roosevelt continued to reply to them after Willkie changed his tactic. FDR's Madison Square Garden speech, itself a reversion to the Jacksonian exemplar in the campaign, thrilled the audience with its repetition of "Martin, Barton and Fish" on national defense. Willkie was also hardly the darling of the powerful Republican right wing. The Willkie clubs reflected the strategy of treating the Republican party "as an allied but somewhat alien power."[37] But by mid-October, Willkie's campaign seemed to have mounted a real challenge. And that challenge was based in part on the liabilities of the Lincoln exemplar.

[36] Ibid., pp. 408, 432-433, 436, 439, 472.

[37] Burns, *Roosevelt: The Lion and the Fox*, p. 433.

After September, Willkie did not move toward a Douglas position, and after Pearl Harbor he was the polar opposite of a Clement Vallandigham. But the Republican candidate attempted to assume the role of the peace candidate, and the only peace candidate, in 1940. In Kansas he said, "I warn you—and I say this in dead earnest—because of some fine speeches about humanity, you return this administration to office, you will be serving under a totalitarian government before the long third term is finished." Three days later in Los Angeles, he told a crowd: "I hope and pray that he [FDR] remembers his pledge [no American participation in foreign wars] better than he did the one in 1932. If he does not, you better get ready to get on the transports. . ." At the end of October he predicted that should FDR be elected America would be at war in six months.[38]

Willkie, early in the campaign, had attempted to make the third term issue a major feature of his strategy for election. FDR had hoped to run as a Lincoln against Hitler. Willkie's shift toward an isolationist position sharpened his third term argument because in part it focused upon the liabilities of the Lincoln exemplar that Roosevelt himself had chosen. We mentioned the critical strand in Lincoln interpreters. While it is difficult to determine if this critique was explicitly part of the American mind when it contemplated Lincoln, it is possible to say that the employment of the Lincolnian exemplar does signal crisis, sacrifice, and the most demanding leadership. The equation of Lincoln with war and a war led against opposition is an inevitable part of the Lincoln symbol. Thus while the Lincoln exemplar amongst the general population probably contains no details about the Civil War president's suspension of habeas corpus and his appropriation of money unauthorized by Congress, by its very nature it does provide an opening for a critique. The president's "oratory, as defender of democracy conceals the fact that by his own meddling in international politics he encouraged the European conflagration," charged Willkie in an attempt to appeal to isolationist sentiment.[39]

[38] *New York Times,* September 17, 1940, p. 11; ibid., September 20, p. 1; ibid., November 1, 1940, p. 18.

[39] Ibid., September 15, 1940.

The organized isolationist forces in 1940 were a disparate group, including Communists, Midwestern progressives and ethnic groups with their own specific loyalties and animosities. The Willkie position permitted a common focus on FDR's use of executive power. The specter of dictatorship that formed a central part of New Deal opposition could not be raised against New Deal policies, which Willkie found had risen to the level of a consensus in 1940, but against participation in foreign wars. Willkie gained the support of Hiram Johnson, nearly gained support from Joe Kennedy, received (and rejected) support from Father Coughlin, gained support from Charles Lindbergh. But Willkie's real catch was the powerful, charismatic labor leader, John L. Lewis. Lewis had been sparring with Roosevelt for several years. It is not clear exactly why Lewis felt driven to support a corporate lawyer. The answer lies partly in Lewis' own Midwestern and immigrant background, his competitive relationship with FDR, his penchant for the big gamble (the CIO president closed his speech with a promise to resign if Roosevelt were re-elected). But Lewis did appear to genuinely feel that the independence of labor would be seriously threatened by war mobilization and that a "personal craving for power" rather than a concern for the worker was the driving force of FDR's policies. His October 25 speech before a national radio audience warned that the president's re-election "may create a dictatorship in this land." The address probably represented the psychological crest of the Willkie campaign.[40]

Willkie's shift from internationalist to isolationist is taken as a classic case of electoral opportunism. When asked by Senator Gerald P. Nye after the election if the Republican candidate still believed that the U.S. would be at war by April, Willkie responded by admitting that his prediction was "a bit of campaign oratory." Yet the fear of war in the fall of 1940 did permit Willkie to directly confront the New Deal in ways that neither Hoover or Landon had been able to do. In general, FDR had responded to charges that he would or had subverted the American system by exposing the attack as a disguised attempt at class domina-

---

[40] For an account of the speech and exploration of the Lewis decision to support Willkie, see Robert H. Zieger, *John L. Lewis: Labor Leader* (Boston, 1988), pp. 123-131, and Steve Neal, *Dark Horse: A Biography of Wendell Willkie* (New York, 1984), pp. 169-172.

tion. They only "seek the restoration of their selfish power" was the theme of the 1936 campaign. But to the extent to which the president had attempted to employ the Lincolnian exemplar of unity such responses were not available.

Willkie raised the parallel to European dictatorships early in the campaign. At Coffeyville he vividly described the bombing of London. "Gas and water mains are ripped open, houses are blown to pieces, women and children lie dead. . . " But something more was under attack in Britain and that was the "philosophy of democracy." Willkie paid tribute to this small town by autobiographically recounting his experiences as a history teacher at Coffeyville High School. He had "learned much more than I taught:"

> I learned that democracy is not what we call government. Democracy is the people. At school we learned these things. We got our first lessons in how to get along with others; we learned also gratitude; we learned how to play fair and we tasted the excitement of competition within the rules. We learned the meaning of companionship as well as the meaning of self-reliance and also in Sunday school and church we learned other things, and many other things in this Western country.[41]

The Coffeyville speech was of course part of the politician's traditional obeisance to the small town, one that both Hoover and Landon had also enacted. Willkie, too, was attempting to capture the Jeffersonian mind for his campaign. But he gave a special cast to this strategy. Hoover had praised the morality of Main Street only to warn against nostalgia for its economic and political forms. Landon focused upon rural and small town commitments to constitutionalism and free enterprise. For Willkie the small town was the repository of "freedom," "equality" and "democracy." The philosophy of democracy was nurtured and taught and preserved across generations at this level. "Our mothers taught us to be honest, polite, to be pleasant and kind. . .our fathers to be brave. . ." The New Dealers spoke in the language of democracy and portrayed themselves as "great 'defenders' of democracy," but they are

---

[41] *New York Times,* September 17, 1940, p. 15.

all "cynics who scoff at our simple virtues. . .and govern us with catch-phrases." They have used relief money to manipulate votes; they "terror-ize" their opponents by leaking untruths to newspapers; they "purge and purge" those who try to be independent of the "New Deal machine." Because they do not trust in a philosophy of democracy they "have concentrated power in their own hands." FDR "may not want dictator-ship," but "in his hands our traditions are not safe." He had "declared forty emergencies in the past seven years."[42]

In Peoria, Willkie argued that whenever democracies had existed in history—"the ancient Roman republic, Sparta, or Athens"—they fell when economic chaos came. So, too, in Germany when economic break-down occurred, the people turned to a paper hanger because their demo-cratic system would not work. Where was FDR when Germany fell?, Willkie asked. He was attacking the Supreme Court: "He tore this coun-try, this great united people to pieces when he might have exercised leadership." The policies of the New Deal set an example for the world and Willkie contended that Leon Blum modeled his policies on Roosevelt's and "took France to its wreckage."[43]

Later in the campaign Willkie suggested that not only had Roosevelt's policy failures promoted dictatorship abroad but that FDR himself was following a path toward dictatorship. Since he had been in office he had repeatedly declared emergencies (the count now was at 67) and "seized more power." "I will leave it to any student of our time whether this pattern I have described is not the pattern and the exact pattern of the decline in democracy in every country in the world where democracy has passed away." Now he was asking for more power, the violation of the "unwritten law" that prohibits a third term. This was a government that "treats our Constitution like a scrap of paper." This was a man who referred to an ambassador of the U.S. as "my ambassador." "Pretty soon it may be 'My Generals'. . . After a while it will be 'My People.'"[44]

[42] Ibid.

[43] Ibid., October 23, 1941, p. 26.

[44] Ibid., November 1, 1940, p. 18.

While Roosevelt was trying to argue that the choice the American people faced was a commitment to a world of democracies versus dictatorships, Willkie was contending that perhaps the president was on the other side. FDR was casting himself as the "indispensable leader," a "tactic used by tyrants throughout history and the world today." Those who opposed the New Deal needed no such urging, but for those who had doubts Willkie repeated the nine million unemployment figure as well as the suspicion that the current crisis in international affairs was, unlike the depression, avoidable. Could the President be trusted? Willkie's Jeffersonian "philosophy of democracy" suggested that Americans rely on themselves rather than indispensable leaders.

FDR recoiled before this ideological assault. In a letter to Rosenman he complained that those who "most loudly cried dictatorship against me would have been the first to justify the beginnings of dictatorship by somebody else." He planned five major campaign speeches between October 23 and November 2. For one, which was incorporated into his Cleveland address, he wrote notes for his writers to state why "FDR could not be a dictator, etc."[45] It would have been a fascinating debate had the president continued to pursue the Lincoln exemplar in the face of Willkie's Jeffersonian inspired one. But FDR did not. Not only did he pledge that "your boys are not going to be sent into any foreign wars," but he largely, although temporarily, abandoned Lincoln to return once again to Jefferson and Jackson. In Brooklyn, FDR returned to his 1936 response to his critics. His opponents had no conception of public happiness because they "measured prosperity only by the stock ticker," and in Cleveland he repeated the domestic themes of his second inaugural and charged that those who criticized the New Deal hoped to "weaken democracy" and "destroy the free man's faith in his own cause."[46]

There emerged in the final days of the campaign a neat oppositional symmetry in the ideological arguments of both candidates, despite the fact that both candidates had given in to opportunism on the question of American participation in the war in Europe. Willkie compared FDR's

---

[45] Rosenman, *Working With Roosevelt,* pp. 236, 245.

[46] *Public Papers* (1940), pp. 531, 532, 544.

motives and tactics to European dictators. FDR compared Willkie (or at least the groups supporting him) to European dictators. Aside from the White House contention that Willkie was the candidate preferred by Berlin, there was a whispering campaign about which the Republican candidate complained bitterly. Willkie was alleged to have a sister who married a Nazi officer and one Democratic senator asserted that the name on the family burial plot bore the German spelling "Wilcke."[47] Both arguments managed to evoke their share of terrors: a president who could not be trusted with American traditions and who regarded the constitution as a scrap of paper, and a reactionary opposition that had allied itself secretly with the far left in an unscrupulous attempt to achieve their dictatorial ends. Those who threatened democracy in both instances spoke as defenders of democracy.

"A nation is like a person"

FDR won the argument. Willkie immediately pledged support for Roosevelt and moved to an internationalist position. FDR had in the last weeks of the campaign portrayed the conflict in Europe as a class war. Immediately he returned to the Lincolnian model of national unity. It would be just over a year before America was to be a major participant in world war, but in the next eight weeks the president completed the application of the Lincoln exemplar to the international crisis.

The December 29, 1940 fireside chat began with the assertion that it was not a speech on war but national security: "the purpose of your President is to keep you now, and your children later, and your grandchildren much later, out of a last-ditch war for the preservation of American independence. . ." While Roosevelt admitted that there was a risk of war in making America "the great arsenal of democracy," the action was justified because "we and our. children will be saved the agony and suffering of war which others have had to endure." He repeated his campaign pledge: "there is no demand for sending an American expeditionary force outside our borders. There is no intention

---

[47] Neal, *Dark Horse,* pp. 161-165.

by any member of your government to send such a force. You can, therefore, nail any talk about sending armies to Europe as deliberate untruth."[48]

Yet despite these disavowals, the arsenal of democracy speech was very much the ideological equivalent of Lincoln's Springfield address. Lincoln had declared that the government "cannot endure permanently half slave and half free," that the discord in the nation would "not cease until a crisis shall have been reached and passed." FDR also spoke of crisis, one as great as that of 1860 (and 1932). Lincoln had argued that Douglas' "care not" policy could not maintain a status quo. Roosevelt stated the belief of some that "wars in Europe and in Asia are of no concern to us." He spoke of those "who want to see no evil and hear no evil, even though they knew in their hearts that evil exists." But the Nazi goal was world conquest. If Britain fell, Hitler would turn to this hemisphere. The U.S. "would be living at the point of a gun." "To survive in such a world we would have to convert ourselves permanently into a militaristic power on the basis of war economy. The U.S. was threatened with a modern form of slavery." The Axis proclamations were correct: "There can be no ultimate peace between their philosophy of government and our philosophy of government."[49]

A week later in his annual message to Congress, the President repeated his argument in military-political terms. The threat of war facing the country was unlike any except the civil war. FDR defended various American military actions in the past but admitted that even in World War I there was "only a small threat of danger to our own American future." But today "the future of all the American Republics is in danger." Without the protection of the British Navy, the U.S. would not immediately be subject to invasion but only because strategic bases would be required to facilitate troop landings. Thus the first phase of invasion would occur in Latin America through the activities of "secret agents and their dupes," just as it had already occurred in Norway. No negotiation is possible, despite those who "with sounding brass and

[48] *Public Papers* (1940), p. 640.

[49] Ibid., pp. 634-636.

tinkling cymbal preach the 'ism' of appeasement," for "no realistic American can expect from a dictator's peace international generosity."[50]

So imminent was the crisis that must be reached and passed in Roosevelt's image of the world situation that he also declared what amounted to war aims: "The first is freedom of speech and expression—everywhere in the world; the second is freedom of every person to worship God in his own way—everywhere in the world; the third is freedom from want. . .everywhere in the world; the fourth is freedom from fear. . .everywhere in the world."[51]

The "four freedoms" included in the Atlantic charter and repeated throughout the war are often interpreted as part of FDR's progressive heritage. The President had "picked up Woodrow Wilson's fallen banner, fashioned new symbols and programs to realize old ideals of peace and democracy. . ."[52] Indeed, FDR had already begun to elaborate a defense of America's participation in the World War as part of his attack on the isolationists and the charge that America had been drawn into the conflict by munitions dealers. But the four freedoms also owed much to the Lincoln exemplar. In his debates with Douglas, Lincoln had insisted that the principles of Jefferson's Declaration of Independence applied to African-Americans over his opponent's objections that he was extending the meaning of the document. Roosevelt's Jeffersonian-inspired freedoms were not only overlaid with New Deal understandings but also involved a globalization of the Declaration. "Everywhere in the world" constituted FDR's expansion of the document. When the president dictated the close of his Annual Message to his secretary, Rosenman was impressed with the way the "words seemed to roll off his tongue as though he had rehearsed them many times over." The first two formulations were derived directly from Jefferson. The "American invention" in 1776 was the key to understanding the current crisis of democracy.[53]

---

[50] Ibid., pp. 665, 666.

[51] Ibid., p. 672.

[52] Burns, *Roosevelt: Soldier of Freedom*, p. viii.

[53] *Public Papers*, (1940), p. 281. In this earlier formulation at a press conference, the president paired the various freedoms against the philosophy of the "corporate state."

"Freedom from want" entailed the New Deal reading of Jefferson that FDR had offered in his 1932 Commonwealth Club speech and freedom from fear was a reiteration of his famous first inaugural injunction.

Thus as Jefferson had been used as the ideological foundation of the early New Deal, his theories were now used as the goals of war. But as there were strains in using Jefferson for Hamiltonian ends in 1932-1933, there would be strains in using Jefferson for Lincolnian ends in 1940-41. Of course, Lincoln himself employed Jefferson for his war aims as well. Certainly Lincoln was confronted with the paradox more intensely and more often. The Civil War always had its critics. But FDR, however, could not escape the contradiction involved in employing Jeffersonian freedoms, however modified by New Deal values, for a challenge that required unity, centralization and national sacrifice.

The two exemplars are artfully merged in the third inaugural. Lincoln as well as Washington are presented as symbols of unity and order. "In Washington's day the task of the people was to create and weld together a Nation. In Lincoln's day the task of the people was to preserve the nation from disruption from within. FDR announced that his task was to save the nation from "disruption from without."[54]

Lincoln's great contribution to political thought centered around his admonition, stated as early as the Lyceum address, that time was the great destroyer of free government. The "jealousy, envy, and avarice, incident to our nature," are only "smothered and rendered inactive" during a crisis. Only a conscious, rational re-dedication to the principles of the regime can defend against the "silent artillery of time."[55] Roosevelt had begun to explore this theme in his third term campaign. "Remember 1932" was important as a simple campaign slogan, but it also served as an occasion to remind Americans that it is in the memory of crisis that a people prolong their freedom. In his inaugural, the president declared that "the lives of nations are determined not by the count of years, but by the lifetime of the human spirit." A man's life was "three

---

[54] *Public Papers* (1941), p. 3.

[55] *Collected Works*, 1, p. 115.

score and ten; a little more, a little less." But the life of a nation is determined by the "measure of its will to live."[56]

The central metaphor of the inaugural was the assertion that a nation was "like a person." The metaphor's long tradition in political thought and all its variations—from Plato's to the medieval concept of a "great chain of being" to Hobbes' mechanistic formulation—is designed to emphasize unity and order as the central aims of politics. The Lincolnian interpretation that a nation could not be divided on basic principles, it could not remain "half slave and half free," was generally consistent with the claim that there are certain elements of a political system that cannot be subject to pluralism. The house divided metaphor employed by Lincoln evoked an image far more complex than that of the literal one of a dwelling. Lincoln himself had experimented with the more literal aspects of architectural imagery before he focused upon the Biblical source which raised the point, spoken by Jesus himself, that confusion and fear are the consequences of conflict and division.[57]

Roosevelt's formulation takes on Hegelian tones. A nation, like a person, has a body that must be "fed and clothed and housed." A nation has a mind that "must know itself" and understand the "hopes and needs of its neighbors." But most of all a nation, like a person, has a soul, "something deeper, something more, larger than the sum of its parts." This aspect of a nation was the most important of the three and requires "the most sacred guarding of its present." A nation that loses its spirit loses its will to live, and FDR asserted that since the spirit of America was "born of the multitude of those who came from many lands" and represented the culmination of democratic struggle from the "ancient life or early peoples," it must speak to other nations—"the enslaved, as well as the free."[58]

Roosevelt was very much aware of the claims that fascism represented a "New Order." He had attacked this idea in his acceptance speech, charging that "tyranny is the oldest and most discredited rule

---

[56] Charles B. Strozier, *Lincoln's Quest for Union* (New York, 1982), pp. 177-181.

[57] *Public Papers* (1941), pp. 4-6.

[58] Ibid.

known to history," and that the rise of dictatorships was "only a relapse, a relapse into ancient history." Sherwood discussed with the president Anne Lindbergh's best seller, *The Wave of the Future,* remarking, "I certainly wish we could use that terrible phrase. . ." FDR replied, "Why not?" and included the Lindbergh argument in the address: "There are men who believe that democracy, as a form of government and a frame of life, is limited or measured by a kind of mystical and artificial fate—that, for some unexplained reason, tyranny and slavery have become the surging wave of the future—and freedom is an ebbing tide."[59]

The third inaugural claimed that the U.S. was, to use Hegelian language, a world historical nation. This was not a new assertion. But now America as "novus ordo seclorum" was interpreted in global terms even more far reaching that the Wilsonian claim that the goal of WWI was to "make the world safe for democracy." Unless the spirit of America defeated the spirit of tyranny, the spirit of America would perish, although the nation's "body and mind" might live on for a while "constricted in an alien world." Here was a position as demanding and crisis-ridden as Lincoln's house divided interpretation of the problem of slavery. But if the spirit of America must become absolute, the spirit itself was a spirit of localism, pluralism, political restraint, and freedom. The spirit was "written into the Magna Carta, the Mayflower Compact, the Declaration of Independence, the Constitution." The spirit of America spoke through "our daily lives, through the processes of governing in the sovereignties of 48 states," through our "counties," "cities," "towns," and "villages." It is true, of course, that there are principles and practices that so affront the nature of a free people that they cannot be tolerated. If fascism (and chattel slavery in Lincoln's time) did not qualify as the outer limit of pluralism then no principles and practices could. But one can still ask if in Roosevelt's formulation, the American spirit that was to protect freedom had become so generalized and so absolute as to become detached from the actual life of a free society which after all is one in which many voices speak.

---

[59] Rosenman, *Working With Roosevelt,* p. 270.

In the months before Pearl Harbor the president repeated his commitment to Jeffersonian ends. He repeated the four freedoms, reminding his audience that should America fail these would "become forbidden things for centuries." He told labor leaders that should fascism fail to be stopped "trade unions would become historical relics and collective bargaining a joke." He assured farmers that "there is no call to plow up the plains." He commended the savings stamp approach to the financing of defense: "It is national and it is homey at the same time." He asked what would a Jeffersonian America look like if Hitler were to defeat Britain: "Will our children, too, wander off, goose-stepping in search of new gods?" He distinguished between "obedience and loyalty." "Obedience can be obtained and enforced in a dictatorship by the use of threat or extortion or blackmail. . ." Loyalty, on the other hand, was far different. "It springs from the mind that is given the facts, that retains ancient ideals and proceeds without coercion to give support to its own government."[60]

But what of those who did question when given the facts, who complained that decisions were being rendered too fast? Here the spirit of America spoke of "appeasers," "defeatists," "back stairs manufacturers of panic," "propagandists, defeatists and dupes, protected as they are by our fundamental civil liberties. . ." In an April press conference he responded to those who questioned the feasibility of Lend Lease thusly: "Now, I don't call that good Americanism." Those asking for negotiation were referred to as "Vallandighams."[61]

In August, the president paused in the middle of a press conference, pulled out Sandburg's *Lincoln: The War Years,* and read two passages. One, made in 1862, was a complaint that "the people have not yet made up their minds that we are at war with the South." The other was reported to take place a year later. It, too, was a complaint directed toward McClellan and his supporters: "They have no idea that the War is to be

---

[60] *Public Papers* (1941), pp. 44, 666, 129, 184.

[61] Ibid., pp. 62, 83, 138. The term "Vallandighams" refers to former Ohio Congressman Clement Vallandigham, who was the most notorious Southern sympathizer in the North. In May 1863, in an effort to obtain the Democratic nomination for governor, he so vehemently attacked "King Lincoln" during his speeches that Maj. Gen. Ambrose Burnside unwisely arrested him.

carried on and put through by hard, tough fighting, that it will hurt somebody; and no headway is going to be made while this delusion lasts." FDR noted what he called an "interesting parallel. . .Lincoln's belief that this country hadn't waked up to the fact that they had a war to win, and Lincoln saw what was going on." When a reporter asked how his lead ought to read, the president answered: "I'd say, 'President quotes Lincoln—And Draws Parallel.'"[62] In September he told the nation that those who ask for negotiation "ask me to become the modern Benedict Arnold. . ." Then there was the language of totality: "single-mindedness," "no divisions of party or section," "total effort" "weapons of freedom," "total defense," "deep duty," "the battle lines of democracy." In March, after the passage of Lend Lease, the president formally declared that the "great debate" was over: "It was not limited to the halls of Congress. It was argued in every newspaper, on every wave length, over every cracker barrel in all the land; and it was finally settled and decided by the American people themselves." Now that the decision had been made there was to be an "end of any attempts at appeasement in our land; the end of urging us to get along with dictators; the end of compromise with tyranny and the forces of oppression." The decision "is binding on us all. And the world is no longer in doubt."[63]

Conclusion

To the extent to which Franklin Roosevelt followed Machiavelli's advice about the prudent archer in 1939-41, his speeches illustrate both the assets and liabilities of Lincoln as an exemplary figure in American political culture and presidential policy making. In aiming high, the president undertook a risk in 1939, not only in terms of his own fortunes as a political leader but in terms of the consequences for the nation at large. That FDR briefly retreated from his gamble late in the 1940 campaign shows how the use of the Lincoln exemplar opened up an

---

[62] Ibid., pp. 328-329. The *New York Times*' headline the following day read: "President Bids Nation Awake to Peril/Roosevelt is Grim/Quotes Lincoln to Show a Parallel."

[63] Ibid., p. 63.

effective critique which was pursued by Willkie. Lincoln's arguments—long term self-interest in principled action, the attack on moral indifference as the basis of public policy, the assertion that armed conflict was an outcome of democratic will (a "people's contest")—may not hold together under either philosophic or historical scrutiny, but they do constitute a formula for creating a national general will in a liberal society. The United States may well have drifted toward war without FDR's use of the Lincoln exemplar but then had it done so, the conflict would have had to have been pursued without the advantages of ideological unity that the Lincolnian model provided.

On the other hand, whatever the individual ideological motivations of those who write in the critical Lincoln tradition may be, they show that the Lincoln exemplar carries with it great risks for a polity. Roosevelt spent his entire public life attempting to create openings in American political culture. He provided a national vision of society based upon the entrance of forgotten men and women into the political system. The liberal community that he created had always showed wear in the connections among groups and often been held together from the fear that he had provoked of economic royalists. But it also had some elements of commitment to the new social contract he had described in his 1932 Commonwealth Club speech. New Deal experimentation may not have been as bold and persistent as was promised, but the New Deal had shown a certain willingness to entertain initiatives never dreamed by other administrations.

With the adoption of the Lincoln exemplar FDR sought to close up alternative visions. Dwight MacDonald's assessment of FDR in 1945 is too harsh. The president, he said, had become "the Commander-in-Chief, the implacable executioner of enemy peoples."[64] But MacDonald had reacted to what amounted to a fundamental moral shift in the president's world view. However demagogic the class rhetoric of 1936 had been, the number of economic royalists was small and readily identifiable. Vallandighams could be anywhere and everywhere. FDR never faced the kind of opposition Lincoln confronted during his war. For a

---

[64] Dwight MacDonald, *Politics Past* (New York, 1957), p. 285.

brief moment in 1944 it appeared that MacArthur might become Roosevelt's McClellan, but the threat never materialized. Dewey did raise the question of "one-man government" in Washington in the election but never centered the critique the way Willkie had in 1940.[65] Even without Copperheads, however, FDR still could react in the mode of the civil war leader. He regarded Biddle's reluctance to evacuate Americans of Japanese descent with bemusement and once told him that when Lincoln's Attorney General refused to initiate legal proceedings against Vallandigham, Lincoln had declared martial law and tried him in a military court.[66]

The legacy of the Rooseveltian use of the Lincoln exemplar is complex, and of course could not be clearly foreseen by the president himself. But William F. Buckley's response to early calls for Nixon's impeachment are illustrative:

> Anything Roosevelt did was all right, and any challenge to Roosevelt's executive prerogatives was reactionary, nihilistic, and anarchistic. Roosevelt used to make secret commitments in behalf of the United States every couple of weeks, with extras on Halloween—armies to Iceland, fleets to the Mediterranean, marines to Singapore. Never mind, what now we are taught to call the military-industrial complex, in those days we called the arsenal for democracy—you couldn't do business with Hitler—we had to shoulder the responsibilities of a great power—had to have a strong President. Impeach Roosevelt? As well impeach the Statue of Liberty.[67]

To the extent to which the crisis presidency as an institution, which had lain fallow with the exception of Wilson who had resorted to the Lincoln exemplar as well, was revived by FDR, Roosevelt's prudent archery has had lasting consequences. The application of the Lincoln

---

[65] Occasionally, FDR compared the 1944 election to 1864. In his acceptance speech he cited Lincoln's second inaugural and in a campaign address he noted that this was the first time a national election had been held during wartime since 1864. *Public Papers* (1944-45), pp. 206, 354.

[66] Francis Biddle, *In Brief Authority* (Garden City, 1962), p. 166.

[67] William F. Buckley, *Inveighing We Will Go* (New York, 1972), p. 266.

exemplar to tensions with the Soviet Union was a relatively simple ideological task. The Nazis had been defeated but the world was still half-slave and half-free. But the use of FDR–Lincoln was ideologically neutral in terms of partisan politics in America. Socio-economically the Republicans could not really present a New Deal or even a Fair Deal, but they could compete ideologically in terms of the FDR-inspired interpretation of Lincoln. Moreover, since the transition from anti-fascism to anti-communism was made under a Democratic administration, and under the protest of the party's left, the questions of Yalta and China and Hiss gave the Republicans a certain initiative. Most troubling in the long term, however, was the fact the apocalyptic structure of the Lincolnian exemplar (of which Truman's inaugural address is a perfect illustration) is incapable of resolution under the constraints of the atomic age. Winning and losing may have been difficult enough ideological categories in regard to Antietam or even Guam. They provided the basis for incoherence in the context of an exemplar that permitted none when applied to the Berlin airlift or Korea. Still, as Lincoln had spoken of the people's war, the opposition to communism could be pursued systematically and ruthlessly at home. And this both parties and presidents and presidential aspirants have done since FDR. The end of the cold war deinstitutionalizes these practices, but the recent experience in the Persian Gulf war illustrates how readily they can be retrieved.[68]

---

[68] In President George Bush's 1991 Air Force Academy address: "The Lessons of the Gulf War," *Vital Speeches* (June 15, 1991), pp. 514-516, the president spoke of his generation's struggles in a "divided world—frozen in the ice of ideological conflict." "As superpower polarization and conflict melt," the United States faces other "challenges" to freedom in the form of "regimes packed with modern weapons and seething with ancient ambitions."

W hile Ford will never receive the homage paid to Lincoln, he did grasp the essence of Lincoln's civility, compassion, composure, and common touch. The influence of the Lincoln legacy on Ford was a salutary one.

Edward L. Schapsmeier &
Frederick H. Schapsmeier

Edward and Frederick Schapsmeier received their doctorates at the University of Southern California in 1964. The former is University Distinguished Professor at Illinois State University; the latter was designated John McN. Rosebush Professor at the University of Wisconsin–Oshkosh. Both teach United States 20th century history and have co-authored *Walter Lippman* (Public Affairs Press, 1966); *Henry Wallace* (Iowa State University Press, 1968), 2 vols.; *Abundant Harvests* (Forum Press, 1970); *American Agricultural History* (Greenwood Press, 1975); *Gerald R. Ford's Date With Destiny* (Lang, 1989); *Political Parties* (Greenwood Press, 1981), *Ezra Taft Benson* (Interstate Printers of Illinois Press, 1985); and *Dirksen of Illinois* (University of Illinois Press, 1985). They have also written articles on Lincoln, Theodore Roosevelt, and Dwight D. Eisenhower.

Gerald Ford and the Lincoln Legacy:
A Time to Heal

Gerald R. Ford will long be remembered for his statement: "I am a Ford, not a Lincoln." This terse utterance was made just after Ford was sworn in as vice president. He was the first nonelected vice president under the 25th Amendment and also would be the first nonelected president. Ford's memorable words were spoken in 1973 when he filled the vacancy left by the resignation of Spiro Agnew. They were widely interpreted by the media primarily as being a frank and self-deprecatory acknowledgement by a truly honest and humble man. Actually, the second and third lines of this so-called profession of humility are overlooked or ignored. They went: "My addresses will never be as eloquent as Lincoln's. But I will do my best to equal his brevity and plain speaking."[1] At that moment Vice President Ford was indicating his intention of emulating Abraham Lincoln's rhetoric in terms of the latter's simple candor and plain talk. This had not been characteristic of Ford's predecessor, Agnew, whose excessively florid speeches (frequently filled with acrimonious barbs) made him highly controversial even before his wrongdoings as governor of Maryland forced him out of office.

The Watergate episode had created a politically explosive situation. Its corrosive effect was causing a steady disintegration of the relation-

---

[1] "Remarks Upon Taking Oath of Office as Vice President," December 6, 1973, Speech File–Gerald R. Ford Library (Ann Arbor, Michigan). Hereafter cited as GRFL.

ship between Richard Nixon, the beleaguered chief executive, and an angry Congress. At his vice presidential confirmation hearings before a Senate committee, Ford indicated that his role would be that of "a ready conciliator and calm communicator between the White House and Capitol Hill. . . ." Ford, still believing at this time that President Nixon was innocent of a cover-up, perceived his prime function as being that of a mediator. He pledged "to support truth and intelligent compromise." Ford furthermore promised to "do it as President Lincoln did, 'with firmness in the right, as God gives us to see the right.'"[2] Ford came to this decision rather naturally, since his entire career in Congress (especially as GOP Minority Leader) was not characterized by inflammatory rhetoric or combative tactics. As a rule his Lincolnesque "modus operandi" was to seek consensus and compromise with members of Congress—not confrontation.

Gerald Ford's admiration of Abraham Lincoln began when he was a youth growing up in Michigan. "Abe Lincoln was one of my boyhood heroes, perhaps the greatest," claimed Ford. He admired Lincoln for "his humility, his devotion to hard work, his dry sense of humor, his generosity of spirit, his love of God and common men." Ford was particularly impressed with Lincoln as "a moral man, a man with the kind of character and integrity and compassion that made him a unique man—a great leader who seemed created for his times."[3]

Gerald Ford's fine character and excellent work habits were developed in Grand Rapids, Michigan where, as a high school student, he gained recognition both as an academic achiever and outstanding athlete. He worked his way through college. After graduating from the University of Michigan in 1934, Ford (a football star) declined an offer by the Green Bay Packers and entered Yale Law School as a part-time student while supporting himself as an assistant coach at Yale University. His decision to pursue a legal career was based on the following rationale, as

---

[2] "Statement by The Honorable Gerald R. Ford, Minority Leader Of The House of Representatives Before The Senate Committee On Rules and Administration," November 1, 1973, Speech File–GRFL.

[3] "Address to Student Body at Illinois Wesleyan University," Bloomington, Illinois, February 10, 1969, Speech File–GRFL.

he put it: "I thought my talents would be those of a mediator and counselor. As Abraham Lincoln once wrote: 'It is as a peacemaker that the lawyer has a superior opportunity.'"[4]

Gerald Ford got the opportunity to serve as a peacemaker even before graduating from law school. Strangely enough he served as an intermediary between his father and mother. Ford's mother, Dorothy Gardner, married Leslie King on September 7, 1912. King's father was a wealthy merchant in Omaha, Nebraska. The young couple lived in the elder King's mansion in Omaha. A son was born to them on July 14, 1913. He was named Leslie King, Jr. Within five months the couple was divorced. Leslie, Sr., who was hot tempered and prone to abuse his wife physically, was directed by the court as the final part of the divorce proceedings to pay child support for young Leslie until he was 21 years of age. In defiance of the court ruling Leslie, Sr. left the state and thereafter defaulted on his child payments.[5]

Dorothy Gardner moved to Grand Rapids, Michigan where she subsequently married Gerald R. Ford. He adopted Leslie King, Jr., and renamed him Gerald R. Ford, Jr. Young Gerald, Jr. never saw his real father until he was seventeen years old. This occurred when Ford's biologic father stopped by Grand Rapids after picking up a new Lincoln Zephyr at Detroit. At the time Gerald Ford was working in a small restaurant catering to high school students. Leslie King, who by this time had inherited his father's wealth, cavalierly invited Gerald to live with him, gave him twenty-five dollars as a gift, but said nothing about being arrears in child support nor did he indicate any willingness to help his son through college.[6]

Leslie King later made the mistake of reentering the state of Nebraska where an outstanding warrant for his arrest awaited him. This

---

[4] Gerald R. Ford, *A Time to Heal: The Autobiography of Gerald R. Ford* (New York, 1970), pp. 53-54.

[5] Docket 126–No. 247 (June 3, 1939), District Court of Douglas County, Nebraska, Copy of Satisfaction of Judgment, Office of Legal Files-GRFL. For more details see our essay, "President Gerald R. Ford's Roots in Omaha," *Nebraska History,* vol. 68 (Summer 1987), pp. 56-62.

[6] Ford describes this experience in *A Time to Heal,* pp. 47-48. It is also covered in Edward L. and Frederick Schapsmeier, *Gerald R. Ford's Date With Destiny: A Political Biography* (New York, 1989), pp. 7-8.

was in 1939 when Ford was still in Yale Law School. Prior to this Gerald Ford had visited his real father in Riverton, Wyoming, and met the father's new wife and children (one son and two daughters). Whereas Ford felt a deep resentment against his biologic father's failure to help him financially, he nevertheless did not want to see Leslie King go to jail. Although the third year law student might have relished some revenge for his father's dereliction of duty and child support delinquency, he followed what he perceived to be the Lincoln model to resolve the issue without taking an additional pound of flesh. He helped end the litigation by mediating a compromise settlement. Leslie King would pay a lump sum cash payment of $4000, after which the pending lawsuit would be dropped. In a sworn deposition before the Commissioner of the Superior Court for New Haven, Connecticut, Ford described his action as an intermediary by claiming "I was simply acting as peacemaker."[7]

Gerald Ford was steeped in the lore associated with the annual celebrations of Lincoln's birthday in the state of Michigan. Since Michigan, along with Wisconsin and Illinois, were claimants to being the birthplace of the Republican party, members of that state's GOP habitually referred to it as the party of Lincoln. During the years Ford served in the U.S. House of Representatives, from 1949 to 1974, he personally gave such formal addresses every year at some gathering of the GOP faithful. It had become part of Michigan's political tradition. The annual Lincoln Day dinners were institutionalized as a time for rededication to basic principles, strengthening party unity, and giving honor to Lincoln as the time-honored symbol of the Republican party.[8] Gerald Ford, sooner than he or anyone else could have anticipated, was thrust upon the path that Lincoln had taken, becoming his party's representative in the nation's highest executive office.

---

[7] Quoted in Peter H. Wood, "The Pardoner's Tale: The Personal Theme of 'Domestic Tranquility' in Gerald Ford's Pardon of Richard Nixon," *Prospects*, vol. 2 (1986), p. 532.

[8] Telephone interview with Penny Circle (President Ford's personal secretary), May 5, 1992. In talking via telephone from the White House to a Lincoln Day Dinner gathering in Grand Rapids, Michigan, in 1976, President Ford asserted: "I have attended Lincoln Day Dinners as far back as 1946." *Public Papers of the Presidents Of The United States, Gerald R. Ford, 1976-77* (Washington, D.C., 1979), p. 722.

When discovery of the incriminating tape (the so-called smoking gun) was made, Richard Nixon resigned the presidency rather than submit to a trial in the U.S. Senate which would follow as the result of impeachment proceedings. Gerald Ford suddenly found himself elevated to the position of chief executive. After taking the oath of office at noon on August 9, 1974 President Ford made a few remarks which he called "just a little straight talk among friends." In the spirit of Abraham Lincoln's Second Inaugural, Ford observed, "But there is a higher power, by whatever name we honor him, who ordains not only righteousness but love, not only justice but mercy." The new President referred to Thomas Jefferson's faith in the people as a sure reliance for preserving liberty, adding: "And down the years Abraham Lincoln renewed this American article of faith, asking: 'Is there any better or equal hope in the world?'" Ford promised to follow his "instincts of openness and candor" and to "bind up the internal wounds" caused by Watergate by striving to restore "the Golden Rule to our political process," thus letting "brotherly love purge our hearts of suspicion and hate."[9] He then asked the American people to pray for him and for the fallen ex-president and his family.

The American public seemed to sigh collectively in relief that the Watergate ordeal was over at last. "It was," Barbara Hinckley wrote in her book, *The Symbolic Presidency,* "as if Gerald Ford inherit[ed] the office of Washington and Lincoln and not one of his predecessor."[10] One opinion poll gave Ford a 71% rate of public approval within the first week of his new administration.

In his first address to a Joint Session of Congress, President Ford asserted, "My administration starts off by seeking unity in diversity." He reminded his audience that "only eight months ago, when I last stood here, I told you I was a Ford, not a Lincoln. Tonight I say I am still a Ford, but I am not a Model T." Ford explained, "I do have some old fashioned ideas, however. I believe in the very basic decency and fairness of America." It was the President's contention that the American people wanted domestic tranquility and that his role was to be that of a

---

[9] "Remarks on Taking the Oath of Office, August 9, 1974," Speech File–GRFL.

[10] Barbara Hickley, *The Symbolic Presidency: How Presidents Portray Themselves* (New York and London, 1990), p. 13.

healer. The post-Watergate period plus the legacy of Vietnam had poisoned the political atmosphere. Ford, in the mode of "with malice toward none and charity for all," wanted to restore the body politic to a state where reason and civility prevailed.[11]

One of Ford's first symbolic acts was to change the portraits that hung in the cabinet room. Nixon had chosen to place the portraits of Dwight D. Eisenhower, Theodore Roosevelt, and Woodrow Wilson. Ike's portrait was there because Nixon had served as Eisenhower's vice president. But T. R. and Wilson represented Nixon's great interest in international relations and diplomacy. Ford retained Ike's portrait, since he too had a longstanding link with Ike. This stemmed from having been one of a small group of House members first to entreat the then general and head of NATO to seek the GOP presidential nomination. But Ford replaced T. R. and Wilson with Abraham Lincoln and Harry S. Truman. Lincoln's presence typified Ford's feeling that just as the former sought to moderate passions at the closing of the Civil War, so must Ford following Watergate and the termination of the Vietnam War. Present in the Oval Office also was a marble pen set on which the final lines of Lincoln's Gettysburg Address were inscribed. Truman was also an inspiration, since Ford knew his bid for a full term on his own in 1976 would involve overcoming the type of obstacles Truman faced in 1948.[12]

To overcome the siege mentality that characterized the White House during Nixon's presidency, Ford sought to make the Oval Office more accessible to all. He did not want a palace guard isolating him from outside contact. To the contrary, Ford encouraged open discussion and solicited ideas even if they ran contrary to his own thinking. To make his point, as related in his memoirs, Ford used the Civil War analogy of the instance when President Lincoln rode out to watch a skirmish on the outskirts of Washington, D.C. Intent on seeing the battle, Lincoln exposed himself dangerously. Ford explained, "A young Union Army lieutenant shouted, 'Get down, you damn fool.'" Ford then revealed that the

---

[11] "Address to a Joint Session of the Congress," August 12, 1974, Speech File–GRFL.

[12] Authors' interview with Gerald R. Ford, September 6, 1983 at Beaver Creek, Colorado. For presidential aide Robert T. Hartmann's account, see his address at Grand Rapids Baptist College, September 17, 1981, copy in Composite General Accession File–GRFL.

young officer who yelled unceremoniously at the president was Oliver Wendell Holmes, Jr., a future member of the U.S. Supreme Court. Lincoln later wrote the brash lieutenant a letter of praise and thanks. Ford drew the lesson for his staff when he declared that "any president—needs to hear straight talk."[13] Ford, like Lincoln before him, valued honest, even blunt, advice. Neither presumed the presidency should exist in splendid isolation nor did they regard the office as being imperial in nature.

Despite President Ford's attempt to make the White House a more open and hospitable place for political adversaries, it eventually became a lonely place for its occupant. Ford even decried the fact he was no longer called Jerry by his friends. As Harry Truman had put it relative to the occupant of the Oval Office, "The buck stops here." The full weight of the presidency soon became evident as Ford was called upon to make important decisions. The Lincoln legacy provided succor and psychological sustenance. The mysterious and pervading spirit of Lincoln seemed to be ever present in the White House. Ford drew strength from the memory of his illustrious predecessor. "Occasionally, at night, I'd step into the Lincoln Cabinet Room on the second floor. . .[where] history permeates the room," President Ford recalled. "I would sit alone and gaze at the paintings and photographs of another time, and I could hear the voice of 110 years before. When I left the room, I always felt revived."[14]

One of the major problems facing Ford dealt with binding up the wounds of a nation having been involved in a long, divisive war. Defense Secretary James Schlesinger first suggested to President Ford that something had to be done about the 50,000 deserters and draft dodgers—many of whom had fled to Canada. Nixon had taken a hard line, feeling such unpatriotic and treasonous action should not go unpunished. In contrast, Ford wanted a more charitable solution. He was inspired by Lincoln's purported action relative to Union Army deserters during the final stages of the Civil War. Ford described it thus: "Lincoln had offered

[13] Ford, *A Time To Heal,* p. 187.

[14] Ibid., pp. 205-206.

deserters restoration of their rights if they withdrew support for the Confederacy and swore allegiance to the Union." Ford noted that Lincoln "was criticized for being too lenient, but his was probably the right decision at the time."[15] Ford, despite expected opposition from veterans' groups, intended to emulate this policy of leniency.

President Ford chose the occasion of the annual convention of the Veterans of Foreign Wars in Chicago on August 19, 1974 to announce his earned reentry plan. He explained:

> Unlike my last two predecessors, I did not enter this office facing the terrible decision of a foreign war, but like President Truman and President Lincoln before him, I found on my desk, where the buck stops, the urgent problem of how to bind up the nation's wounds. And I intend to do that.
>
> In my judgment, these young Americans should have a second chance to contribute their fair share to the rebuilding of peace among ourselves and with all nations. So I am throwing the weight of my presidency into the scales of justice on the side of leniency.
>
> I will act promptly, fairly, and very firmly in the spirit that guided Abraham Lincoln and Harry Truman. As I reject amnesty, so I reject revenge. [16]

Notwithstanding criticism from hawkish veterans as being too lenient and anti-war doves as being too harsh, Ford stuck by his policy of earned reentry.

It was in the spirit of Lincoln also that President Ford faced the issue of pardoning Richard Nixon. He did so one month after becoming president. Ford felt deeply that the healing process needed to bind up the psychic wounds of the nation would be delayed unnecessarily until he disposed of the Nixon problem. Despite any political repercussions, Ford felt it needed to be done immediately to promote domestic tranquility. If the ex-president were indicted, there would be a long and messy trial. Wounds would be reopened and hatreds revived. Daily headlines

[15] Ibid., p. 142.

[16] "Remarks to the Veterans of Foreign Wars Annual Convention," Chicago, Illinois, August 19, 1974, Speech File–GRFL.

would renew passions. The prospect of seeing a former president imprisoned seemed repulsive to Ford even as Abraham Lincoln never wished to see Jefferson Davis behind bars.

Ford very much feared that a protracted trial, with Nixon in the dock, would be extremely divisive and detract from resolving the nation's current problems. And, in the fashion of Lincoln, Ford was motivated also by compassion. The latter was not a commonly expressed sentiment at that time. Ford's decision was his own. He hoped it would bring an end to the nightmarish aftermath of Watergate. After attending a service at St. John's Episcopal Church, Ford returned to the Oval Office to announce his decision. He called a press conference to make a public announcement. In giving his reasons for the pardon, President Ford referred to the Nixons as an "American tragedy." He then explained:

> After years of bitter controversy and divisive national debate, I have been advised and I am compelled to conclude that many months and perhaps more years will have to pass before Richard Nixon could obtain a fair trial in any jurisdiction of the United States under governing decisions by the Supreme Court.
>
> During this long period of delay and protracted litigation, ugly passions would again be aroused. And our people would again be polarized in their opinions. And the credibility of our free institutions of government would again be challenged at home and abroad.[17]

President Ford concluded his remarks by giving his personal reasons for granting the pardon:

> My conscience tells me clearly and certainly that I cannot prolong the bad dreams that continue to reopen a chapter that is closed. My conscience tells me that only I, as President, have the constitutional power to firmly shut and seal this book. My conscience tells me it is my duty not merely to proclaim domestic tranquility but to use every means that I have to insure it. . . .[18]

---

[17] "Remarks on Signing a Proclamation Granting Pardon to Richard Nixon," September 8, 1974, Speech File–GRFL.

[18] Ibid.

President Ford expected some criticism, but not the avalanche of condemnation that descended upon him. He was stunned by the horrendous outcry from the media. Ford regarded the pardon as justifiable in terms of the nation's overall welfare, and even as an act of mercy it seemed charitable. Unfair charges were hurled at Ford. Some claimed cynically that a deal had been made. Ford's Gallup poll rating plummeted from 71 to 49.

Despite Ford's repeated attempts at press conferences to quell the fire storm of criticism, he realized the best way to refute the allegations of a deal was for him to appear before a congressional committee. The President's advisers counseled him not to do so.

No Chief Executive since George Washington had done so officially. But it was reported to Ford that Abraham Lincoln had done so informally in order to deny allegations his wife was a Confederate spy.[19] While this was unsubstantiated, Ford nevertheless decided on his own volition to appear before the Subcommittee on Criminal Justice of the House Committee on the Judiciary. He vehemently denied any involvement whatsoever in any kind of deal relative to the pardon. Partisan passions were high. Ford's testimony was challenged by some but was accepted by most. Nixon haters were not satisfied by any explanation. The issue of the pardon subsequently became a significant factor in Ford's defeat in 1976.

Believing his action served the nation's best interests, Ford took the onslaught of criticism with stoic resignation. In retrospect Ford has indicated he would do the same thing again even knowing it would cost him the election. He recalled an article in the *Wall Street Journal* that mildly chastised his first Hundred Days with the following humorous story:

> It seems there was this immigrant taking his citizenship examination before a judge. The judge was calling out famous names, and the immigrant was trying to identify their place in American history. "Abraham Lincoln," said the judge.
>
> "President of the United States," said the immigrant.

[19] Ford, *A Time To Heal*, p. 197.

"But what did Lincoln do?" the judge persisted, waiting, of course, for "he freed the slaves" or "he preserved the Union."

"He do the best he can," the immigrant replied.[20]

In looking back on his presidency, Ford's response to this chiding anecdote was: "That, I thought, was no small accomplishment, and if the immigrant in the story had wanted to say the same thing about my first hundred days, I wouldn't have minded at all."[21]

When first elected to Congress in 1948 Gerald Ford spoke to a group of young Republicans at Michigan State University. He told them:

> History is a river of circumstances whose currents and eddies take us through the present and drive us into the future with irresistible momentum. History is the controlling channel through which the present runs, and its twistings and turnings are bound to effect the plans of our leaders and parties. Therefore, it behooves us to ask first of all, where does our nation stand in the broad sweep of history?[22]

Just before the advent of the nation's bicentennial, President Ford utilized the New Year's Eve celebration on December 31, 1975 to project a theme for his upcoming bid for election on his own in 1976. Just as Abraham Lincoln linked the preservation of the Union to the survival of democracy in the world, so Gerald Ford likened the Cold War to a great global struggle for the preservation of human freedom. Ford counseled the American people:

> Behind us lie 200 years of toil and struggle, 200 years of accomplishments and triumphs. We remain, in Lincoln's words, "the last, best hope of the earth." But what lies ahead? Shall we let the coming year slip into the record books virtually unnoticed and undistinguished except for the fanfare of a gigantic birthday party? Or shall we make 1976 the beginning of a very special time, a time

---

[20] Ibid., pp. 207-208.

[21] Ibid.

[22] "Speech by Representative Gerald R. Ford, Jr., Michigan State College (now University), East Lansing, Michigan, October, 1948," Speech File–GRFL.

that sparks a renaissance to liberty and justice for all Americans, a time that revives and strengthens the universal human yearnings for freedom all over the world.[23]

Gerald Ford was not a spellbinding orator. He spoke plainly and without fanfare or fake posturing. He felt he was patterning his mode of communication after that of Abraham Lincoln while realizing his efforts in no way approached the latter's literary quality. Speaking at the Lincoln Memorial on February 12, 1976, President Ford identified closely with Lincoln when he said:

> Among his many gifts of greatness, Abraham Lincoln had almost a mystic ability to find deep meaning in the tumultuous events that swirled about him. His expression of these insights in words—that some called dull and dish-watery when they were spoken—are inscribed on these walls and in the hearts of his countrymen.
>
> But it is less for the power of his words that we honor Lincoln than for the force of his faith in America and in the people of this great Republic. [24]

Early in 1976, Ford not only continued to be on the receiving end of a barrage of criticism leveled by Democrats, but from Ronald Reagan, who challenged him for the GOP nomination. Amid this season of political cant and castigation Ford utilized the occasion of dedicating the Lincoln Home National Visitor's Center in Springfield, Illinois, to once more identify with the Lincoln legacy. He reminded the audience about the essence of Lincoln's greatness:

> His amazing ability to communicate some of his own calm courage, his own calm compassion to his fellow countrymen across more than a century sets Abraham Lincoln apart from all great Americans whose names we honor. Others are legend; Lincoln is real.[25]

---

[23] "New Year's Day Message," December 31, 1975, Speech File—GRFL.

[24] "Remarks at a Ceremony Commemorating the Birth of Abraham Lincoln," February 12, 1976, Speech File–GRFL.

[25] Press Secretary and Speech File, GRFL (Ann Arbor, Michigan).

President Ford acknowledged that while he did not believe in the Lincoln ghost or some mysterious apparition in the White House, he did feel in a very real way the presence of Lincoln. In relating the value of this personal experience, Ford asserted: "It is a comforting presence, gently reminding his successors that no matter how worrisome, none of their problems can be worse than he faced, none of their critics more cruel, none of their decisions more difficult."

Surely uppermost in Ford's mind was the resultant hail of criticism for his pardon of Nixon. He told the gathered crowd before him, "I know you will appreciate how much encouragement I find myself today in Lincoln's philosophical reply to political attacks on his leadership." According to Ford, "Lincoln told a visitor at the White House":

> If I were to try and read, much less answer all the attacks made on me, this shop might well be closed for any other business. I do the very best I know how—the very best I can; and I mean to keep doing so until the end. If the end brings me out all right, what is said against me won't amount to anything.[26]

*   *   *

Gerald Ford won the Republican nomination for the presidency, but lost the election to Jimmy Carter in a very close race. When living in retirement, Ford was asked how he felt about the defeat. "I'm a good loser as long as I feel I did my best," he replied. "The biggest pride that I have is the fact that we healed the wounds and restored confidence in our government."[27] It is possible that Jerry Ford also thought to himself, "Old Abe would nod in agreement."[28]

---

[26] "Remarks at the Cornerstone Unveiling Ceremony for the Lincoln Home National Visitor's Center in Springfield, Illinois," March 5, 1976, Speech File—GRFL.

[27] Quoted in Maury De Jonge, "Happy Retiree Ford Keeps 'Options Open,'" *Ann Arbor News,* January 21, 1979.

[28] I thought former President Ford might object to this conjectural sentence, so I sent him a finished copy of this chapter for comment. He replied: "I like and approve of what you have written," Letter, GRF to ELS, July 20, 1992.

While Ford will never receive the homage paid to Lincoln, he did grasp the essence of Lincoln's civility, compassion, composure, and common touch. The influence of the Lincoln legacy on Ford was a salutary one. It helped make Gerald Ford the ideal president during a period when the nation truly needed a time to heal.

Photograph by Mathew B. Brady, Washington, January 8, 1864. (The Frank and Virginia Williams Collection of Lincolniana)

> Lincoln's legislative correspondence contributed to his presidential achievements that transformed him into "the supreme myth, the richest symbol in the American experience."

Samuel B. Hoff

Samuel Hoff is the ROTC Director and an associate professor of history and political science at Delaware State University in Dover. He holds a B.A. from Susquehanna University, M.A. from American University, and M.A. and Ph.D. from the State University of New York at Stony Brook, all in political science. His previous academic appointments have been at New York Institute of Technology, Ohio Wesleyan University, Whittenberg University, SUNY-College at Geneseo, and Wichita State University. Dr. Hoff has published articles in numerous professional journals, including *American Politics Quarterly, Congress and the Presidency, Presidential Studies Quarterly, Southeastern Political Review, Midsouth Political Science Journal,* and the *Journal of Policy History,* as well as in several edited volumes. He has extensive political experience, including three positions with the U.S. Congress, and served as an elected party committeeman from 1984-1986 in Suffolk County and Long Island, New York.

The Legislative Messages
of the Lincoln Administration

The public correspondence between the chief executive and Congress is an important element in gauging relations of these governmental branches. This written record documents and preserves historic transactions and provides scholars with tangible evidence upon which to evaluate the relationships—and sometimes adversarial Constitutional forces. These communications also may "express the nation's heritage and aspirations" and "prepare the ground" for support of an administration's actions.[1]

Official communications between the President and the Congress serve as political mileposts for the public. According to Philip Abbott, "presidential statements are widely cited as models of American political thought."[2] An examination of the public correspondence reveals that this communication functions on at least two levels by carrying both the stated message as well as an unstated message. Recent studies have characterized presidential messages as rhetoric, conversation, vehicles

---

[1] James C. Humes, ed., *My Fellow Americans: Presidential Addresses That Shaped History* (New York, 1992), p. xiii; Harold J. Laski, *The American Presidency: An Interpretation* (New York, 1940), p. 147.

[2] Philip Abbott, *The Exemplary Presidency: Franklin D. Roosevelt and the American Political Tradition* (Amherst, 1990), p. 7.

for policy statements and initiatives, and as indicators of job performance.[3]

This study examines the written interaction between President Abraham Lincoln and the national legislature, ascertaining in the process how
messages to Congress in the 1800s differed in number and content from
those transmitted in this century. It also surveys the reasons why the
Civil War period "is marked by a shift in the historical positions of
Congress and the presidency vis-a-vis one another."[4] In order to accomplish this multi-faceted objective, a three-prong approach was utilized.
First, Lincoln's approach to Congress is probed. Next, a comprehensive
analysis of his presidential messages sent to Congress—including annual, special, and veto messages—is undertaken. Finally, an assessment
of the contribution of the Lincoln administration to later patterns of
executive-legislative communication is offered.

Lincoln's Relations With Congress

Scholars dispute the manner Abraham Lincoln used to approach
Congress and the consequences of presidential-legislative battles during
the Civil War years. One image is of a "tough wartime President, flexing
his executive muscles and expanding his war powers whenever necessity
demanded." According to one Lincoln biography, he "invoked his presidential powers in heretofore undreamed-of-ways. . ."[5] Two other Lincoln scholars suggest that, according to Lincoln's prerogative view of
the office, "the president was empowered to take any action, regardless

---

[3] Stephen A. Borrelli, "Presidential Rhetoric as a Means of Shaping Public Perceptions of
Events," a paper delivered at the 1989 Annual Meeting of the Southern Political Science
Association, Memphis, TN; Robert E. Denton, Jr. and Mary E. Stuckey, "Presidential
Communication as Conversation: Media Effects on Presidential Speech," a paper delivered at the
1990 Annual Meeting of the Midwest Political Science Association, Chicago, IL; Matthew C.
Moen, "The Political Agenda of Ronald Reagan: A Content Analysis of the State of the Union
Messages," *Presidential Studies Quarterly*, vol. 18, 1988; Roderick P. Hart, *The Sound of
Leadership*, (Chicago, 1987).

[4] Jeffrey K. Tulis, *The Rhetorical Presidency* (Princeton, 1987); Mary E. Stuckey, *The
President as Interpreter-in Chief* (Chatham, 1991), p. 22.

[5] Stephen B. Oates, *Abraham Lincoln: The Man Behind the Myth* (New York, 1984), pp. 120,
122.

of its constitutionality, if conditions warranted such action. The threat to the Union manifested by the Civil War provided such justification."[6] From other perspectives, Robert DiClerico declares that "Lincoln was not at all reluctant to take actions that far exceeded his constitutional powers," while Louis Fisher contends that Lincoln "took emergency actions he thought necessary and called upon Congress to provide the legal sanction by statute."[7] Offering yet another interpretation is presidential scholar James G. Randall, who states that "Lincoln tended toward the view that in war the Constitution restrains Congress more than it restrains the President. . . .The national legislature was merely permitted to ratify these measures, or else to adopt the futile alternative of refusing consent to an accomplished fact." Lincoln, concluded Randall, "simply took over certain powers without regard to Congress."[8]

Other students of Lincoln, citing his acts as evidence, supported these conclusions. Stephen Wayne notes that besides calling Congress into special session, President Lincoln "waited until the adjournment of Congress to issue his Emancipation Proclamation in 1864."[9] Obviously Lincoln was not reluctant to exercise presidential authority as he saw it. As the war dragged on, "Lincoln proclaimed even more comprehensive powers for the military authorities, without any apparent thought of seeking authorization from Congress," writes Sidney Milkis and Michael Nelson.[10] To find a basis for these assertions, scholars cite Lincoln's own acts. Louis Koenig echoed these declarations with his contention that President Lincoln regarded the legislature "as a nuisance to be avoided if at all possible."[11] Lincoln's actions, however, must be

[6] Lester G. Seligman and Cary R. Covington, *The Coalitional Presidency* (Chicago, 1989), p. 152.

[7] Robert E. DiClerico, *The American President* (Englewood Cliffs, 1990), p. 64; Louis Fisher, *The Politics of Shared Power: Congress and the Executive* (Washington, 1983), p. 160.

[8] James G. Randall, *Constitutional Problems Under Lincoln* (Urbana, 1964), pp. 514-515; James G. Randall, *Midstream: Lincoln the President* (New York, 1953), p. 142.

[9] Stephen J. Wayne, *The Legislative Presidency* (New York, 1978), p. 12.

[10] Sidney M. Milkis and Michael Nelson, *The American Presidency: Origins and Development, 1776-1990* (Washington, 1990), p. 150.

[11] Louis W. Koenig, *The Chief Executive* (San Diego, 1986), p. 340.

viewed in their wartime context. Michael Benedict believes that because of the war, Lincoln "unquestionably established presidential powers beyond those his predecessors had ever found occasion to claim, and he exercised those powers with a vigor that would not be equaled by any nineteenth century successor."[12] "Lincoln's success in defending his position is demonstrated by the fact that neither the Congress nor the courts placed any significant limits on his actions," observed Richard Watson and Norman Thomas.[13]

According to other researchers, however, President Lincoln's legislative orientation in areas not affiliated with the Civil War was quite restrained. In a speech in Pittsburgh, Pennsylvania in February 1861, the president-elect outlined his philosophy of governing:

> My political education strongly inclines me against a very free use of any of these means, by the Executive, to control the legislation of the country. As a rule, I think it is better that congress should originate, as well as perfect its measures, without external bias.[14]

Stephen Oates postulates that once he took office, "Lincoln maintained close ties with Congress, for he needed its support if the war was to be won and the future of popular government guaranteed."[15] Where "ordinary affairs of state were concerned, he seemed willing to let the government run itself without much direction from the White House. He exerted little control over Congress."[16] Another writer perceives that Lincoln "seldom initiated legislation on Capitol Hill and used his veto

[12] Michael Les Benedict, "The Constitution of the Lincoln Presidency and the Republican Era," in Martin Fausold and Alan Shank, eds., *The Constitution and the American Presidency* (Albany, 1991), p. 48.

[13] Richard A. Watson and Norman C. Thomas, *The Politics of the Presidency* (New York, 1983), p. 143.

[14] Roy P. Basler, ed., *The Collected Works of Abraham Lincoln,* 8 vols. (New Brunswick, 1953), vol. 4, p. 214.

[15] Stephen B. Oates, "Abraham Lincoln: Republican in the White House," in John Thomas, ed., *Abraham Lincoln and the American Tradition* (Amherst, 1986), p. 105.

[16] Don E. Fehrenbacher, ed., *Abraham Lincoln: A Documentary Portrait Through His Speeches and Writings* (Stanford, 1964), p. xxviii.

less than any other important American President."[17] David Donald claims that "in weakly deferring to Congress, he was following the Whig creed in which he was raised."[18]

Attempting to reconcile these ostensibly polar conceptions of Lincoln's use of power, Arthur Schlesinger postulates that despite being forced to implement "extreme policies by unprecedented emergency, he incorporated within himself written and unwritten checks on presidential absolutism."[19] Lincoln's apparent inconsistency in his approach to Congress represents a paradox which is concomitantly a characteristic of the presidency itself, at least according to James MacGregor Burns:

> The more the President becomes a captive to the immediate pressures on him, the more he may be drawn away from the more significant but more remote and long-run problems of his time. The more practical, pragmatic, and operational he becomes, the more he is a victim of events rather than a shaper of events.[20]

In a similar vein, Thomas Cronin, in his examination of the presidency, contends that, not unlike the era in which Lincoln lived, "the ultimate paradox of the modern presidency is that it is always too powerful and yet it is always inadequate."[21] A twentieth century theory which may be applied retrospectively to explain Lincoln's contradictory congressional orientation is the two-presidencies thesis, which holds that chief executives will be more assertive and successful in foreign and military policy initiatives than those in the domestic arena.[22]

[17] Oates, *Abraham Lincoln: The Man Behind the Myth*, p. 92.

[18] David Donald, *Lincoln Reconsidered: Essays on the Civil War Era* (New York, 1956), p. 207.

[19] Arthur M. Schlesinger, Jr., *The Imperial Presidency* (New York, 1974), p. 75.

[20] James MacGregor Burns, *Presidential Government: The Crucible of Leadership* (New York, 1965), p. 60.

[21] Thomas E. Cronin, "The Presidency and its Paradoxes," in Harry Bailey, Jr., ed., *Classics of the American Presidency* (Oak Park, IL., 1980), p. 122.

[22] Stephen A. Shull, ed., *The Two Presidencies: A Quarter Century Assessment* (Chicago, 1991).

Lincoln's Legislative Messages

This section examines the writing style, number and subject matter of, together with various influences on, legislative communication during the Lincoln presidency. In describing the chief executive's correspondence, Preston Brooks divulges that Lincoln "wrote slowly, and with the greatest deliberation, and liked to take his time; yet some of his dispatches, written without any corrections, are models of compactness and finish."[23] Despite Lincoln's writing skills and his unsurpassed ability to evoke emotion through his words, Tulis propounds that "Lincoln wished to provide the conditions for effective command by focusing the citizenry's attention on carefully crafted rhetoric presented 'officially.'"[24]

Several researchers have investigated the content of President Lincoln's legislative dispatches. In their joint study of Lincoln, Mario Cuomo and Harold Holzer find that "Lincoln's writing was nearly all of a 'political kind'. . .Lincoln's rhetoric consecrated in high relief the crucible of the Civil War, and gave majesty to the ethic of majority rule."[25] Randall discovers that "a great deal of space in his messages to Congress was devoted to the Union cause, to the distress and challenge of war making, to the undoing (partially) of the effects of the war, to slavery and emancipation, and to the high ideal of 'freedom disenthralled.'" [26]

That Lincoln sought to employ the written word as an effective tool in dealing with Congress and that he successfully wielded words to achieve his communications goal can not be doubted. David Anderson, in reviewing Lincoln's writings, asserts that "much of his prose is rhythmic in the great tradition of the King James Bible, reflecting his keen ear

---

[23] Herbert Mitgang, ed., *Lincoln As They Saw Him* (New York, 1956), p. 508.

[24] Tulis, *The Rhetorical Presidency,* p. 81.

[25] Mario M. Cuomo and Harold Holzer, eds., *Lincoln on Democracy* (New York, 1990), pp. xxxiv-xxxv.

[26] Randall, *Midstream: Lincoln the President,* p. 147.

for the music of words. Alliteration, assonance, imagery, and analogy, together with phrases of succinct vividness, abound in his mostly deeply felt works."[27] One nineteenth century critic found that Lincoln's writings "always addressed the intelligence of men, never their prejudice, their passion, or their ignorance."[28] But for those who look only at Lincoln's writing, there is cautionary advice: Professor Fehrenbacher reminds us that "In the letters, speeches, and public papers of Abraham Lincoln, one finds the real man, but not the whole man."[29]

The following subsections analyze various types of written messages sent to Congress by President Lincoln.

Special Session Message

Shortly after his inauguration as president, Abraham Lincoln convened a special session of Congress to address the Civil War. In the message forwarded to the legislature, Lincoln "outlined the first few steps that the Government had taken to meet the rebellion against it; he answered the Southern arguments on the right of secession; and he went out of his way to speak to the people of the nation in order to make it clear to them that the War was 'essentially a people's contest.'"[30] His dispatch reflected on the past and future of the American experiment:

> Two points in it our people have already settled—the successfully establishing and the successful administering of it. One still remains—its successful maintenance against a formidable internal attempt to overthrow it. It is now for them to demonstrate to the world that those who can fairly carry an election can also suppress a rebellion; that ballots are the rightful and peaceful successors of bullets, and that when ballots have fairly and constitutionally de-

[27] David D. Anderson, *Abraham Lincoln* (New York, 1970), p. 187.

[28] James Russell Lowell, "Abraham Lincoln," in Charles Eliot, ed., *Essays English and American* (New York, 1938), p. 449.

[29] Fehrenbacher, *Abraham Lincoln: A Documentary Portrait Through His Speeches and Writings,* p. xxix.

[30] Philip Van Doren Stern, ed., *The Life and Writings of Abraham Lincoln* (New York, 1940), p. 126.

cided there can be no successful appeal back to bullets; that there can be no successful appeal except to ballots themselves at succeeding elections. Such will be a great lesson of peace, teaching men that what they can not take by an election neither can they take it by a war; teaching all the folly of being the beginners of a war.[31]

Lincoln's message to Congress was a compelling position statement by the chief executive that some authorities believe represented a more significant communication than if issued contemporaneously. Watson and Thomas state that the power of the chief executive "to call Congress into special session is less important today than it has been in the past. The principal reason for the reduced significance of special sessions is the tendency of Congress, since the 1930s, to remain in session for much of the year, taking periodic short recesses."[32]

Annual Messages

Nineteenth century State of the Union messages differed from those offered by chief executives in the contemporary era of American politics. James Davis declares that:

from Jefferson's time to Taft's—a span of more than a century—this message was merely transmitted to Capitol Hill by courier. Not until Woodrow Wilson resurrected George Washington's practice of addressing a joint session of both Houses of Congress in person was the potentially powerful impact of the State of the Union Message upon the general public as well as Congress again fully realized.[33]

---

[31] James D. Richardson, *A Compilation of the Messages and Papers of the Presidents,* 10 vols. (New York, 1897), vol. 8, p. 3231.

[32] Richard Watson and Norman C. Thomas, *The Politics of the Presidency* (Washington, 1988), p. 245-246. One study examining the dates and duration of special sessions from 1801 to 1974 reveals that Congress met for parts of eleven years and for 922 total days in the 1800s. Harvey C. Mansfield, Sr., "The Dispersion of Authority in Congress," in Mansfield, ed., *Congress Against the President* (New York, 1975), pp. 245-246.

[33] James W. Davis, *The American Presidency: A New Perspective* (New York, 1987), p. 150.

Roland Egger explains that pre-Wilsonian annual messages contained "mostly secondhand prose salvaged from department reports, with legislative recommendations sandwiched in at more or less appropriate points. The inevitable operation of a sort of Greshan's law of political communication tended to obscure the pertinency and blunt the urgency of the President's legislative proposals."[34] Richard Pious postulates that presidents in the 1800s "followed the custom [George] Washington established and simply listed in their annual message to Congress subjects on which new legislation might be required, without offering an administration position."[35]

In keeping with that custom, President Lincoln's first annual message, transmitted to Congress on December 3, 1861, was fourteen pages in length. It included an update on the progress of the war, a report on the treasury, and a proposal that all states have circuit courts. As with all of his annual messages, Lincoln used the opportunity to offer observations on various topics. For instance, in emphasizing the need for authority, he stated that, "In a storm at sea no one on board can wish the ship to sink and yet not unfrequently all go down together because too many will direct and no single mind can be allowed to control."[36] Lincoln likewise praised the value of a humble background: "No men living are more worthy to be trusted than those who toil up from poverty; none less inclined to take or touch aught which they have not honestly earned."[37] The message concluded with the following statements:

> The struggle for to-day is not altogether for to-day; it is for a vast future also. With a reliance on Providence all the more firm and earnest, let us proceed in the great task which events have devolved upon us.[38]

---

[34] Roland Egger, *The President of the United States* (New York, 1967), pp. 142-143.

[35] Richard Pious, *The American Presidency* (New York, 1979), p. 157.

[36] Richardson, *A Compilation of the Messages and Papers of the Presidents,* vol. 8, p. 3257.

[37] Ibid., p. 3259.

[38] Ibid.

The chief executive's second annual message, numbering seventeen pages, was submitted to Congress on December 1, 1862. Besides information on the war and fiscal affairs, this correspondence contained reports of Indian relations and the newly established Department of Agriculture. But perhaps the most critical parts of the 1862 message concern the president's comments on slavery. In what was an eloquent prelude to the Emancipation Proclamation—issued exactly a month later—Lincoln proposed several constitutional amendments pertaining to the abolition of slavery.[39] He justified the recommended changes in the following manner:

> In giving freedom to the slave we assure freedom to the free—honorable alike in what we give and what we preserve. We shall nobly save or meanly lose the last best hope of earth. Other means may succeed; this could not fail. The way is plain, peaceful, generous, just—a way which if followed the world will forever applaud and God must forever bless.[40]

President Lincoln's twelve-page third annual message was forwarded to the national legislature on December 8, 1863. Other than fiscal and military references, this communication mentioned U.S. policy with other nations, Indian relations, and the process of reconstruction after the Civil War. According to historian Richard Current, the reconstruction plan which Lincoln offered to reconquered states—readmission to the Union when 10 percent of voters took an oath of loyalty, repudiated secession, and eliminated slavery—had two purposes: "One was to hasten the end of the war by encouraging Southerners still in rebellion to give up the fight; many of them would have comparatively little to lose by doing so. The other purpose was to hasten reunion once the war was over."[41]

[39] Ibid., p. 3337.

[40] Ibid., p. 3343.

[41] Richard N. Current, "Abraham Lincoln," in Morton Borden, ed., *America's Ten Greatest Presidents* (Chicago, 1961), p. 150.

Before this plan could be implemented, however, the war had to be won. The president cautioned Congress and the nation against losing sight of that goal:

> Hence, our chiefest care must still be directed to the Army and Navy, who have thus far borne their harder part so nobly and well; and it may be esteemed fortunate that in giving the greatest efficiency to these indispensable arms we do also honorably recognize the gallant men, from commander to sentinel, who compose them, and to whom more than to others the world must stand indebted for the home of freedom disenthralled, regenerated, enlarged, and perpetuated.[42]

The final annual message of Abraham Lincoln's administration, delivered to Congress on December 6, 1864, echoed the themes of the previous message while also calling for Congress to reconsider passing a constitutional amendment to eradicate slavery. President Lincoln advanced a single condition for peace: "the war will cease on the part of the Government whenever it shall have ceased on the part of those who began it."[43]

It is evident that Lincoln anticipated an end to hostilities between North and South; he offered several insights about the promise and potential of America following the conflict. In the area of trade with foreign powers, Lincoln hoped "that with the return of domestic peace the country will be able to resume with energy and advantage its former high career of commerce and civilization."[44] Lincoln viewed those who would come from abroad to settle in America as vital to postwar prosperity: "I regard our immigrants as one of the principal replenishing streams which are appointed by Providence to repair the ravages of internal war and its wastes of national strength and health." [45] In perhaps

---

[42] Richardson, *A Compilation of the Messages and Papers of the Presidents,* vol. 8, p. 3392.

[43] Ibid., p. 3456.

[44] Ibid., p. 3445.

[45] Ibid., p. 3447.

the most telling sign that a Union victory was at hand, the president even commented on how his own authority would change:

> The Executive power itself would be greatly diminished by the cessation of actual war. Pardons and remissions of forfeitures, however, would still be within Executive control. In what spirit and temper this control would be exercised can be fairly judged of by the past.[46]

Special Messages

Special Messages are a type of presidential correspondence sent to one or both chambers of Congress, and include reports on departmental activities, responses to legislative resolutions, and requests for action on nominations, treaties, or policy initiatives. These messages constituted the bulk of public dispatches in the 1800s. Tulis delineates how patterns of communication between the executive and legislative branches have evolved over the last two centuries:

> Virtually all nineteenth century communication was written. By contrast, 42 percent of presidential rhetoric today is spoken. . . Written communications to Congress have dwindled to 19 percent of the president's total persuasive effort.[47]

The chart in the Appendix following this essay lists the number of special messages transmitted to the House of Representatives, to the Senate, and to Congress generally, from the administration of George Washington through the second Grover Cleveland administration, divided by each term served. From this, we can deduce that Abraham Lincoln ranks eighteenth in the frequency of House messages, fourth in number of Senate dispatches, and is tied for fifth in the amount of letters sent to both chambers simultaneously over his term in office. A 1983

---

[46] Ibid., p. 3455.

[47] Tulis, *The Rhetorical Presidency,* p. 139.

empirical study of presidential messages submitted to the legislature found a significant positive relationship between percentage of members sharing the president's party affiliation and frequency of both House and Senate special messages, whereas the number of letters addressed to both chambers at once was best explained by the passage of time.[48]

A content analysis of each kind of special message issued by the Lincoln administration was conducted by Hoff, who determined that of the twenty-eight special messages sent to the House of Representatives, virtually all were reports on policy matters, most of which were requested by the House in the form of resolutions. President Lincoln sent more than four times as many messages to the Senate than to the House. Theoretically, this imbalance may be explained by the greater constitutional affinity between the Senate and the chief executive. Indeed, the content analysis reveals that of the 126 total messages sent to the Senate between 1861 and 1865, forty-nine were proposed treaties, nineteen were requests to confirm nominations to executive and judicial positions, and fifty-eight were reports forwarding information. However, the impact of partisan support in each chamber on the number of messages cannot be discounted: there was a clear plurality of Republicans serving in both houses during Abraham Lincoln's entire tenure in office.[49]

The sixty-nine special messages which President Lincoln addressed to Congress as a whole fulfilled several functions, including reports on policy matters (thirty-eight), recommendations on presidential proposals (twenty-six), messages accompanying the signing of legislation (three), an announcement of the death of President Lincoln's son, and a protest over a congressional resolution criticizing the administration's war policy. The aforementioned empirical study of presidential messages sent to Congress over the first century of our constitutional government found that party and electoral factors had an insignificant influence on the release of this type of presidential correspondence.[50] The effect which

---

[48] Samuel B. Hoff, "Electoral and Party Influence on Presidential Messages, 1789-1897," a paper delivered at the 1983 Annual Meeting of the Northeastern Political Science Association, Philadelphia, PA.

[49] Ibid.

[50] Ibid.

time displayed in increasing this category of message is consistent with the growing institutional power of the presidency in relation to Congress, together with the steady growth in the size of the federal government.

Veto Messages

Abraham Lincoln's use of the veto as president may be traced to his pre-presidential philosophy, determined largely by his Whig party affiliation. For instance, he supported a resolution adopted at the 1844 Whig nominating convention which called for "a practical restriction of the veto power, so that it may not be wielded to the centralization of all power in the hands of a corrupt and despotic Executive. . . "[51] Four years later in a June 1848 campaign speech in Wilmington, Delaware, Lincoln criticized the "high-handed and despotic exercise of the veto power" by Democratic President James Polk.[52] In a speech supporting Whig presidential nominee Zachary Taylor delivered in July 1848, Lincoln compared the views of Thomas Jefferson and Taylor on the use of the presidential veto:

> It is. . .Mr. Jefferson's opinion, if on the constitutionality of any given bill, the President doubts, he is not to veto it. . .but is to defer to congress, and approve it. And if we compare the opinions of Jefferson and Taylor, as expressed in these paragraphs, we shall find them more exactly alike, than we can often find any two expressions, having any literal difference.[53]

In a September 1848 speech at Tauton, Massachusetts, Lincoln stated that Taylor "had promised not to veto any measure unless it was unconstitutional or passed in haste and acknowledged that to be constitutional which had been established by long usage and acquiesced by the people." In a debate the following month in Jacksonville, Illinois, Lin-

---

[51] Basler, *The Collected Works of Abraham Lincoln*, vol. 1, p. 339.

[52] Ibid., p. 476

[53] Ibid., p. 503.

coln attempted to show that Zachary Taylor opposed the veto. The 1860 Republican platform criticized Democratic territorial governors in Kansas and Nebraska for vetoing legislative acts prohibiting slavery.[54]

As chief executive, Abraham Lincoln utilized the veto sparingly, applying it to only two bills by regular means. In areas where Congress was granted authority, such as in counting and determining the legality of electoral votes, Lincoln considered it "not competent for the Executive to defeat or obstruct that power by a veto, as would be the case if his actions were at all essential in the matter."[55] President Lincoln's first public bill veto occurred on June 23, 1862, when he returned unsigned an act designed to repeal legislation forbidding the circulation of bank notes of less denomination than $5.00 within the District of Columbia. A pertinent section of his message reads as follows:

> In my judgment it will be found impracticable in the present condition of the currency to make such a discrimination. The banks have generally suspended specie payments and a legal sanction given to the circulation of irredeemable notes of one class of them will almost certainly be so extended in practical operation as to include those of all classes, whether authorized or unauthorized.[56]

Lincoln's second and final veto by regular means was issued less than a month later, on July 2, 1862. In a short, two-paragraph message, the president negated an act to provide for additional medical officers of the volunteer service because "I have approved an act of the same title passed by Congress after the passage of the one first mentioned for the express purpose of correcting errors in and superseding the same, as I am informed."[57]

---

[54] Ibid., pp. 7, 12; Donald Bruce Johnson, *National Party Platforms,* vol. 1 (Urbana, 1978), p. 33.

[55] Richardson, *A Compilation of the Messages and Papers of the Presidents,* vol. 8, p. 3461.

[56] Ibid., p. 3288.

[57] Ibid., p. 3289.

Abraham Lincoln pocket vetoed five bills during his administration, including one in 1863, two in 1864, and two in 1865.[58] In the only message accompanying a pocket veto, released on January 5, 1865, the president specified his reasons for not signing a joint resolution to correct clerical errors in a recently passed internal revenue act: "Since the adjournment of the last session of Congress other errors of a kind similar to those which this resolution was designed to correct have been discovered in the law, and it is now thought most expedient to include all the necessary corrections in one act or resolution."[59]

On at least one occasion Lincoln used the draft of a veto message as a way to revise the wording of legislation. Karlyn Campbell and Kathleen Jamieson note that when Lincoln's objections to a bill authorizing seizure of the property of Confederate office-holders became known, the offending language was deleted. The result, according to the aforementioned authors, was that "Lincoln not only altered the character of that act but also laid out the principles that he thought should guide policy in this area and that would inform his decisions about future legislation."[60] In other instances, he "used the threat of a veto to successfully force or prevent changes in pending legislation."[61]

In general, the veto was employed infrequently by presidents before 1865. Of the fifty-nine total vetoes issued from the Washington through the Lincoln administrations, thirty-six were by regular means, while twenty-three were pocket vetoes. Conversely, 561 vetoes were exercised by presidents over the 1865 to 1889 time frame, of which 175 were of the pocket veto variety. Presidents serving between 1865 and 1889 also suffered nineteen overrides of their public bill vetoes, more than three times the number of overturns before 1865.[62]

---

[58] U.S. Senate Library, *Presidential Vetoes, 1789-1976* (Washington, 1978), pp. 27-28.

[59] Richardson, *A Compilation of the Messages and Papers of the Presidents,* vol. 8, p. 3472.

[60] Karlyn Kohrs Campbell and Kathleen Hall Jamieson, *Deeds Done in Words: Presidential Rhetoric and the Genres of Governance* (Chicago, 1990), p. 86.

[61] Wayne, *The Legislative Presidency,* p. 12.

[62] Samuel B. Hoff, "The Presidential Pocket Veto: Its Use and Legality," a paper delivered at the 1991 Annual Meeting of the Northeastern Political Science Association, Philadelphia, PA.

The reasons for increased use of the veto after Lincoln's tenure are varied. One researcher contends that alteration in the scope of national legislation, such as the battle over reconstruction during Andrew Johnson's administration and pension and relief bills common during the presidencies of Ulysses Grant and Grover Cleveland, led to more bills being vetoed.[65]

Other scholars identify modifications in congressional procedure, such as attaching riders to appropriations bills, or policy differences between Congress and the president on specific issues.[66] Perhaps the most basic trend in post-Civil War presidential vetoes was their utilization for other than constitutional reasons. Henry Lewis asserts that the change from unconstitutionality to expediency as the primary ground for issuing a veto augmented its use.[67]

Discussion

The legislative messages transmitted by Abraham Lincoln not only contributed to his success as our sixteenth chief executive, but influenced the pattern of executive–congressional relations for many decades. Anderson applauds Lincoln's "greatness as a man and as a writer." Oates asserts that "this was no latter-day Whig in the White House. It was no Whig who wrote those magnificent state papers about the purpose of the war and the mission of the American experiment." A century after his death, President Lyndon Johnson recognized the value of Lincoln's writings for contemporary times, stating that Lincoln's "words have become the common covenant of our public life." Cuomo and

---

[65] Edward C. Mason, *The Veto Power, 1789-1889* (New York, 1890).

[66] Charles J. Zinn, *The Veto Power of the President* (Washington, 1951); John L.B. Higgins, "Presidential Vetoes, 1889-1929," Ph.D. dissertation, Georgetown University, Washington, D.C., 1952. See also, Carlton Jackson, *Presidential Vetoes, 1789-1945* (Athens, 1967); John C. Metz, *The President's Veto Power, 1889-1968*, Ph.D. dissertation, University of Pittsburgh, Pittsburgh, PA, 1971; Albert C. Ringelstein, *Presidential Vetoes: Motivations and Classifications,* and *Congress and the Presidency,* vol. 12 (1985), for further explanations for heightened veto use after Lincoln's presidency.

[67] Henry M. Lewis, *The Veto Power of the President* (D.C.L. dissertation, American University, Washington, D.C., 1927).

Holzer observe that "Lincoln's written legacy continues to transcend both time and place, holding relevance for today as well as tomorrow."[68]

Douglas Hoekstra asserts that Lincoln's writings show that he "was an unusually thoughtful president, one whose deepest convictions challenged important aspects of the regime and shaped his purposes and politics during the War. . . ."[69] Yet, as Richard Current detects, Lincoln "had a knack of appealing to fellow politicians and talking to them in their own language."[70] Such diverse skills would lead, after his death at the hands of an assassin, to exemplary assessments of his abilities and character. Historians Harry Carman and Reinhard Luthin contend that had Lincoln "not displayed his ability as a politician with such single success, it is doubtful whether he would be regarded today as a statesman."[71] Benjamin Thomas finds that the people "looked upon Lincoln as embodying the nation's commendable traits. He came to be regarded as the true American."[72] Similarly, Victor Searcher states that, "As the merit of his leadership unfolded it became increasingly clear he was the greatest American America had produced."[73]

After Lincoln's presidency was cut short by John Wilkes Booth, "Congress grew to dominate relations with the president until the end of the century."[74] Still, Mary Stuckey states that Lincoln helped to insure the power of the executive branch by "emphasizing the legitimating possibilities of the presidency and away from a strict understanding of the office as a predominantly administrative entity."[75] Richard Ellis ex-

---

[68] Anderson, *Abraham Lincoln,*, p. 192; Oates, "Abraham Lincoln: Republican in the White House," p. 107; Alex Ayres, ed., *The Wit and Wisdom of Abraham Lincoln* (New York, 1992), p. xiv; Cuomo and Holzer, *Lincoln on Democracy,* p. xi.

[69] Douglas J. Hoekstra, "Neustadt, Barber, and Presidential Statesmanship: The Problem of Lincoln," *Presidential Studies Quarterly,* vol. 19 (1989).

[70] Richard N. Current, *The Lincoln Nobody Knows* (New York, 1984), p. 211.

[71] Harry J. Carman and Reinhard H. Luthin, "Lincoln Distributes the Spoils," in James Rawley, ed., *Lincoln and Civil War Politics* (New York, 1969), p. 23.

[72] Benjamin Thomas, *Abraham Lincoln* (New York, 1952), p. 521.

[73] Victor Searcher, *Lincoln Today* (New York, 1969), p. 16.

[74] Wayne, *The Legislative Presidency,* p. 12.

[75] Stuckey, *The President as Interpreter-in-Chief,* p. 22.

plains that even as Abraham Lincoln's political situation was similar to that of other presidents, his success in gaining support from competing groups stands as an enduring legacy.[76]

Conclusion

It is apparent from the evidence presented in this essay that President Lincoln's legislative correspondence contributed to his presidential achievements that transformed him into "the supreme myth, the richest symbol in the American experience."[77] Equally apparent is that Lincoln's legacy of heroic leadership endures in the American public. It is a legacy largely shaped by his own words, writings that transcend time and capture for all generations the democratic principles of the Founding Fathers. In Lincoln, each successive generation finds a new meaning that appeals to the loftiest instincts of the individual. As Frank Williams asserts, he is our ever-present contemporary.

[76] Richard J. Ellis, "What Can 19th Century Presidents Teach Us About the Twentieth Century Presidency?" a paper delivered at the 1990 Annual Meeting of the American Political Science Association, San Francisco, CA.

[77] Clinton Rossiter, *The American Presidency* (Baltimore, 1987), p. 94.

APPENDIX

Frequency of Special Messages Sent
to Congress, by Term, 1789-1897

PRESIDENT	TO HOUSE	TO SENATE	TO BOTH HOUSES
Washington	2	41	61
Washington	5	22	69
J. Adams	10	29	45
Jefferson	16	25	53
Jefferson	14	33	71
Madison	30	37	63
Madison	15	26	31
Monroe	38	55	26
Monroe	97	66	34
J. Q. Adams	67	65	40
Jackson	41	87	40
Jackson	43	71	42
Van Buren	77	85	42
Tyler*	77	123	21
Polk	43	115	23
Fillmore*	31	130	36
Pierce	56	168	47
Buchanan	41	102	21
Lincoln	28	126	69
A. Johnson*	133	181	49
Grant	53	123	37
Grant	40	46	38
Hayes	31	66	28
Arthur*	74	105	228
Cleveland	31	95	118
Harrison	11	29	113
Cleveland	21	57	39
TOTALS	**1125**	**2108**	**1484**

*succeeded a president who died in office.

"Tousled hair" pose by Alexander Hesler, Chicago, February 28, 1857—a year before the Lincoln–Douglas debates. (The Frank and Virginia Williams Collection of Lincolniana)

> The primary issue in the presidency is not one of whether a president should obtain advice, but how to most effectively and efficiently do this. More attention should be given to the construction and administration of the cabinet in successful administrations.

Arthur R. Williams

Arthur Williams, a professor at L. P. Cookingham Institute, Henry R. Bloch School of Business and Public Administration, University of Missouri at Kansas City (UMKC), was born in Dayton, Ohio, where his interest in Lincoln was stimulated as a youth during brief conversations with Carl Sandburg and Lloyd Ostendorf. He received a Ph.D. in government from Cornell University in 1981, a M.A. in economics from University of the Philippines in 1975, and a M.P.A. from the University of Pittsburgh in 1971. Living in the Philippines for ten years, Dr. Williams worked with the Rockefeller and Ford Foundations and conducted a study of central-local government relations under the martial law regime. He has published extensively in the areas of American colonial government in the Philippines and in health services research.

Amanda Noble

Amanda Noble received her undergraduate degree in Social Work at Michigan State University in 1989. She received her M.P.A. in 1992 at the L. P. Cookingham Institute where she worked as Research Associate. Ms. Noble is an auditor with the Office of the Auditor, City of Kansas City, Missouri.

From Poltroons and
Apes to Diamonds in Their Setting:
Lincoln's Practice of Cabinet Alchemy

Four and a half decades ago, in his *Autobiography of Seventy Years*, Senator George F. Hoar held it "one of the chief proofs of the kindness of divine Providence to the American people in a time of very great peril that their leaders were so different in character. . . .A circle in which Lincoln shines like a diamond in its setting."[1] The point which Hoar emphasizes is that a signal strength of the Union was the diversity of opinion in Congress and also in the Lincoln cabinet, which enabled the government to make difficult but well-considered policy choices.

This is not an opinion of the Lincoln Administration commonly shared by professional historians of the Civil War.[2] Much of this writing emphasizes military necessity, conflict between the Committee on the Conduct of the War and the Administration, or criticisms of decisions (made with perfect hindsight by analysts) often portraying Lincoln as an

---

[1] George F. Hoar, *Autobiography of Seventy Years*, 2 vols. (New York, 1903), vol. 2, pp. 77-78.

[2] See, for example, Bruce Catton, *Mr. Lincoln's Army* (Garden City, 1962), pp. 197-200.

uninformed or misinformed, easy-going, unduly imposed upon, or less than competent administrator.[3]

Scholarship on Lincoln as president and leader has swung from hagiography to vitriolic criticism. Professor Don Fehrenbacher, in his study of Lincoln's image in American historiography, notes that "during the very years of the greatest achievements in Lincoln studies, general interpretation of the Civil War was taking an anti-Republican and therefore anti-Lincoln direction. Furthermore, several of the most important Lincoln scholars were in the vanguard of revisionist historians."[4] For example, one thesis advanced by revisionists was that the war was unnecessary because the extension of slavery was economically infeasible or not economically viable in the South over the long-run. Such scholarship de-emphasizes the moral, ethical, and political-democratic implications of the Civil War, which figure so prominently in Lincoln's own public statements and correspondence.[5]

While prevailing opinion now recognizes that "the Civil War was pre-eminently a political war, a war of peoples rather than of professional armies, [and that] political leadership and public opinion weighed heavily in the formation of strategy," emphasis on the "political" nature of the war also is consistent with both an earlier and more recent literature which emphasizes Lincoln's alleged powers of manipulation and ambition for advancement. Much of this literature searches Lincoln's

[3] David McCullough, *Truman* (New York, 1992), pp. 256-280, 287-291, points out that objections were raised to the Senate Special Committee to Investigate the National Defense Program (Truman Committee) on the basis of the "well known" Civil War "experience" of Lincoln with Radical members of the Committee on the Conduct of the War. Interestingly, despite initial reservations, Franklin D. Roosevelt supported the work of the Truman Committee, and later, during World War II, refused to acquiesce in the dissolution of the Committee in the face of advisors who cited the alleged negative Civil War experience of Lincoln with congressional "interference." This is an interesting topic for further examination, and it illustrates the influence of interpretation of historical events on subsequent presidential policy discussions; it may also illuminate Roosevelt's appreciation for multiple sources of information about programs and policies.

[4] Don E. Fehrenbacher, *The Changing Image of Lincoln in American Historiography* (Oxford, 1968), p. 17.

[5] Roy Basler, ed., *The Collected Works of Abraham Lincoln* (New Brunswick, 1953), has been consulted for this chapter, but notations are not given since the brevity of this report precludes direct citations. Lincoln's works, using texts from the Basler edition, are now available to the wider public in two volumes through excellent Library of America editions edited by Don E. Fehrenbacher, *Abraham Lincoln, Speeches and Writings, 1832-1858* (New York, 1989) and *Abraham Lincoln, Speeches and Writings, 1859-1865* (New York, 1989).

early life for clues or examples of behavior consistent with later patterns. Manipulation and ambition have been cited as key to understanding Lincoln's selection of his cabinet. The argument proceeds along these lines: Lincoln chose his cabinet as any president would, balancing geographic and political factors. Members were chosen from scattered geographic areas for regional balance. Furthermore, Lincoln selected powerful figures in the Republican Party for his cabinet because the party was disunited, and he achieved unity in the party by sacrificing some unity in the Administration. Lincoln did this because he was certain of his ability to handle contentious members of his cabinet.[6]

William E. Barringer's *A House Dividing: Lincoln as President Elect*, an example of this literature, asserts that "politics and politicians were not essentially different on the Potomac and on the Kaskaskia. In Washington, as in Vandalia, he won his victory, using in his handling of national affairs a skill in practical politics which he had begun to develop three decades earlier in the [Illinois] frontier capital."[7] *Voila!* Lincoln is a backwoods politician transformed into a mixture of Cooper's Hawkeye and Nietzsche's *Ubermensch*. He has the will to dominate, but he does it with a smile on his face and a twinkle in his eye.

During the Civil War, however, contemporary opinion of decision-making in the White House ranged from critiques of presidential "indecisiveness" to utter contempt. In the words of one contemporary, "I never since I was born imagined that such a lot of poltroons and apes could be gathered together from the four corners of the Globe as Old Abe had succeeded in bringing together in his Cabinet."[8]

---

[6] James M. McPherson, *Battle Cry of Freedom* (New York, 1988), p. 332; Gore Vidal, *Lincoln* (New York, 1984).

[7] William E. Barringer, *A House Dividing: Lincoln as President Elect* (Springfield, 1945), p. 126.

[8] David Donald, ed., *Inside Lincoln's Cabinet: The Civil War Diaries of Salmon P. Chase* (New York, 1954), p. 12. In Donald T. Phillips, *Lincoln on Leadership: Executive Strategies for Tough Times* (New York, 1992), the author attempts to explicate "executive strategies for tough times" for American business leaders with a presentation of Lincoln's leadership behavior and beliefs. While his book achieves considerable balance, perhaps more than Ballinger's, and touches on some topics treated in this chapter, the brevity, aphoristic style, and direction to business application oversimplifies a number of important issues. Not the least of which is the political-democratic context within which Lincoln articulated his "strategies." For example, it is not clear that close correspondence exists between public and private [business] conduct in the United States—though

The fundamental thesis of this chapter is that Lincoln did practice cabinet "alchemy" by transforming a cabinet of contentious rivals into one of diamonds in their setting. Indeed, three of these bitter rivals—William Seward, Salmon P. Chase, and Edwin Stanton—are often regarded as among the best Secretaries of State, Treasury, and War (Defense) who have served the nation. The cabinet strongly influenced decision-making for the better through its unity in diversity—so well noted by Senator Hoar but ignored by many scholars. Furthermore, Lincoln's decision-making style, as Phillips correctly indicates, is consistent with the modern theory of well functioning or "excellent" organizations.

Modern management research has shown that group decisions are superior to individual ones when pertinent information is distributed among group members, when problems are unstructured, and when group members share a common goal.[9] Lincoln's cabinet represented diverse interests but maintained within it an emphasis on preserving the Union, acting as a collective body that effectively contributed to Lincoln's ability to make difficult, complex decisions. Professor McPherson has argued that "whatever flaws historians might find in Lincoln's military strategy, it is hard to find fault with his national strategy. His sense of timing and his sensitivity to the pulse of the Northern people were superb."[10]

Building consensus from a diversity of interests—this taking the people's pulse—also is fundamental to democratic theory, practice, and leadership. As Lincoln understood, he who gets too far in front of a parade quickly finds himself with no followers and no parade. He also understood intuitively that group consultations including those within the cabinet could develop into smoking clubs or circles of yes-men, victims of "groupthink," in the modern parlance, and that leaders need to

---

one may wish this were so. Nevertheless, Phillips' book could be indicative of the new direction which Lincoln scholarship may take in an America where decent executive leadership—both public and private—has been lacking for more that three decades.

[9] Examples of this literature are abundant. Well-known works dealing with leadership, reporting some empirical findings, include such authors as Victor H. Vroom, Warren Bennis, Rensis Likert, Tom Peters, Robert Waterman, and Donald T. Phillips.

[10] McPherson, "Abraham Lincoln and the Second American Revolution," in Gabor S. Boritt, ed., *Lincoln the War President* (Oxford, 1992), p. 61.

be active in facilitating open discussions within councils. Even Lincoln's usual practice of opening cabinet meetings with humor—a joke, story, or aphorism—has been prescribed by modern management theorists as a way of breaking down tensions to ease the exchange of information and ideas within decision-making groups. Lincoln clearly did not study management theory and no theorist has to our knowledge looked closely at Lincoln.

Interestingly, Lincoln's practice of "cabinet alchemy" is not unique. Both George Washington and Thomas Jefferson, two other presidents often described as "great," interacted with their cabinets in a manner similar to Lincoln's. By comparison, James Buchanan—generally recognized as one of the weakest chief executives—behaved in a way that has become conventional or standard within the recent Imperial Presidency. The nature of interactions within the cabinet is a key to understanding presidential "greatness."[11]

In this vein, this essay briefly examines the status and relevance of the cabinet in political analysis and practical politics, reviews the selection and operation of Lincoln's cabinet, notes comparisons among the Lincoln cabinet and the cabinets of Washington, Jefferson, and Buchanans, and discusses Lincoln's decision-making and leadership styles. While these topics are sufficient for several monographs, it is our hope that this limited discussion will be provocative, particularly after the 1992 presidential election, won by President Clinton with less than a majority of the popular vote.[12]

Cabinet Government?

The American cabinet has been little studied as a political institution. One of the few books about the cabinet written by a professional political scientist notes its "decline" in the face of the development of

---

[11] The term "Imperial Presidency" was used by Arthur M. Schlesinger, who penned an interesting article in Boritt, ed., *Lincoln the War President,* Arthur M. Schlesinger, Jr., "War and the Constitution."

[12] President Bill Clinton was elected to office at 46 years of age; Lincoln was elected at age 50. Both men would be considered "young" for the presidency; Lincoln was also elected by a plurality of the popular vote.

other consultative bodies such as the National Security Council, special presidential advisors, and a growing, bureaucratized presidential staff.[13] Currently, the Cabinet appears of little interest to political scientists, and it is doubtful that the proverbial man-on-the-street could name more than one or two (at most) of the members of the current cabinet.

Even historians, as hard as they are pressed for fresh topics, have neglected this one. Only two substantial books have been written about Lincoln's cabinet, and both are more than fifty years old.[14]

Interest in the cabinet as an institution has arisen in primarily two contexts: presidential succession and governmental reform.[15] Since the order of succession act in 1947 and the ratification of the 25th Amendment to the Constitution twenty years later, the importance of the cabinet in presidential succession is essentially moot. On the other hand, while reforming the presidency by formal inclusion of cabinet officials in executive or legislative decision-making still surfaces periodically, the informal status of the cabinet in the Constitution, the difficulties of constitutional amendment, and, perhaps, American pride in the uniqueness of its divided institutions, generates little if any enthusiasm for presidential reform through more formalized cabinet responsibilities. In addition, cabinet "reform" generates little sustained public attention or enthusiasm.

A recent 136-page report entitled *Beyond Distrust*, produced by a panel of the National Academy of Public Administration (NAPA), which focused on "Building Bridges Between the Congress and the Executive," makes only three passing references to the cabinet.[16] While this may not be surprising in view of earlier comments, the NAPA report

•

[13] Richard F. Fenno, Jr., *The President's Cabinet: An Analysis of the Period from Wilson to Eisenhower* (New York, 1956).

[14] Clarence E. Macartney, *Lincoln and His Cabinet* (New York, 1931), and Burton J. Hendrick, *Lincoln's War Cabinet* (Boston, 1946).

[15] Still of interest is Henry Barrett Learned, *The President's Cabinet: Studies in the Origins, Formation, and Structure of an American Institution* (New Haven, 1912). Also, Mary L. Hinsdale, *History of the President's Cabinet* (Ann Arbor, 1911).

[16] National Academy of Public Administration, *Beyond Distrust: Building Bridges Between Congress and the Executive* (Washington, 1992), pp. 11, 75, 108.

ignores the essential role that the cabinet has played in legislative-executive liaison and in government decisions.

Ignoring this historic role of the cabinet and its members has contributed to a plethora of presidential biographies dominated by lonely office holders carrying the entire burdens of office on broad or narrow presidential shoulders. While such a viewpoint may add to the drama of the biography—and certainly eases the archival burden of the biographer—such work is both historically and organizationally naive.

A more meaningful role for the cabinet in executive decision-making consistent with Lincoln's leadership behavior and principles, as well as with management theory, as it is now being written, is suggested below. Tenets of modern management theory emphasize an organization's need for customer or client-centeredness, *quality* in information gathering and processing, and participation in decision-making by those directly affected by decisions.

For example, among these management tenets is the concept of Management By Walking Around (MBWA), which maintains that an administrator should spend time with service providers and the public rather than rely on reports from secondary or tertiary sources. Cabinet members, as directors of executive departments, are in a unique position to represent diverse constituencies while bringing a wealth of relevant information to bear on policy problems and discussions. Strengthening the role of the cabinet in executive decision-making through increased consultation and the selection of representative, qualified members requires no change in the formal role of the cabinet in American government. But it does require a president who takes great care in selecting cabinet members, carefully weighing partisan and parochial interests, and who is unafraid of criticism—a President who both has an ego and who knows when to suppress it. In policy discussions, a cabinet of faithful but deaf and blind friends can be the President's worst enemy as recent history has demonstrated, not once but on several occasions.

The Selection of the Cabinet

Not only is Lincoln's cabinet unique by modern standards, but its selection was seen as unique in his own day. Nineteenth-century presidential policy analysis, whether conducted by Democrats or Whigs, was dominated by what can be called the "Happy Household Theory of the Cabinet." The cabinet was to be unified, and act as a family under the chief executive as patriarch. The Lincoln cabinet, in contrast, looked like one of warring factions made up of politicos too prone to give conflicting advice. What Lincoln's contemporaries failed to realize was that the composition of his cabinet in terms of diversity of opinion resembled that of both Washington and Jefferson, two presidents whom Lincoln greatly admired (in fact, his admiration for Washington was unbounded). The contentiousness of individuals within Lincoln's cabinet was certainly equalled or exceeded within Washington's.

Indeed, today one can look back on Lincoln's cabinet as perhaps the most remarkable of any president. Only three of its seven members were of the same party as the president (the cabinet was composed of three Whigs and four Democrats).[17]

At least four of the seven members of the cabinet thought they deserved to be President more than Lincoln. William H. Seward, Lincoln's secretary of state, had expected to be nominated on the first ballot at the 1860 Republican Convention, but was shoved aside when Governor Andrew Curtin of Pennsylvania decided that Seward would probably defeat the entire ticket in his state. The other three presidential hopefuls—Salmon P. Chase, Edward Bates, and Simon Cameron—were all figures of long standing national reputations, although Cameron's was stained by Philadelphia machine politics and financial irregularities. After the election of 1860, John W. Bunn saw Chase leaving Lincoln's room and recorded the following exchange:

"You don't mean to put that man in your cabinet, I hope?"

"Why do you say that," asked Lincoln.

"Because," said Bunn, "he thinks he is a great deal bigger than you are."

---

[17] Lincoln had been a leading Whig in Illinois in both the state legislature and in electoral politics within the state. The Republican Party was organized in 1854 out of the remains of Whig, dissenting Democrat, Free Soil, American Party ("Know Nothings"), and other political factions. Lincoln "reentered" politics as a Republican following the signing of the Kansas-Nebraska Act by President Franklin Pierce on May 30, 1854. Lincoln once remarked that he was the fourth Whig, and, therefore, his cabinet was "nicely balanced."

"Well," replied Lincoln, "do you know of any other men who think they are bigger than I am?"

"I cannot say that I do," replied Bunn. "But why do you ask me that?"

"Because," said Lincoln. "I want to put them all in my cabinet."[18]

Among cabinet appointees, there was consensus on only one of the great questions of the day: the preservation of the Union. The cabinet held different opinions with varying degrees of intensity from the abolitionist Chase to the border state aristocrat Montgomery Blair. In fact, Lincoln searched for a Southern Unionist, but found none willing to accept a cabinet appointment.

Lincoln chose men about him with vastly more governmental experience than his. Simon Cameron, secretary of war, had been active in national politics for twenty-seven years, built one of the most influential political machines in the nation, and was a United States senator. Secretary of the Interior Caleb Smith had served three terms in Congress and established a reputation, despite a lisp, as one of the outstanding stump orators of Republicanism. Edward Bates, attorney general, had served in Congress, been elected attorney general of Missouri, and delivered in 1844 at the Internal Improvements Convention one of the most stirring addresses in American history, sky-rocketing himself to national fame.[19]

William H. Seward, secretary of state, served as governor of New York and U.S. senator, and was generally acknowledged as the creator of the Republican Party. Gideon Welles, the secretary of the navy, had been

---

[18] Recounted in Macartney, *Lincoln and His Cabinet*, p. xi.

[19] It may be difficult for us to imagine today how such sharp interest could have arisen over internal improvements, now called "public works." First, the development of these improvements was closely linked with the American System advocated by Henry C. Clay and the Whigs; therefore, both partisanship and sectional interests were embedded in these issues. Second, arguments over internal improvements became linked in debates between Jacksonians and Whigs over the role of state and national governments; ideology became part of the debate. Third, in an expansive frontier society internal improvements were linked to economic growth and development which favored some owners of capital (at that a large part of capital was land-holdings) and provided additional disposable income to laborers outside the planting-harvesting cycle in a primarily agrarian economy. Advocacy of internal improvements is closely associated with Lincoln's political career in both the Illinois legislature and the White House. This intense political mobilization over internal improvements may be better appreciated in low-income developing countries than in our own, although these improvements were of great political importance in the United States as recently as the New Deal.

an advisor to Andrew Jackson, candidate for the governorship of Connecticut, and a nationally influential newspaper editor. Treasury secretary Salmon P. Chase was a senator and two term governor of Ohio who, because of his abolitionist zeal, proudly wore the epithet "Attorney General of Slaves." Montgomery Blair, at age 48 the youngest member of the cabinet, was a federal judge who as an attorney had argued the Dred Scott case before the Supreme Court. His father, Francis P. Blair, Sr., served as an informal advisor to Lincoln and had been one of the members of Andrew Jackson's "Kitchen Cabinet." In addition, Montgomery's brother Frank was a political power in Missouri.[20] Edwin Stanton, who entered the cabinet upon Cameron's resignation in January 1862, was acknowledged to be one of the outstanding attorneys in the nation and had been a pro-Union member of Buchanan's administration. Stanton was appointed to the cabinet despite Lincoln's overhearing Stanton's ridicule of him some years earlier, and open knowledge within Washington of Stanton's widely known personal dislike of the "gorilla" Lincoln.

At the time the cabinet was announced many saw it as an absurd attempt of a disunited administration to maintain Union in the face of Southern secession. After the inauguration, Seward wrote his wife:

> The President is determined to have a compound cabinet and that it shall be peaceful, and even permanent. I was at one time on the point of refusing—nay, I did refuse for a time, to hazard myself in the experiment. But a distracted country appeared before me, and I withdrew from that position.[21]

---

[20] In the opinion of the primary author of this chapter, the condition of politics in Missouri, its political factionalism, in the formation of Lincoln's cabinet and attitudes toward the Border States has not been adequately appreciated or analyzed. Hendrick, *Lincoln's War Cabinet,* and other studies have interpreted Lincoln's appointment of Montgomery Blair as an attempt to win over Maryland through the powerful Blair family. This was likely the case, but possibly not the entire story. The division of Missouri into Bates, Fremont, Price, and Blair factions, intensified by the "war" on the Kansas border, was well-known in Springfield, Illinois, to Lincoln who owned property in Council Bluffs, Iowa. As noted by Cullom Davis, the Lincoln Legal Documents Project has discovered that Lincoln's law practice extended into Missouri. Through Bates and the Blairs, Missouri had dual but sometimes conflicting representation in the cabinet.

[21] Hendrick, *Lincoln's War Cabinet,* p. 122.

Lincoln's own explanation for the selection of the cabinet was recorded by Gideon Welles several years later. According to Lincoln, after the election results of 1860:

> I went home, but not to get much sleep, for I then felt, as I never had before, the responsibility that was upon me. I began at once to feel that I needed support—others to share with me the burden. This was on Wednesday morning, and before the sun went down I had made up my cabinet. It was almost the same that I finally appointed.[22]

It is characteristic of Lincoln that he chose the "biggest men in the country" to share the burden with him. Warren Harding, in point of contrast, once said that he thought the cabinet had been created so there would be places for his friends.[23] Not one of Lincoln's close associates was appointed to the cabinet; in fact, he refused an appointment to Henry Winter Davis, the illustrious cousin of David Davis, Lincoln's friend and campaign manager, and gave the solicited appointment to Montgomery Blair, Davis' bitter political adversary in Maryland.

Lincoln's Personality

One must wonder why Lincoln would undertake, to utilize Seward's words, the "experiment" of a "compound" government. Biographers often describe him as moody, melancholy, and needing approval, an array of personality characteristics that would seem incongruent with a contentious, disunited official family.[24] Few historians have taken Lincoln at his word—at least as presented by Welles above. A review of some aspects of Lincoln's personality is illuminating.

---

[22] Barringer, *A House Dividing*, p. 7

[23] Macartney, *Lincoln and His Cabinet*, p. xi; Barringer, *A House Dividing*, p. 77.

[24] Stephen B. Oates, *With Malice Toward None: The Life of Abraham Lincoln* (New York, 1977), pp. 71ff. Oates' biography is much more balanced than many which attempt psychological diagnosis with a self-assurance that is sometimes shocking. Allowing documentary sources to speak for themselves, Oates' work admirably captures a more human, complex Lincoln.

Lincoln possessed a keen analytical mind, perhaps the finest of any of our presidents, including Jefferson. Two dimensions of Lincoln's thinking are particularly important: a continual search for information, and a dedication to logic. In 1892, Alexander McClure wrote that Lincoln "sought information from every attainable source. He sought it persistently, weighed it earnestly, and in the end reached his own conclusions."[25]

As an attorney in Springfield, Lincoln subscribed to a large number of newspapers, and while President, his secretaries, John Hay and John G. Nicolay, continually clipped articles from various newspapers and passed them on.[26] It is also interesting that Lincoln actively solicited opinions from those in opposition. As historian Allan Nevins noted, Lincoln's wartime letters are striking in two characteristics: first, they are frequently addressed to opponents and critics, and second, they refuse to assert that Lincoln has been right or his opponent wrong.[27]

During his administration, Lincoln spent more hours at the War Department telegraph office than any other place except the White House.[28] A telegraph operator speculated that the office was the only place where Lincoln could escape official cares. More likely, the war telegraph was one of the paths Lincoln followed in his continuous search for information. Another was regular White House openings to the public. Members of the official family tried to encourage him to spend less time with the public, but he consistently refused, once telling the portraitist Carpenter that these sessions were his "public opinion baths."

---

[25] Alexander K. McClure, *Abraham Lincoln and Men of War Times* (Philadelphia, 1892), p. 78. A contradiction is obvious, if one sought information from every available source and carefully weighed it, the extent to which any decision is based on one's "own conclusions" becomes problematic. Implicit in the argument of this chapter is that Lincoln's decision-making style was highly consultative and "synergistic." Jay Hall's "Decisions, Decisions," *Psychology Today*, November, 1971, is an early discussion of group decision-making processes and "synergism"—results superior to the best solution offered by a single member of a group.

[26] Emmanuel Hertz, ed., *The Hidden Lincoln: From the Papers of William H. Herndon* (New York, 1938). The newspapers were: *Chicago Tribune, New York Tribune, The Anti-Slavery-Standard, Charleston Mercury, Richmond Enquirer*, and *National Era*.

[27] Allan Nevins, *The Statesmanship of the Civil War* (New York, 1953), p. 66.

[28] David Homer Bates, *Lincoln and the Telegraph Office* (New York, 1907), p. 3.

Lincoln thoroughly believed that by absorbing all the information he could and by interacting with others he could come to the right conclusion. He saw truth, which was to him always tentative, emerging from a process similar to debate.[29] Instructive in this regard is part of Lincoln's reply to Stephen Douglas at Ottawa, Illinois, August 21, 1858:

> I want to call your attention to a little discussion on that branch of the case, and the evidence which brought my mind to the conclusion which I expressed as my belief. If, in arraying that evidence, I had stated anything which was false or erroneous, it needed but that Judge Douglas should point it out, and I would have taken it back with all the kindness in the world. I do not deal in that way. If I have brought forward anything not a fact, if he will point it out, it will not even ruffle me to take it back. But if he will not point out anything erroneous in the evidence, is it not rather for him to show by a comparison of the evidence that I have reasoned falsely, than to call the "kind, amiable, intelligent gentleman" a liar? [Cheers and laughter] If I have reasoned to a false conclusion, it is the vocation of an able debater to show the argument that I have wandered to an erroneous conclusion.[30]

While this inquisitiveness and willingness to debate issues is well-known, and even the subject of folk-tales, Lincoln's dedication to logical-deductive reasoning is less widely appreciated. David C. Mearns, one of the curators of the Library of Congress, has pointed out that "Mr. Lincoln had a mathematical bent."[31] It is possible that Lincoln read the *Elements of Euclid* as early as 1839-1840. And, it is known that he studied both Abel Flint's *System of Geometry and Trigonometry with a Treatise on Surveying* and Robert Gibson's *Theory and Practice of Surveying* to teach himself the trade of surveying after the Lincoln-Berry store in New Salem went bust, or "winked-out," in Lincoln's words.

---

[29] Hertz, *The Hidden Lincoln,* p. 45. Herndon wrote that "Mr. Lincoln, in my opinion, according to my recollection, thought all evil *apparent* evil in the end, not absolute evil."

[30] Fehrenbacher, *Speeches and Writings,* p. 519.

[31] David C. Mearns, "Mr. Lincoln and the Books He Read," in David C. Mearns, ed., *Three Presidents and Their Books* (Urbana, 1955).

Herndon, Lincoln's law partner, reported the incident of Lincoln's three-day attempt to "square the circle," a problem that had baffled mathematicians for centuries. Lincoln took a copy of Euclid with him during his one term in the U.S. Congress to improve his discipline in "demonstrating," not merely proving, a point in debate. One need not assume that Lincoln was a prairie Pythagorean to understand the key importance of deductive logic in his thinking.[32] It is no fluke that the earliest surviving Lincoln documents are from his grammar school sum book (1824-1826), that the Lincoln–Douglas debates often read like demonstrations of principles expounded in Blackstone's *Commentaries*, and that Lincoln was the only president awarded a U.S. patent (1849).

Despite stories to the contrary, the adult Lincoln was not an avid reader—outside of newspapers. It is known that between 1861 and 1865 more than 125 loans were made to Lincoln's account at the Library of Congress; however, this included not only himself but his family and staff.[33] The youthful Lincoln of legend has been depicted as an avid reader of varied materials, and while the evidence is that he did go out of his way to acquire reading materials, these were scarce on the frontier.[34] Reading on the frontier would have been characterized by the reading of limited materials and their memorization by those with that skill.[35]

---

[32] A discussion of this is used by Sandburg to close his first volume, Carl Sandburg, *Abraham Lincoln: The Prairie Years,* 2 vols. (New York, 1926), pp. 475-480. The best source on Lincoln's boyhood is Louis A. Warren, *Lincoln's Youth: Indiana Years, 1816-1830* (Indianapolis, 1991).

[33] Mearns, *Three Presidents and Their Books,* p. 68. McPherson, "Lincoln," asserts that Lincoln was an avid reader. There is no evidence to document this for the adult Lincoln, and statements of Herndon, Nicolay and Hay, Carpenter, and others suggest a preoccupation with newspapers and continuous perusal of a few favorite sources, such as the Bible and Shakespeare. The Library of Congress records certainly do not document heavy reading on the part of the president.

[34] Warren, *Lincoln's Youth,* pp. 164ff. Also, Douglas L. Wilson, "What Jefferson and Lincoln Read," *Atlantic Monthly* (January, 1991).

[35] See, for example, Ulysses S. Grant's description of his father, Jesse, on the Ohio frontier: "During the minority of my father, the West afforded but poor facilities for the most opulent of youth to acquire an education, and the majority were dependent, almost exclusively, upon their own exertions for whatever learning they obtained. . . .Books were scarce in the Western Reserve during his youth, but he read every book he could borrow in the neighborhood where he lived. This scarcity gave him the early habit of studying everything he read, so that when he got through with a book, he knew everything in it." Ulysses S. Grant, *Memoirs and Selected Letters* (New York, 1990), p. 19. Other parallels with Lincoln's life are striking: a total of six months formal schooling, reading of newspapers, ability in debate, and activity in Whig politics. Many of the stories about Lincoln represent a frontier type who was unusual but not uncommon during this period. The

This accounts for Lincoln's prodigious memory which was commented on by all who knew him and, perhaps, also for his attention to detail, analysis, and logical construction. Many have commented on the ability of Lincoln to concentrate his attention. For example, James McPherson, citing Archilochus, described Lincoln as a "hedgehog": "The fox knows many things, but the hedgehog knows one big thing."[36]

What has sometimes been characterized as Lincoln's "fixity" of purpose or "steady policy" rests on Lincoln's faith in being able to deduce "true" principles from debate which could be then be appraised in an orderly, logical manner.[37] This is implied in the comments above from the Lincoln–Douglas debates, in his own correspondence, and in public statements.

Since debate and discussion (conversation) played such a large role in Lincoln's understanding of right thinking, it is not surprising that the search for truth was constrained by maintaining the good feelings and opinions of others. After the inauguration, he told the Pennsylvania delegation: "Have it understood that if we ever have a Government on the principles we prefer, we should remember while we exercise our opinion, that others also have these rights, and act in such a manner as to create no bad feelings."[38]

As a member of the Illinois Legislature, Lincoln was known to go to considerable lengths to avoid bad feelings. William Butler, Clerk of Sangamon County Circuit Court, once wrote letters to members of the Sangamon County delegation claiming they were not only selling out him but the county. Representative Edward Baker's reply was:

---

networks established through book-lending and the cultivation of *critical* conversational arts is unfortunately a topic on which either too little has been published or we have too little archival information.

[36] James M. McPherson, "The Hedgehog and the Foxes," in *Abraham Lincoln and the Second American Revolution* (Oxford, 1990).

[37] For "fixity," see McPherson, "The Hedgehog and the Foxes," pp. 113-130, and for "steady policy," see William S. McFeely, *Frederick Douglass* (New York, 1991), citing a letter from Douglass to Luther Stearns of August 12, 1863.

[38] Cited in Edward J. Kempf, *Abraham Lincoln's Philosophy of Common Sense* (New York, 1965), p. 970.

If you believe the charges you make to be true, I say most flatly you are a fool. . . .This is a short letter, but it is longer than one having so little truth or reason or justice as yours, deserves an answer.[39]

Lincoln's reply read:

You were in an ill-humor when you wrote that letter, and, no doubt, intended that I should be thrown in one also; which, however, I respectfully decline being done. All you have said. . .I know you would not say seriously in your moments of reflection; and therefore do not think it worth while to attempt seriously to prove the contrary to you. I only say now, that I am willing to pledge myself in black and white to cut my own throat from ear to ear, if, when I meet you, you shall seriously say, that you believe me capable of betraying my friends for any price. . . .Your friend in spite of your ill-humor.[40]

Alexander McClure once wrote that "of all the public men I have met, he [Lincoln] was the most difficult to analyze."[41] In a number of letters and papers, Herndon admitted that despite his close association with Lincoln, he never actually understood him. Edward Kempf, a psychologist, wrote an ambitious psychoanalytical biography of Lincoln in 1965. In one place he states that Lincoln "held that the equalitarian Christian moral principle of treating other people as you wish to be treated was. . .[the] true basis of democracy."[42] Eight pages later the following cryptic statement appears:

His [Lincoln's] weakness lay in his excessive patience and kindness in listening to advice lest he might treat someone unjustly by not hearing him through—by not tolerating impositions on his time and energy as long as he could bear them. He indulged his cabinet

[39] Paul Simon, *Lincoln's Preparation for Greatness: The Illinois Legislative Years* (Norman, 1965), p. 163.

[40] Ibid., p. 163.

[41] McClure, *Abraham Lincoln and Men of War Times,* p. 72.

[42] Kempf, *Abraham Lincoln's Philosophy,* p. 959.

officers and generals, his political affiliates, office seekers, the horde of obsessed advisors, until he spoiled them, like his wife and sons, into imposing on his generosity.[43]

It is a legitimate to question if the "allowing of impositions on his time" was a weakness. Probably not, in view of recent results of an American romance with the "best and the brightest" or experience with a president who wishes to make everything but the truth "perfectly clear," both tactics designed to limit critical input into policy decisions. As Donald Phillips correctly notes, Lincoln developed a consultative style of leadership which is now advocated by modern organization theorists.[44]

There are few examples of greater contrast between two persons' leadership philosophies while serving in the same government than illustrated by Lincoln's remarks to Grenville Dodge, and Salmon P. Chase's to the Reverend J. Leavitt. Lincoln's remarks reflect a democratic leadership style, while those of Chase are clearly authoritarian:[45]

> You are theoretically right but practically wrong. If I am to lead these people I must not separate myself from them. Whatever my individual thoughts may be, whatever the logical conclusions of my mind, based upon the premises which I admit to be sound and true, nevertheless I must not separate myself from the people. If I am to lead, I must stay with the procession.[46]

[43] Ibid., p. 967.

[44] Phillips, *Lincoln on Leadership,* refers to Thomas J. Peters and Robert H. Waterman, *In Search of Excellence* (New York, 1982), a popularized version of some existing management literature, which was released at an opportune time. Many of these issues have been more thoroughly examined at the Institute for Social Research, University of Michigan, and in other behavioral science studies. An early, seminal discussion of such work is Rensis Likert, *New Patterns of Management* (New York, 1961).

[45] This contrast between management styles has been discussed in the management and organizational behavior literature since the 1950s. The classic statement is Douglas McGregor, *The Human Side of Enterprise* (New York, 1961.)

[46] Grenville M. Dodge, *Personal Recollections* (Denver, 1965), p. 30. An interesting example of how "Lincolnisms" pervade American thought—at least at better moments. Phillips, *Lincoln on Leadership,* p. xiii, cites the following from James MacGregor Burns, *Leadership* (New York, p. 427), what often passes for leadership "is the behavior of small boys marching in front of a parade, who continue to strut along Main Street after the procession has turned down a side street toward the fairgrounds." We are not certain if Phillips and Burns are aware of the use of this image in

While a member of Lincoln's cabinet, by contrast, Chase wrote to the Reverend Leavitt:

> Had there been an administration in the true sense of the word, a President conferring with his cabinet and taking their united judgments and with their aid enforcing activity, economy, and energy in all departments of public service we could have spoken boldly and defied the world.[47]

The cabinet was one of Lincoln's more important sources of advice and information, and he chose, therefore, colleagues not only accepted by him as most capable of giving advice, but by constituencies in the country at large. Bates, Seward, Chase, and Cameron all received delegate votes at the nominating convention in Chicago, while Lincoln was a darkhorse. These cabinet members and Blair and Welles represented well-defined political constituencies.

While Lincoln is often depicted as extraordinarily self-confident, there is little documentary evidence to support such an assertion.[48] In fact, Lincoln was acutely aware of his ungainly appearance, lack of formal education, and sensitive to his "backwoods" family background. The evidence does support Horace Greeley's statement that "there was probably no year in his life when he was not a wiser, cooler, and better man than he had been the preceding year."[49] Lincoln was aware that he

---

Dodge's memoirs or other sources which report variants of the Dodge statement such as: "If you want to lead a parade, you can't get too far out in front." One problem is that Lincoln is so imbedded in American folklore, as Phillips correctly notes, that it is often difficult to discern a genuine Lincoln statement. More importantly, the sources of Lincoln's documented statements sometimes have a folk origin. For example, the "house divided" metaphor used in Lincoln's speech of June 16, 1858, is often attributed to the Bible with Lincoln's first usage during the Lincoln-Douglas debates. However, Lincoln used this metaphor at least as early as March 4, 1843, in a Whig campaign circular. He attributed the statement to Aesop, one of Lincoln's favorite sources. Copies of the *Fables* which circulated in the United States at that time contained not only Aesop's work but that of others (particularly Franklin) and anonymous folk sources.

[47] Hendrick, *Lincoln's War Cabinet*, p. 373.

[48] Phillips, *Lincoln on Leadership*, p. 171.

[49] Benjamin P. Thomas, *Abraham Lincoln* (New York, 1952), p. 524, which is also cited in Phillips, *Lincoln on Leadership*.

was elected by only a plurality of the popular vote and that he at age 51, was a young and inexperienced president. Up to that time only James K. Polk and Franklin Pierce had been *elected* at younger ages. Lincoln possessed little experience in national affairs, and was not a nationally recognized figure.[50]

Lincoln's cabinet acted as more than a sounding board, and Lincoln made substantial concessions to keep the cabinet together, including interpersonal mediation among members who were long time political rivals. David Homer Bates watched Lincoln and Stanton over a number of years in the War telegraph office: "Each knew how far to yield without a sacrifice of prerogative."[51]

In Lincoln's first four years there were only two changes in the cabinet. Simon Cameron resigned more or less against his will, while Caleb Smith eagerly accepted a federal judiciary post. This low turnover can be compared with previous administrations. Only two cabinets were as stable as Lincoln's: James Polk's and Franklin Pierce's, both of which did not contain leaders of the national reputation or political following of Bates, Cameron, Chase, or Seward. During Andrew Jackson's eight years, there were five secretaries of treasury, two secretaries of war, four secretaries of state, three attorneys general, three secretaries of the navy, and two postmasters general. Martin Van Buren had four changes in his cabinet. All of Tyler's cabinet except Webster resigned in 1841. The Taylor–Fillmore cabinet had three secretaries of state, two treasury, two

---

[50] Both Tyler and Fillmore had entered the presidency from the vice-presidency at 51 and 50 years of age, respectively. Pierce was elected to office at age 48, but this was on the basis of a somewhat questionably valorous Mexican War record. On this, see the generous comments penned by Grant, *Memoirs,* pp. 99-100. Polk was elected at age 49. Ages of the preceding presidents upon taking office are Washington, 57; Adams, 62; Jefferson, 58; Madison, 58; Monroe, 59; J.Q. Adams, 58; Jackson, 62; Van Buren, 56; Jefferson, 58; Madison, 58; Taylor, 65; Fillmore, 50; Pierce, 49; and Buchanan, 66. These data suggest that age or longevity was clearly an asset for election to national political office in the early period of the United States. The ages of the presidents are particularly striking when one recalls that average life expectancy at birth was only about 40 years. The ages of Lincoln's cabinet members in 1861 were: Welles, 59; Seward, 60; Bates, 68; Cameron, 62; Chase, 52; Smith, 53; and Blair, 48. Hannibal Hamlin, the vice-president, was 52. Blair was seen by other cabinet members as representative of the Blair family, and "Old Man Blair," Francis Preston Blair, was 70. This was an accurate perception. Even among his own cabinet, Lincoln was comparatively an uneducated, backwoods youngster. During the election of 1860, the ages of the candidates were Lincoln, 51; Douglas, 47; Breckinridge, 39; and Bell, 63. The election of 1860 had a group of very young candidates.

[51] Bates, *Lincoln and the Telegraph Office,* p. 390.

war, three navy, three interior, three postmasters general, and two attorneys general. Buchanan's cabinet completely fell to pieces during his last months in office.[52]

Richard Fenno, in one of the few books written about the cabinet as an institution, maintains that Lincoln wanted only to hold periodic meetings of the cabinet.[53] This is not true, but it supported Fenno's argument that "a gross distinction" should be made "between Presidents who require a great deal of advice and those with a greater intellectual self-sufficiency."[54]

A cursory examination of primary materials indicates that Seward desired only periodic meetings of the cabinet, convened by himself. Lincoln considered the convening of meetings the president's prerogative, which it clearly is in the Constitution. A cabinet debate was held on the frequency of meetings, and it was decided the meetings would be held every Tuesday and Friday noon. Lincoln concurred and acknowledged that this decision did not restrict him from calling special cabinet meetings.

These cabinet meetings were extremely informal. They usually began with a humorous anecdote told by Lincoln or a reading from Artemus Ward or Petroleum V. Naseby, and occasionally cabinet members joined in frivolity. Carpenter attended a meeting where the dour Bates precipitated a joke.[55] After the levity, the cabinet usually got down to business with Lincoln making any comments about latest news received and broaching a subject for discussion. Cabinet members also brought

---

[52] The count of cabinet members is in Leonard D. White, *The Jacksonians: A Study in Administrative History, 1829-1861* (New York, 1954), p. 94.

[53] Fenno, *The President's Cabinet*, p. 92. The recent photographic biography of Lincoln by the Kunhardts notes that the cabinet "was meeting almost daily" in the first seven months of the administration. Philip B. Kunhardt, Jr., Philip B. Kunhardt III, and Peter W. Kunhardt, *Lincoln* (New York, 1992), p. 160. The latter study, however, leaps to the conclusion that the administration "was in disarray." This seems to be based on "bickering" within the cabinet and frustration "at the slow pace of events." This conclusion represents a misunderstanding of group processes, and what Lincoln got and presumably expected from the cabinet. Later events speak for themselves, as the cabinet remained essentially intact through the first administration.

[54] Fenno, *The President's Cabinet*, p. 36.

[55] Francis Bicknell Carpenter, *Six Months at the White House with Abraham Lincoln* (New York, 1867), p. 55.

questions for discussion, often with spirited debates ensuing. One of Seward's friends once complained that Seward's failure to keep a diary was depriving posterity of an important record of cabinet meetings. Seward replied that it would contain little but quarrels which would disgrace the nation if ever exposed to public view.[56]

Apparently, no written minutes were kept of the meetings. John Hay and John Nicolay scarcely mention cabinet meetings in their multi-volume biography of Lincoln.[57]

As suggested above, the atmosphere of the meetings, even in times of crisis, was usually informal. Lincoln often leaned back on his chair, and propped his feet out the White House window, and Seward once delivered a report while reclining on a couch. Not infrequently, meetings broke down into a number of simultaneous (and acrimonious if Seward is believed) discussions over different matters.

Writers who prefer to build Lincoln's image as a great-man-in-office rarely devote much time to contributions of specific cabinet members to important decisions.[58] Even writers discussing the cabinet tend to de-emphasize the contribution of its members to policy decisions. Hendrick makes the statement, for example, that John P. Usher, the successor to Caleb Smith at Interior, "counted for nothing in the cabinet" in discussions of postwar policy.[59] One is left with the clear impression that Usher was a nonentity.

However, there is an interesting mention of Usher's contribution to a cabinet decision. On August 3, 1862, a highly-excited and disturbed Lincoln called an emergency meeting to announce that the Cherokee Indians had signed a treaty with the Confederates, and that he was considering the use of Federal troops to invade Indian Territory. Usher advised the cabinet to "deal indulgently with deluded Indians, and make

[56] Hendrick, *Lincoln's War Cabinet,* p. 370.

[57] John G. Nicolay and John Hay, *Abraham Lincoln: A History,* 10 vols. (New York, 1890).

[58] An example of this genre is Jay Monaghan, *Diplomat in Carpet Slippers: Abraham Lincoln Deals With Foreign Affairs* (Indianapolis, 1945). The often-cited counter example is the credit given to Seward for advising Lincoln to delay the Emancipation Proclamation until a Union victory. Both Blair and Seward advised this course, and the cabinet as a group fully debated it.

[59] Hendrick, *Lincoln's War Cabinet,* p. 457.

their deluders feel the weight of the Federal authority."[60] After discussion, most of the cabinet concurred with Usher. It is interesting to speculate what a diversion of these forces might have meant to the victorious and advancing Union forces in the Western Theater.

On July 22, 1862, Lincoln read the Emancipation Proclamation to the cabinet in substantially the same form which was to be announced two months later. According to Hendrick: "The cabinet had really little to do with the conception or formulation of this measure. It was, except for a few minor suggestions, exclusively Lincoln's work. None of his acts so completely embodied his conception of presidential responsibility."[61]

Hendrick, however, neglects the fact that slavery had been the object of numerous debates within the cabinet (Chase urged immediate and unrestricted emancipation, while both Blair and Bates urged caution). In fact, immediately before Lincoln read his draft of the Emancipation Proclamation, the cabinet unanimously agreed to drop the question of the colonization of ex-slaves, while Chase suggested the arming of slaves.[62]

Questions relating to Lincoln's draft were discussed at meetings on August 3 and possibly as early as August 1.[63] On September 22, Lincoln said, "I do not wish your advice about the main matter—for that I have determined for myself."[64] However, in reading the document, Lincoln was careful to note where the opinions of each of the cabinet members had been taken into account. There can be little doubt that Lincoln considered the proclamation expressive of collective discussions within

---

[60] Donald, ed., *Inside Lincoln's Cabinet,* p. 105.

[61] Hendrick, *Lincoln's War Cabinet,* p. 351.

[62] Donald, *Inside Lincoln's Cabinet,* pp. 98-99. The July 22 meeting left the question of the proclamation open for discussion. Lincoln's proclamation proposed the freeing of all slaves within the areas in rebellion, a move which would exclude the border states and previously recovered territory.

[63] Ibid., p. 103. Chase, on August 1, notes "a good deal of talk took place, but no results." He does not mention further discussion of the draft on August 8, August 19, September 2, September 5, and September 9. It is difficult to believe Chase's August 1 reference to the proclamation, given the heat of other discussions leading up to the Battle of Antietam.

[64] Ibid., p. 150.

the cabinet, though his primary Constitutional responsibility. In response to a serenade on September 24, Lincoln emphasized the extent to which the proclamation was made after "full deliberation [with the cabinet]."

During cabinet discussions, the opinions of participants frequently shifted, clear evidence of collective decision-making. The first important decision confronting the new administration was whether to provision Fort Sumter, the imposing masonry bastion guarding the approaches to Charleston, South Carolina. At a meeting on March 15, 1861, all but Blair and Chase opposed the provisioning of the fort, and Lincoln requested that all bring opinions in writing to the next meeting. The written opinions were discussed the following day. Although Blair stood firm, Chase began to waiver in his belief about the provisioning of the fort. Stephen A. Hurlbut, Ward H. Lamon, and Gustavas V. Fox were sent to Charleston to obtain further information for the president. Early on the morning of March 29, 1861, following the first state dinner, Gen. Winfield Scott proposed to an emergency session of the cabinet that the government abandon not only Fort Sumter, but also Fort Pickens, which guarded Pensacola, Florida. That afternoon, the cabinet met and discussed Scott's proposal and intelligence gathered by Hurlbut, Lamon, and Fox. Every member of the cabinet except Seward and Smith advised immediate relief of the forts, and the expedition to provision them was thus ordered.[65]

Another crucial decision was made December 26, 1861.[66] The cabinet meeting held that day after Christmas centered around the release of Confederate commissioners James Mason and John Slidell, who were taken from the *HMS Trent*, an English ship, on November 8, 1861, by the *USS San Jacinto*. This controversy had been a matter of heated debate for well over a month, and on December 25, it seemed that war with Great Britain was imminent. According to Hendrick, the idea of backing down to British threats "rankled in Lincoln's breast."[67] On

---

[65] This discussion follows Hendrick, *Lincoln's War Cabinet*, pp. 170-172.

[66] Salmon Chase mentions only that a meeting was held on December 25, an example of the incompleteness of the available diary sources. Ibid., p. 150.

[67] Hendrick, *Lincoln's Cabinet*, p. 205.

Christmas Day, Charles Sumner attended a cabinet meeting and presented letters from his influential British friends urging the president to
seek a peaceful solution. Seward delivered an impassioned argument for
the release of Mason and Slidell. Discussion was postponed until the
following day, when the cabinet decided to release Mason and Slidell.
Lincoln told Seward, "I found that I could not make an argument that
would satisfy my own mind. That proved to me that your ground was the
right one."[68]

A clue to the amount of discussion and debate preceding decisions is
the constant criticism of Bates and Chase that Lincoln lacked "will."
Welles, despite his admiration for the president, criticized his indecision
as well, and Horace Greeley, in his *New York Tribune*, was often causti-
cally critical.[69]

---

[68] Ibid., p. 208. See Macartney, *Lincoln and His Cabinet*, pp. 142-148, for a discussion of the
affair. There are other examples of group process within the cabinet. Except for Chase, the cabinet
presented in December 1862 a well-united front to Senate Radicals seeking Seward's removal.
Hendrick, *Lincoln's Cabinet*, p. 334. Among topics discussed at cabinet meetings for which we
have documented evidence were: prisoner exchanges, orders to troops in hostile territory,
conscription, Maj. Gen. John Pope's operations in northern Virginia, the reappointment of
McClellan to command the Army of the Potomac after Pope's thrashing at Second Bull Run, the
condemnation of McClellan's timid employment of his army by fellow officers (such as Phil
Kearney and John Pope), the creation of military districts or departments, certificates of trade with
Confederates, the colonization of ex-slaves, naval operations, the opening of the port of Norfolk,
Virginia, and the suspension of habeas corpus, to name just a few. Even this abbreviated
list—stretching only to September 15, 1863—is impressive, particularly considering the erratic
record-keeping of participants.

[69] Welles diary is particularly impressive in that, though a curmudgeon in many ways, he was
the first of the cabinet members to accurately foresee Lincoln's place in American history. Gideon
Welles, *Diary of Gideon Welles,* 2 vols. (Boston, 1911), vol. 1, p. 37. Lincoln often referred to his
secretary of the navy as "Father Neptune." It is a great misfortune that Welles did not maintain a
scrupulous record of cabinet meetings. One must remember that he and other heads of departments
were certainly more than fully occupied most of the time. They were the first secretaries of an
administration to confront daily large bureaucracies created to run the expanding war machinery.
Greeley obtained inside information from Chase and other Radicals who often obtained their
information, in turn, from Greeley (Greeley's newspaper, nevertheless, remained among Lincoln's
favorite pieces of reading material.) The discussion of Chase's relationship with Lincoln and other
members of the cabinet is a story in itself, but too lengthy to discuss here. Despite Chase's
personal idiosyncracies, his management of the Treasury Department during the war was
considered excellent by Lincoln, an opinion concurred with by most historians. When Lincoln had
to appoint a successor, he appointed a friend of Chase's from Maine who was chairman of the
Senate Finance Committee, William P. Fessenden, who also proved to be a good choice for this
critical position. Despite Chase's disloyalty to Lincoln personally, Lincoln appointed him to the
Supreme Court, where Chase later continued to maneuver for opportunities to enter the White
House as president, as Lincoln accurately foresaw that he would.

Comparison With Other Cabinets

The doctrine of a unified (not "compound") cabinet that was explicitly articulated by many of the presidents preceding Lincoln either ignored or misinterpreted the experience of the most brilliant cabinet up to that time. George Washington's cabinet during his first and part of his second administration was as brilliant and as contentious as any in American history. The rivalry of Alexander Hamilton and Thomas Jefferson, both members of Washington's cabinet, has been called the "Struggle of Titans."[70] The other members of the cabinet, all tested in public affairs, were Henry Knox, Edmund Randolph, and Samuel Osgood, with Vice President John Adams also playing an active role in cabinet discussions. Virtually all historians agree that Washington's first administration was a brilliant success, despite political and personal divisions within the cabinet and Congress.

Sufficient scholarship exists to suggest that in peace as in war "Washington depended heavily on his advisors."[71] Gordon Wood recounts an episode prior to the presidency in which Washington was offered shares of the James River and Potomac Canal Company by the Virginia legislature. A decision on this matter involved Washington in "more distress," agony, and soul-searching than seems warranted when the shares could be viewed as either modest compensation for services rendered or a pension. "The situation would seem comic today but it was not to Washington"; he consulted a wide spectrum of acquaintances—many of whom were political rivals of each other—on the virtue of his acceptance of such an offer: Thomas Jefferson, Patrick Henry, William Grayson, Benjamin Harrison, George Fairfax, Nathaniel Greene, and even Lafayette, who was in France.[72]

---

[70] Alf J. Mapp, Jr., *Thomas Jefferson: A Strange Case of Mistaken Identity* (New York, 1987), pp. 275-343.

[71] See the sources in Barry Schwartz, "George Washington and the Whig Conception of Heroic Leadership," *American Sociological Review* (February 1983).

[72] Gordon S. Wood, *The Radicalism of the American Revolution* (New York, 1992), p. 208.

Meetings of Washington's cabinet have been described by many as "stormy councils" which often provided conflicting advice.[73] In fact, the cabinet as a formal body developed unobtrusively during Washington's administration through his desire to consult advisors in council.[74] Washington, an avid fact gatherer, exhibited a keen interest in logical argument. Perhaps this is consistent with his reputation for having a "somewhat plodding mind of little imagination." His highest level of intellectual attainment as a young man was the mastery of surveying, and his first public office was surveyor of Culpeper County.[75] Washington, legendary for his reticence and shyness, often lamented his lack of formal education in both public and private correspondence, and eagerly asked for advice of those with whom he differed. He anxiously cultivated gentlemanly behavior which consisted of giving no unintended offense to others, and he was more than willing to share success—but never blame—with colleagues. Brissot de Warville noted, "His modesty is astonishing, particularly to a Frenchman. He speaks of the American War as if he had not been its leader."[76]

Thomas Jefferson also constructed a cabinet of exceptional individuals from "radical" and "moderate" wings of the nascent Democratic-Republican party: Albert Gallatin, often considered among the best secretaries of the treasury, James Madison, Henry Dearborn, Robert Smith (Benjamin Stoddert, a Federalist, remained until Smith came on board), Levi Lincoln, and Gideon Granger.[77] Jefferson's cabinet is often viewed as exceptionally "harmonious." Indeed, in a letter to A. L. C. Destutt de Tracy, dated January 26, 1811, Jefferson said that his administration "presented an example of harmony in a cabinet of six person[s], to which perhaps history has furnished no parallel. There never arose

[73] Robert M. Johnstone, *Jefferson and the Presidency: Leadership in the Young Republic* (Ithaca, 1978), p. 85.

[74] Marcus Cunliffe, *George Washington: Man and Monument* (New York, 1958), p. 135.

[75] James T. Flexner, *George Washington, 1732-1775* (Boston, 1965), p. 251.

[76] Wood, *The Radicalism of the American Revolution*, p. 199.

[77] Abraham Lincoln was distantly related to Levi through a common ancestor, Samuel, who came to America in 1633. See Warren, *Lincoln's Youth*, p. 3

during that whole time, an instance of an unpleasant thought or word between members."[78]

This clause of Jefferson's letter is often used as evidence that he selected members of his cabinet to assure "harmony."[79] A more careful analysis shows that the selection of Jefferson's cabinet was influenced by philosophical diversity within party ranks, regional interests, and Jefferson's own appraisal of the rectitude of potential members.[80] Considerable evidence exists for vigorous debate among cabinet members over such issues as the participation *b*of Vice President Aaron Burr in executive decision-making (Jefferson considered Burr untrustworthy and venal), the Louisiana Purchase, and issues surrounding decommissioning ships in the navy. These debates frequently evoked passionate responses within Democratic-Republican ranks, since they involved ideological differences surrounding interpretations of the Constitution, as well as sectional economic and political interests.[81]

Some of the evidence for vigorous debate exists within the Destutt de Tracy letter itself, which is rarely quoted in full. The context of the letter also is important: Jefferson was writing about the translation and printing of de Tracy's work in Philadelphia. Before he left the White House, Jefferson had begun negotiations in this regard for de Tracy. The letter written from Monticello dealt with a number of issues, the most important of which (for the purposes of this discussion) was Montesquieu's and de Tracy's high regard for a plural executive. Jefferson

[78] The entire letter is published in Thomas Jefferson, *Writings* (New York, 1984), pp. 1241-1257.

[79] See, for example, Johnstone, *Jefferson and the Presidency,* p. 86, and Alf J. Mapp, *Thomas Jefferson: Passionate Pilgrim* (Lanham, 1991). Mapp, while not citing the letter directly, is clearly influenced by it.

[80] Henry Adams, *History of the United States of America During the Administrations of Thomas Jefferson* (New York, 1986), pp. 148-168.

[81] It is not too difficult for us to understand today how some of these issues can be associated with strong sectional and economic interests. Decreasing the size of the navy and the substitution of low draft vessels for frigates has obvious modern parallels with cuts in current defense spending. The warship was one of the major national government expenditures of Jefferson's day, with agrarian interests in the South and West less concerned with bearing this cost than merchants in New England and the mid-Atlantic states. Likewise, the primary beneficiaries of the Louisiana Purchase were the West and traders on the Mississippi. The cost of the "purchase" would be largely borne by tariffs in the South and middle Atlantic states.

believed that a plural executive would not work on the basis of (1) the experience of the Directory during the French Revolution, and (2) his experience in both the Washington and his own administration. Jefferson believed shared executive power would fail "due to internal jealousies and dissensions. . .which will ever arise among men in equal power." He then offered as a solution to this problem of executive authority among "men constituted with the ordinary passions" the American "counsels of cabinets of heads of departments." According to Jefferson, only such a counsel under the "power of decision of the President" in Washington's administration was able to reconcile "monarchism" and "republicanism." Only after this discussion did Jefferson make the above-cited earlier comment about harmony in his administration. He also added, however: "We sometime met under differences of opinion, but scarcely ever failed, by conversing and reasoning, so to modify each other's ideas, as to produce a unanimous result. Yet, able and amicable as these members were, I am not certain this would have been the case, had each possessed equal and independent powers." [82]

Jefferson and Benjamin Franklin are America's personifications of the Age of Reason. Jefferson's studies in science are well known, but what may be less well known is his love of logic, which often expressed itself in classifications or typologies: the best known of these are his work in library classification and the Anglo-Saxon language, which were used well into recent times. Jefferson was noticeably reticent or shy in crowds, but very open during small dinner conversations. Ironically, Jefferson, who had one of the best educations then available in the colonies, often bemoaned his lack of knowledge and understanding. Unlike many geniuses, Jefferson was not deluded by his brilliance, for he appreciated how much he did not know. One of the characteristics often noted of Jefferson was his kindliness. Despite hyperbole in some of his personal correspondence, not meant for others eyes, he had a reputation for helpfulness and, unfortunately for his personal finances,

---

[82] The complete text of this letter is reprinted in Jefferson, *Writings,* pp. 1241-1247. The emphasis that Jefferson gives for unanimity of decisions is questionable, and may have arisen from a rosy retrospection after his retirement. See also, Adams, *History of the United States,* p. 301, for an example of a cabinet decision. Unfortunately, documentation for cabinet meetings is sparse.

being an easy touch. One of his favorite sayings was "things should be taken by the smooth handle."

In contrast to Lincoln, Washington, and Jefferson, James Buchanan would have nothing to do with a "compound" cabinet. Instead, he advised Franklin Pierce:

> The cabinet ought to be a unit. . . .I undertake to predict that whoever may be President, if he disregards this principle in the formation of his cabinet, he will have committed a fatal mistake. He who attempts to conciliate opposing factions by placing ardent and embittered representatives of each in his cabinet, will discover that he only has infused into these factions new vigor and power for mischief. [83]

After his election, Buchanan tried to build his cabinet around trusted personal friends. Only one of these would accept an appointment; thereafter, he proceeded to a second list of friends with whom he was less familiar. He finally settled on Howell Cobb, John B. Floyd, Isaac Toucey, Lewis Cass, Jacob Thompson, Aaron Brown, and Jeremiah Black. Historian Kenneth Stampp concludes that "Buchanan thus succeeded in forming a harmonious cabinet that would loyally support his plans to suppress slavery agitation and undermine the sectional Republican party. It was a cabinet of Democratic moderates, containing no true representative of the northern free-soil wing or of the southern fire-eaters. But it was a far from distinguished body."[84]

To the country as a whole, the cabinet appeared to be one of Southern doughfaces. Northern Democrats (such as Stephen A. Douglas), who were occasionally critical of the South and the administration, were viewed as "malcontents" and systematically excluded from cabinet discussions. Complaints of cabinet members—up until the end of the administration mostly good-natured—focused on Buchanan's stubbornness and unwillingness to listen to them. "We meet in Cabinet, and 'discuss' very much; but I believe we all feel it to be a sort of game of soli-

---

[83] White, *The Jacksonians*, p. 90. The underlining appears to be in the original correspondence.

[84] Kenneth M. Stampp, *America in 1857* (New York, 1990), p. 62.

taire—the play of Hamlet with the part of Hamlet left out."[85] Many cabinet meetings were held without Buchanan present. These were often presided over by Cobb, despite the fact that Cass was Secretary of State. Buchanan and his friend, John Appleton, often signed Cass' name to documents, which he left unread.

The failure of Buchanan's administration has been attributed to his character weaknesses and his puppet role in the hands of proslavery interests. Buchanan often found himself in agreement with Southern politicians; therefore, he can hardly be called a puppet. Stampp suggests that while some of the premises underlying Buchanan's policies may have been correct, neither fact nor delusions were challenged within the administration. Unfortunately for Buchanan and the country, his ill-chosen policy of cynical political manipulation was inappropriate for the time and well beyond the capacity of his presidency.[86]

Ironically, on paper a James Buchanan résumé would have radiated high qualifications for the presidency. Five terms in Congress, a decade in the Senate, Secretary of State under Polk, and Minister to Great Britain, were supplemented by long experience in party politics in Pennsylvania. These achievements, however, were matched by some character deficits including a local and regional political reputation as a party hack, a long legislative career lacking in association with any legislative initiatives, and complicity in the Ostend Manifesto, which was a cynical attempt to acquire Cuba as a slave state without appropriate congressional knowledge or approval.

Conclusions

Much of the discussion of the presidency focuses on the personality of the officeholder, and clearly character can be important in shaping institutions.[87] Indeed, Lincoln, Washington, and Jefferson had well-de-

---

[85] Ibid., p. 70.

[86] Ibid., pp. 284-285.

[87] We agree with James Q. Wilson that it is truly unfortunate that "character" is so little discussed, particularly moral and ethical implications. James Q. Wilson, *On Character* (Washington, D.C., 1991).

served reputations for honesty, kindliness, and inquisitiveness. Honesty and kindliness have been emphasized in the "mythology" constructed around them. What has been less recognized, with the possible exception of Jefferson, is the degree to which all three engaged in lifetime learning, which to them also included moral self-improvement.

A common characteristic of all three was their amazing capacity to sublimate ego. Washington rarely replied to personal criticism, and when he did he deeply regretted it. Jefferson and Lincoln often wrote angry letters; in the latter case, he usually did not send them. Jefferson frequently did the same, but when one was sent it was clearly noted as confidential. Yet, all three men took criticism to heart.[88]

Alfred Mapp has argued that modern critiques of Jefferson based on his alleged inconsistencies or even hypocrisy by some social scientists fail to recognize that Jefferson was a dynamically growing person who changed opinions and beliefs as he aged and more information became available to him.[89] This also was true of Washington and Lincoln. Regrettably, for both historical accuracy and the understanding of political institutions, Washington, Jefferson, and Lincoln, especially, have been subjected to a Great Man theory of history. In one version of treatment, they arise from Zeus' head like Athena fully armored with Wisdom. In the case of Lincoln, perceptions of the Man and Policy are altered readily in versions to fit circumstances defined by critics. The most recent examples of this are two articles by Garry Wills: a laudatory article in the wake of Desert Storm, and another entitled "Dishonest Abe," which appeared one month prior to the 1992 presidential election.[90]

Such debunking, though perhaps inevitable, distracts the public and leads to few standards by which presidents can be judged. In the case of

---

[88] Interestingly, Harry Truman was noted for writing lengthy angry memos and letters which he never sent. Truman was very well read historically, but we have seen no evidence that he was aware of this pattern in Lincoln. McCullough, *Truman.*

[89] Alf J. Mapp, *Thomas Jefferson: A Strange Case of Mistaken Identity* (New York, 1991), pp. 1-7.

[90] Garry Wills, "Lincoln," *Life* (February, 1991), pp. 22-28, and Garry Wills, "Dishonest Abe," *Time* (October 5, 1992), pp. 41-42. The latter article is notable for its extreme inaccuracies, i.e."he was nominated by one of the most corrupt conventions ever held," the discussion of the Crittenden amendment is ahistorical, and so forth.

Jefferson, for example, his alleged affair with a mulatto slave was resurrected in a best-selling psychobiography to demonstrate Jefferson's hypocrisy.[91] While no basis in fact for such an affair exists, the scholarly refutation is unlikely to find as wide an audience as Brodie's "scandal."[92] In the meantime, as the stock of presidents rises or falls on the basis of perceived consistent or inconsistent moral righteousness, the organizational context in which presidential, or any public, policy is made and the dynamic effects of institutions on the man-in-office are ignored. It is unlikely that any man, for better or worse, has left the presidency the same as he entered it.

The cabinet was an important, and currently neglected, source of information, criticism, and, perhaps, wisdom for three great presidents, and a source of poor or wrongly ignored advice for Buchanan and many others. The distinction between presidents who need a great deal of advice and those who do not is fatuous in view of the size and diversity of the United States and complexity of presidential decision-making. It is difficult to imagine a president who does not need a great deal of advice. It is easier to imagine a president, like Buchanan, who will not seek unbiased opinion, particularly in view of the recent history of this country. Current scholars are sensitive to the danger of a chief executive who has a court "mass of intrigue, posturing, strutting, cringing, and pious commitment to irrelevant windbaggery."[93]

Nevertheless, much of the writing on the post-New Deal presidency emphasizes the degree to which the president has to be his own man and represent broader interests in the country than can be articulated in a heterogenous Congress. Perhaps, the Great Man theory of leadership rises like a specter from Hyde Park. Some of this writing is frightening: "And mere experience, however relevant, is no assurance that a President will find the confidence he needs just when he needs it most. Such confidence requires that his image of himself in office justify an unre-

---

[91] Fawn Brodie, *Thomas Jefferson: An Intimate History* (New York, 1974).

[92] Virginius Dabney, *The Jefferson Scandals* (New York, 1981). It is likely that the brother of Jefferson's beloved wife, Martha Wayles, was the father of Sally Hemings.

[93] George E. Reedy, *The Twilight of the Presidency* (New York, 1970), p. xi, cited in Harold Seidman and Robert Gilmour, *Politics, Position and Power* (New York, 1986), pp. 77ff.

mitting search for personal power."[94] Although written a hundred years
later, this sounds more like Chase or Buchanan than Lincoln, Jefferson,
or Washington, who would have emphasized "virtue" in public office.

The cabinet rarely, if ever, emerges from these discussions except as
an "adversary" of the president. A commonly cited admonition attributed to Charles G. Dawes, the first director of the budget, is, "cabinet
members are the natural enemies of the President." However, as Seidman and Gilmour note, the quotation is incomplete and taken out of
context. Dawes' complete statement was, "cabinet members are vice
presidents in charge of spending and as such are the natural enemies of
the President" [emphasis added].[95] In fact, Seidman and Gilmour argue
that members of the cabinet are the president's "natural allies," even
while they may be the bane of presidential staffers.

In view of the successful experiences of three great presidents with
their cabinets (and the string of recent mediocrities, or worse), one may
suspect that a growing and entrenched presidential staff too often plays
the court sycophant. Even if flattery should be the exception and not the
rule, the privileged position of a large staff will insulate the president
from his cabinet. As Matthew Holden, Jr., and Martha Derthick clearly
point out in their dissent from the NAPA report discussed earlier, the
president can have personal knowledge of the competence and character
of no more than twenty persons; therefore, consultation processes must
be limited by such a constraint.[96]

The primary issue in the presidency is not one of whether a president should obtain advice, but how to most effectively and efficiently do
this. More attention should be given to the construction and administration of the cabinet in successful administrations. The current resort to
large presidential staffs may represent a resurrection of Tory government
and special privilege antithetical to the American Revolution and gov-

---

[94] Richard E. Neustadt, *Presidential Power* (New York, 1964), p. 172.

[95] An example of the misuse of this citation appears in Neustadt, *Presidential Power,* pp. 47-48.

[96] National Academy of Public Administration, *Beyond Distrust,* pp. 133-135. As in so much of
the management literature, one has to ask about the number: Why twenty? The relevant point in
this chapter and by the two authors cited is that this number must be quite modest compared to the
responsibilities of office.

ernment by the people. Pervasive public cynicism is a natural conse-
quence of such an unrepresentative system of government.

The world appears more complex today than a century or two ago.
While a suggestion to look backward for examples or prototypes of
presidential decision-making may appear on the surface profoundly reactionary, recent work in modern management theory indicates that behavior of at least some of the great presidents is consistent with both
current theory and research findings. All three of the great presidents
discussed in this article sought advice from representatives of diverse
constituencies and continually searched for information—the picture of
Lincoln at the telegraph office is an indelible one. Lincoln, Washington
and Jefferson each used a consultative leadership style, consistent with
principles of modern management theory that stress participation in decision-making by those directly affected.

These principles mentioned briefly in the opening sections of this
essay would seem to argue that the chief policy advisors of the president
ought to be the heads of executive departments in cabinet. Only these
individuals—and not staffers—have a direct service-provider relationship with the public, and only they have a clear vested interest in the
successful implementation of a policy or program. Lincoln himself re-
lieved Maj. Gen. John C. Fremont when it became clear that "he [was]
losing support of men near him, whose support any man in his position
must have to be successful. His cardinal mistake is that he isolates
himself & allows nobody to see him; and by which he does not know
what matter he is dealing with."[97]

More work needs to be done in this area. Although literature is
available, it is slim and often focuses on why poor group decisions have

---

[97] Letter dated September 9, 1861, to Maj. Gen. David Hunter, reprinted in Basler (ed.), *The Collected Works,* vol. 4, p. 513. The annotations also make it clear that Frank Blair and his brother, the Attorney General, were involved in this policy outcome. General Winfield Scott had written on this matter five days earlier, and it seems highly probable that the Fremont situation was discussed in the cabinet. No doubt political motives were involved, but clearly these are not evident on Lincoln's part from this correspondence. Kunhardt, *Lincoln,* p. 160, emphasizes the role mismanagement of funds played in Fremont's relief. This matter is not alluded to in the correspondence cited above. In fact, the decision is based solely on a principle that modern managers would understand.

been made by the presidential staff in council, not the cabinet.[98] Admittedly, this chapter focuses on the efforts of three extraordinary men. Whether more "ordinary" leaders are potentially as capable is a reasonable question. The democratic principle embedded in "cabinet alchemy" calls on the better angels of our nature and the control of Faustian ones.

[98] See, for example, Frederick Thayer, "Presidential Policy Processes and 'New Administration': A Search for Revised Paradigms," *Public Administration Review* (September/October, 1971); Irving L. Janis, *Victims of Groupthink* (Boston, 1972); and Graham Allison, *The Essence of Decision* (Boston, 1971).

In the long term, Lincoln's coordinate review legacy could promote total disaster for constitutional democracy as we know it. Judge Learned Hand observed that without the Supreme Court as ultimate arbiter as required by traditional judicial review, finality would be unattainable and the whole system would collapse.

William D. Bader

Attorney William Bader is a 1974 Phi Beta Kappa graduate of Vassar College. He pursued graduate studies at Cornell University and in 1979 received his Juris Doctorate from the Hofstra University School of Law. Between 1988 and 1990 he was Attorney–Editor at West Publishing Company and a major contributor to *Corpus Juris Secundum,* among other West publications. He has authored several papers and chapters on constitutional history and constitutional jurisprudence, including *Great Justices of the U.S. Supreme Court* (Lang, 1993), and "The Jurisprudence of Levi Woodbury" in the *Vermont Law Review* with Henry J. Abraham (1994). His practice specialty is constitutional law, and he teaches psychiatry and law at the University of Virginia Medical School.

Abraham Lincoln and Judicial Review

Traditional judicial review, as understood in this essay, is the power of the U. S. Supreme Court to declare acts of the Congress and the executive unconstitutional. As such, the Court is the supreme and final arbiter of the Constitution. After the Supreme Court's decision in the *Dred Scott Case,*[1] Abraham Lincoln began to espouse a controversial philosophy which was hostile to traditional judicial review.

One of the seminal exercises of judicial review occurred in Dr. Bonham's Case in 1610.[2] Invoking natural law, Sir Edward Coke, the Lord Chief Justice, wrote: "When an act of Parliament is against common right and reason, or repugnant, . . . the common law will control it and adjudge such act to be void."[3]

Although judicial review did not firmly take hold in England, it has become a cornerstone of our constitutional government in the United States. There are numerous theories which seek to legitimize judicial

---

[1] 19 How. 393 (1857).

[2] 8 Co. 188a (1610).

[3] Ibid.

review, and a few which attempt to deny its existence. While interesting, critical analysis of all these theories is beyond the scope of this chapter. It will suffice to say that despite the lack of explicit language in Article III, there is much evidence that the Framers at the Constitutional Convention, both Federalists and Anti-Federalists, overwhelmingly favored judicial review and feared government by a totally unrestrained popular majority who might not respect the minority's constitutional rights.[4] Furthermore, it has been shown that such a power of judicial review was explicitly acknowledged in the First Congress.[5] Some scholars have also suggested that judicial review is inherent in the very structure of our Constitution.[6] Judge Learned Hand believed that the traditional rules pertaining to the legal construction of documents dictated an engrafting on of judicial review to prevent the Constitution from failing as a legal instrument.[7]

The issue was squarely settled, however, in 1803 by Chief Justice John Marshall in the important case of *Marbury v. Madison*.[8] Declaring section 13 of the Judiciary Act of 1789 unconstitutional, Marshall held:

> If a law be in opposition to the Constitution; if both the law and the Constitution apply to a particular case, so that the court must either decide that case conformable to the law, disregarding the Constitution, or conformable to the Constitution, disregarding the law; the court must determine which of these conflicting rules governs the case; this is of the very essence of judicial duty.[9]

Thus, Marshall reasoned that the Court must interpret the Constitu-

---

[4] Charles A. Beard, *The Supreme Court and the Constitution* (Englewood Cliffs, 1962).

[5] Alexander M. Bickel, *The Least Dangerous Branch: The Supreme Court at the Bar of Politics* (New Haven, 1986), p. 21.

[6] Ibid.

[7] Learned Hand, *The Bill of Rights* (New York, 1964), p. 29.

[8] 1 Cranch 137 (1803).

[9] Ibid.

tion and apply it to strike down any act by a coordinate branch which it adjudges to be in noncompliance.[10]

Marbury v. Madison set a precedent that has been followed so closely ever since, that it has become the seminal case in our legal culture. As Henry Abraham writes, ". . .the issue has been decisively settled by history—the debate over the legitimacy of judicial review is now an academic exercise." [11]

Under our regime of traditional judicial review, the accepted manner for presidential challenge of a law's constitutionality has been to submit the contested issue in case form to the Supreme Court for a final decision. As Chief Justice William Rehnquist noted when he headed the Office of Legal Counsel at the U.S. Justice Department, the power of the president in this respect does not extend beyond his right ". . .to take appropriate steps to have the law [judicially] tested."[12]

One gains insight regarding Lincoln's later thinking about judicial review after examination of his career as a trial and appellate attorney on the American frontier. In such a practice he encountered his share of lay judges, and only a few members of the bench who had formal law school educations. As Carl Sandburg notes ". . .having eaten many meals with judges and having slept in the same hotel bedrooms with judges, and having himself on a few occasions sat on the bench by appointment during the absence of a judge for a day or two," he was decidedly underawed by those who donned the black robes.[13] Furthermore, Lincoln likely viewed traditional legal doctrines such as *stare decisis*, or respect for precedent, as ad hoc and informal, due to the fact that great rhetoric about basic principles counted for more than learned utilization of legal precedent in most frontier tribunals. Robert A. Ferguson writes:

[10] Ibid.

[11] Henry J. Abraham, *Freedom and the Court* (New York, 1988), p. 7.

[12] 2 Moorhead Hearings 381.

[13] Carl Sandburg in Paul M. Angle, ed., *The Lincoln Reader* (New Brunswick, 1947), pp. 222-223.

> Lincoln speaks with the voice of a circuit-riding lawyer. He argues
> from ideas presented as fundamentals, from principles rather than
> precedent. . . .His essential medium is the speech. . . .On the Illinois
> court circuits of the 1840s, eloquence still counted. . .How one
> spoke was at least as important as what one knew, and it was hardly
> a coincidence that [his] law partners, Ward Hill Lamon and William
> Herndon, shared his fondness for Shakespearean declamation.[14]

The 1857 *Dred Scott Case* gave Lincoln the opportunity to put forth his theory of judicial review. He vehemently disagreed with the Supreme Court's holding in the *Dred Scott Case,* which declared the Missouri Compromise unconstitutional and prohibited the federal government, on due process grounds, from proscribing slavery in any territory. First in the context of his senatorial campaign against Stephen A. Douglas, and later in the opening days of his presidency, Lincoln criticized the Court's decision and propounded the controversial general principle that "judicial decisions are of greater or less authority as precedents according to circumstances."[15] Thus, he believed that decisions of great authority essentially require unanimity of the Court or judicial reaffirmation over a long period of time, widespread public agreement, and a history of concurrent support from the other branches of government. Otherwise, according to Lincoln, a case has no binding effect on anyone except the particular litigants at bar.[16]

The essence of Lincoln's theory of judicial review can be characterized as a "coordinate review," where each branch of government makes its own constitutional determination of the issues before it, and no one branch has supremacy over the others with respect to such judgements. Thus Lincoln could state that if he were in Congress and a vote came up on the question of whether slavery should be prohibted in a new territory, "in spite of that *Dred Scott* decision, I would vote that it should."[17]

---

[14] Robert A. Ferguson, *Law and Letters in American Culture* (Cambridge, 1984), pp. 308-309.

[15] Roy P. Basler, ed., *Abraham Lincoln: His Speeches and Writings* (New York, 1946), p. 355.

[16] Ibid.

[17] Bickel, *The Least Dangerous Branch,* p. 260.

Lincoln regarded such independent judgment by a coordinate branch of government as not merely permissible, but required absolutely. He essentially believed that traditional judicial review by an unelected judiciary undesirably thwarted a great fundamental of our democracy, the majority's political will as expressed through their elected leaders. He stated in his first Inaugural Address:

> . . .the candid citizen must confess that if policy of the government, upon vital questions, affecting the whole people, is to be irrevocably fixed by decisions of the Supreme Court, the instant they are made, in ordinary litigation between parties, in personal actions, the people will have ceased, to be their own rulers, having to that extent, practically resigned their government, into the hands of that eminent tribunal.[18]

Lincoln could not appreciate, however, the Framers' desire to protect the minority's basic constitutional rights from the immediate political realm through the institution of traditional judicial review, and thereby restrict majority will to its constitutional bonds. The Framers certainly realized, in Charles McIlwain's words, that:

> . . .even in a popular state. . .the problem of law versus will remains the most important of all practical problems. We must leave open the possibility of an appeal from the people drunk to the people sober, if individual minority rights are to be protected in the periods of excitement and hysteria from which we are unfortunately not immune.[19]

Lincoln, however, did not agree with this interpretation, asserting instead that:

> A majority. . .is the only true sovereign of a free people. Whoever rejects it does, of necessity, fly into anarchy or to despotism. Unanimity is impossible; the rule of a minority, as a permanent arrange-

---

[18] Basler, *Abraham Lincoln,* pp. 585-586.

[19] Charles McIlwain, *Constitutionalism: Ancient and Modern* (Ithaca, 1947), pp. 145-146.

ment, is wholly inadmissable; so that, rejecting the majority principle, anarchy or despotism in some form is all that is left.[20]

As Alexander Bickel notes, Lincoln's coordinate review was considered a "heresy against the theoretical basis of *Marbury v. Madison*" by
his contemporaries.[21] In fact, the role of the Supreme Court as final
arbiter in our constitutional system has long enjoyed widespread acceptance among members of the polity despite some controversial grum-
bling from Andrew Jackson in the 1830s.[22] In conjunction with the
"Executive Prerogative" power which President Lincoln also claimed
for himself, his theory of coordinate review was an essential aberration
which held great potential for danger.

Specifically, Lincoln exercised a prerogative, which he believed in-
hered in the presidency, to take extra-constitutional and unconstitutional
actions as exigencies of state demanded.[23] Scholars such as Mark Rozell
argue that the judiciary provides a safety check on excesses in the exercise of such presidential prerogative.[24] Of course, no such check really
existed in Lincoln's use of unbridled prerogative since his theory of
judicial review led him to believe that his interpretation of the Constitution had as much binding validity as the Supreme Court's. Thus, for
example, when Chief Justice Taney declared Lincoln's suspension of the
right of habeas corpus unconstitutional in *Ex parte Merryman*, the president simply ignored the justice's declaration.[25]

Lincoln's legacy of coordinate review has been a special favorite of
those who wish to change the course of constitutional law, but who have

---

[20] Roy Basler, ed., *Collected Works of Abraham Lincoln*, 8 vols. (New Brunswick, 1953), vol. 4,
p. 268.

[21] Bickel, *The Least Dangerous Branch*, p. 261.

[22] Alfred H. Kelly and Winfred A. Harbison, *The American Constitution: Its Origins and
Development* (New York, 1976), p. 317.

[23] Richard M. Pious, *The American Presidency* (New York, 1979), p. 57.

[24] Mark J. Rozell, "Executive Prerogative and American Constitutionalism: In Defense of the
Lincolnian View." This paper was presented at LSU, Shreveport, Louisiana, September 18, 1992,
and is published as the following essay in this volume.

[25] 17 Fed. Cases 487 (1861); Kelly and Harbison, *The American Constitution*, 24, p. 413.

lost rather decisively in the Supreme Court. Early in the New Deal, for example, President Franklin Roosevelt initiated a political juggernaut to attack a recalcitrant Supreme Court, threatening its very role in our governmental process, while invoking Lincoln on judicial review as his. primary justification.[26] Similarly, during the 1930s, the American Communist party and its allies, unable to further their program through the Court, launched, in Daniel J. Boorstin's words, a "radical attack on the doctrine of judicial review. . .by way of a labored two-volume treatise, Louis Boudin's *Government by Judiciary.*"[27] In the 1950s, die-hard segregationists based their nearly successful political disruption of Court mandated school integration on the Lincolnian constitutional philosophy.[28] Today, some opponents of abortion who are frustrated by the unsuccessful attempts to overrule *Roe v. Wade* advocate anti-abortion political action based upon coordinate review theory.[29] More political free-for-alls over our basic rights, which are disruptive of the traditional separation of powers, and are legitimized by the Lincolnian perspective on judicial review, can be expected in the immediate future.

In the meantime, the Lincoln legacy, which denies the validity of traditional judicial review, would deprive our political-legal culture of the generalized principled restraining influence that such review can provide by its mere existence. Justice Benjamin Cardozo, in *The Nature of the Judicial Process*, wrote eloquently of the constitutionally salutary effects on the political branches of such a restraining influence brought about by judicial review:

> By conscious or unconscious influence, the presence of this re-
> straining power [of judicial review] aloof in the background, but
> none the less always in reserve, tends to stabilize and rationalize the
> legislative judgment, to infuse it with the glow of principle, to hold
> the standard aloft and visible for those who must run the race and
> keep the faith. . .[It manifests its chief worth] in making vocal and

[26] E. Roosevelt, ed., *FDR: His Personal Letters, 1928-1945*, vol. 1 (1950), pp. 459-460.

[27] Daniel J. Boorstin, *Hidden History: Exploring Our Secret Past* (New York, 1989), p. 83.

[28] Bickel, *The Least Dangerous Branch,* p. 259.

[29] 410 U.S. 113 (1973).

audible the ideals that might otherwise be silenced, in giving them
continuity of life and expression, in guiding and directing choice
within the limits where choice ranges.[30]

In the long term, Lincoln's coordinate review legacy could promise
total disaster for constitutional democracy as we know it. Judge Learned
Hand observed that without the Supreme Court as ultimate arbiter as
required by traditional judicial review, finality would be unattainable
and the whole system would collapse.[31] It is also likely that when the
conflicts are of a particularly contentious nature, the branch of government with access to the military would have the final word. Note that in
Ex parte Merryman, President Lincoln commanded the Union Army,
while Chief Justice Taney merely possessed his pen and paper.

Abraham Lincoln proved to be one of the most brilliant leaders in
United States history. His masterful political skills, tempered by a be-
nevolent disposition, helped preserve the Union. It is clear, however, that
our destiny as a nation must not be dependent on the benevolence of one
man or woman, but on the rule of law. As Raoul Berger writes:

> The historical records make clear that the Court was made the
> 'ultimate interpreter' of the Constitution; and as a corollary it was
> contemplated that its 'final' interpretations would be obeyed. Dis-
> obedience by either Congress or the President would set at naught
> the carefully wrought constitutional 'limits.' To make effectiveness
> of those limits turn on the likelihood of disobedience to a decree is
> to feed defiance of law.[32]

---

[30] Benjamin N. Cardozo, *The Nature of the Judicial Process* (New Haven, 1921), pp. 93-94.

[31] Hand, *The Bill of Rights,* pp. 29-30.

[32] Raoul Berger, *Executive Privilege: A Constitutional Myth* (New York, 1975), pp. 378-379.

The famous Mathew B. Brady photograph used on the five dollar bill, taken by Anthony Berger of Brady's studio on February 9, 1864, and considered "the most satisfactory likeness" by Lincoln's son, Robert T. Lincoln. (The Frank and Virginia Williams Collection of Lincolniana)

The president has a prerogative to act as Lincoln did, in times of emergency, and to do so unfettered by any specific statutory restraints. A proper understanding of the constitutional framers' notion of the separation of powers provides all the necessary restraints against presidential excesses and also ensures the chief executive the latitude and discretion to act in emergencies.

Mark J. Rozell

Mark Rozell, an associate professor of political science at Mary Washington College, was awarded his doctorate in American Government from the University of Virginia in 1987. He is the author of *The Press and the Carter Presidency* (Westview, 1989), *The Press and the Ford Presidency* (University of Michigan Press 1992), and *Executive Privilege: The Dilemma of Secrecy and Democratic Accountability* (Johns Hopkins University Press, 1994), as well as numerous book chapters and articles in journals including *Political Science Quarterly*, *Polity*, and *Presidential Studies Quarterly*.

Executive Prerogative: Abraham Lincoln and American Constitutionalism

Although Abraham Lincoln is revered as one of the nation's greatest presidents—if not *the* greatest—his extraordinary exercise of presidential powers remains mired in constitutional controversy. As is often the case, historical hindsight vindicates the extraordinary measures that Lincoln adopted to preserve the Union. But as a matter of constitutionalism, retrospective assessments that a president's actions worked do not alone provide justification for such actions. The constitutional stamp of approval is not automatically conferred on decisions that produced the desired results. Such decisions must be firmly based in recognized, proper constitutional principles.

The constitutional controversy over Lincoln's wartime measures is not primarily a results-oriented debate. This debate specifically concerns whether Lincoln in the first place had the authority to exercise the prerogative powers of the presidency and, more generally, whether any U.S. president has such authority.

The argument presented here is that Lincoln's extraordinary wartime measures were both necessary and constitutionally proper. A careful reading of the writings of the Framers, the Constitution, case law, and of influential theorists, makes clear that the president indeed may adopt extra-constitutional—and even perhaps unconstitutional—measures under the most extraordinary circumstances. There is no principle higher than that of self-preservation because, as Lincoln understood, without achieving that goal no other valued societal ends—particularly those guaranteed by the Bill of Rights—can be secured.

The presidential prerogative power can be exercised only under the most extraordinary circumstances and for the most compelling reasons. The Lincolnian view is not that of the completely unfettered presidency as expressed by former president Richard M. Nixon in his assertion that "when a president does it, that means that it is not illegal."[1] A proper view of presidential prerogative recognizes the legitimacy and normally co-equal status of the other governmental branches. The Framers' notion of the separation of powers provides the vital mechanisms for Congress and the judiciary to contest—and eventually control—presidential excesses in the exercise of prerogative powers.

This essay will examine Lincoln's exercise of prerogative powers. It presents the arguments against presidential prerogative, provides a defense of Lincolnian prerogative, and demonstrates how prerogative powers fit comfortably within a republican regime based on separated and balanced powers.

Lincoln and Executive Prerogative

According to Lincoln, the president possesses independent authority under the Constitution's Commander-in-Chief clause (Article II, Section 2) and the responsibility, as set forth in Article II, Section 3, "to take care that the laws be faithfully executed." Lincoln employed these constitutional measures in the twelve week period between the outbreak of hostilities at Fort Sumter and the convening on July 4, 1861, of a special session of Congress. According to Richard M. Pious, by adopting unilateral actions during this period Lincoln had "in effect created a form of *constitutional dictatorship*: constitutional because the ultimate checks of

---

[1] "Nixon: A President May Violate the Law," *U.S. News & World Report,* May 30, 1977, p. 65.

elections and impeachment remained, but a 'dictatorship' because he disregarded the proximate checks and balances in the emergency."[2]

Lincoln's extra-constitutional actions included a blockade of Southern ports without a congressional declaration of war, an increase in the regular army by 22,714 officers and men, 18,000 in the Navy, and a call for 42,034 volunteers for three years of service. Lincoln adopted these actions without specific constitutional or statutory authorization, even though the Constitution grants to Congress power to "raise and support armies." Lincoln then sought retroactive authority from Congress for what he already had done.[3] The president told Congress:

> These measures, whether strictly legal or not, were ventured upon, under what appeared to be popular demand and a public necessity, trusting then as now, that Congress would ratify them. It is believed that nothing has been done beyond the constitutional competence of Congress.[4]

Lincoln adopted other extraordinary measures that he later reported to Congress. He had the U.S. Treasury issue, without congressional appropriation, $2,000,000 to three citizens to purchase military supplies. Lincoln issued proclamations authorizing the commanding general of the armed forces to suspend the writ of habeas corpus "at any point or in the vicinity of any military line which is now or should be used between Philadelphia and the city of Washington."[5]

The coordinate branches of government responded by legitimizing Lincoln's prerogative presidency. *The Prize Cases* gave constitutional sanction to presidential exercise of the war powers.[6] Lincoln's issuance of the Emancipation Proclamation under his power as the Commander-

---

[2] Richard M. Pious, *The American Presidency* (New York, 1979), p. 57.

[3] Wilfred E. Binkley, *The Man in the White House: His Powers and Duties* (New York, 1964), pp. 192-193.

[4] Ibid.

[5] Ibid., pp. 193-194; Pious, *The American Presidency,* p. 58; Louis W. Koenig, *The Chief Executive* (New York, 1986), pp. 235-236.

[6] *The Prize Cases,* 2 Black 635 (1863).

in-Chief has never been constitutionally challenged, even though the Constitution explicitly had protected slavery.[7] The Congress retroactively accepted Lincoln's unilateral military actions by passing an act that stated that the president's "acts, proclamations, and orders. . .are hereby approved and in all respects legalized and made valid, to the same effect as if they had been issued and done under the previous express authority and direction of the Congress of the United States."[8] Congress continued to ratify the president's measures. For example, in 1862 Congress retroactively approved Lincoln's censoring of telegraph lines and passed the Militia Act to allow the president to draft more troops. In 1863, Congress passed a law giving Lincoln authority to suspend the writ of habeas corpus and also approved a draft law that legitimized the president's earlier unilateral issuance of the draft.[9]

Nevertheless, Congress did try to establish for itself a share of the war power. A Joint Committee on the Conduct of the War went beyond normal investigatory powers as its members actually visited the military front, interrogated generals, and tried to advise Lincoln's officers on wartime measures. But as Wilfred E. Binkley wrote: "Lincoln's extraordinary resourcefulness in outmaneuvering Congress, together with his support by loyal public opinion, enabled him to maintain unimpaired the authority of the president throughout his incumbency."[10]

Lincoln also established wartime military tribunals for trials of civilians. These tribunals eventually were held unconstitutional, but only after the war and the assassination of the president.[11] Nonetheless, Clinton Rossiter wrote that "the law of the Constitution is what Lincoln did in the crisis, not what the Court said later."[12]

---

[7] Binkley, *The Man in the White House,* p. 194.

[8] Pious, *The American Presidency,* p. 58.

[9] Ibid.

[10] Binkley, *The Man in the White House,* p. 196.

[11] *Ex parte Milligan,* 4 Wall. 2 (1866).

[12] Rossiter quoted in Binkley, *The Man in the White House,* p. 195.

Although Lincoln's actions speak loudly about his view of the prerogative power, the president best articulated that view in his famous letter to A. G. Hodges on April 4, 1864:

> My oath to preserve the Constitution to the best of my ability, imposed upon me the duty of preserving, by every indispensable means, that government—that nation, of which that Constitution was the organic law. Was it possible to lose the nation and yet preserve the Constitution? By general law, life and limb must be protected, yet often a limb must be amputated to save a life; but a life is never wisely given to save a limb. I felt that measures otherwise unconstitutional might become lawful by becoming indispensable to the preservation of the Constitution through the preservation of the nation. Right or wrong, I assumed this ground, and now avow it. I could not feel that, to the best of my ability, I had even tried to preserve the Constitution, if, to save slavery or any minor matter, I should permit the wreck of government, country, and Constitution all together.[13]

In assessing Lincoln's measures, several facts must be kept in mind. First, the president adopted many of his measures when Congress was out of session and unable to convene. A major defense of presidential prerogative is the practical matter of Congress not always being in session and the president always being capable of acting. Second, Congress approved Lincoln's measures. If it chose to do so, Congress instead could have challenged those measures and even impeached the president. Third, by seeking congressional approval for his measures, Lincoln exercised extraordinary powers under the republican notion of the consent of the governed. Fourth, Lincoln's measures were directed to the purposes of the war. His "constitutional dictatorship" pertained to the war powers. Congress carried on its normal legislative responsibilities in other areas. In no sense was Lincoln acting as an absolute dictator.

---

[13] "Letter to A.G. Hodges," in Carl Van Doren, ed., *The Literary Works of Abraham Lincoln.* (Norwalk, 1980), p. 261. Consider Thomas Jefferson's defense of extraconstitutional powers, which is similar to Lincoln's view: "To lose our country by scrupulous adherence to written law would be to lose the law itself with life, liberty, and property. . .thus absurdly sacrificing the ends to the means." Quoted in Aaron Wildavsky, *The Beleagured Presidency* (New Brunswick, 1991, p. 248).

Despite the necessity and successes of Lincoln's prerogative presidency, the exercise of prerogative powers remains controversial. Therefore, it is necessary to identify and discuss the leading arguments against prerogative powers.

The Opposing Arguments

To many analysts, the doctrine of executive prerogative is of questionable validity. They cite a number of arguments refuting the existence of a prerogative power in our constitutional system. The most common argument is that the president does not have the power to violate the Constitution in order to save it. As David Gray Adler maintains, "the president possesses no prerogative power to violate the law in an emergency."[14] According to Adler's view, the president's formal powers are contained in the executive articles of the Constitution and are strictly limited to what those articles specify. This view was best stated in the memoirs of the former president and Supreme Court chief justice William Howard Taft:

> The true view of the executive function is, as I conceive it, that the president can exercise no power which cannot be fairly and reasonably traced to some specific grant of power or justly implied and included within such express grant as proper and necessary to its exercise. . . .There is no undefined residuum of power which he can exercise because it seems to him to be in the public interest.[15]

Taft's strict reading of the Constitution refutes the notion of residual presidential power associated most often with Lincoln and the two Roosevelts. Nonetheless, throughout history, the legislative branch has

---

[14] David Gray Adler, "Presidential Prerogative and the National Security State: The Corruption of the Constitution," a paper delivered at the annual meeting of the American Political Science Association, San Francisco, California, August 30, 1990, p. 6. See also Adler's "The Constitution and Presidential Warmaking: The Enduring Debate," *Political Science Quarterly,* vol. 103, no. 1 (Spring 1986), pp. 1-36.

[15] William Howard Taft, *Our Chief Magistrate and His Powers* (New York, 1916), p. 138. But see the opposing "stewardship" view of the presidency of Theodore Roosevelt in, Wayne Andrews, ed., *The Autobiography of Theodore Roosevelt* (New York, 1958), pp. 197-200.

often deferred to presidents claiming broad constitutional authority to confront crises. Consequently, the second argument against prerogative power is that illegal actions are not validated after they have been committed a number of times. As former U.S. senator J. William Fulbright stated, "usurpation is not legitimized simply by repetition, nor is a valid power nullified by failure to exercise it."[16] From this perspective, every president who has exercised the prerogative power has acted unconstitutionally. The fact that many presidents have done so, and that Congress has accepted such executive authority, is of no moment.

That conclusion leads to the third argument against the prerogative power: Congress cannot delegate its own authority—or even extra-constitutional authority—to the president, even if it wanted to do so. To a large extent, the defense of an executive prerogative power rests on the proposition that the constitutional Framers were influenced by John Locke, who provided for such a power. Thomas S. Langston and Michael E. Lind protest: "The claim that the President possesses an extralegal plenary 'Lockean prerogative' cannot survive a close reading of Locke."[17] They interpret Locke as having provided for a separation of powers in which the supreme lawmaking branch—the legislative—"cannot legitimately delegate discretion to the executive in areas of legislative responsibility."[18] Under the nondelegation doctrine, the members of a particular branch of government cannot consent to alter constitutional arrangements to achieve some temporary gain. A proper understanding of the separation of powers is one in which each branch has constitutionally defined responsibilities. Hence, the exercise of an extra-constitu-

---

[16] J. William Fulbright, "Statement Before the Subcommittee on Separation of Powers of the Committee on the Judiciary," *Executive Privilege: The Withholding of Information by the Executive,* U.S. Senate, 92nd Congress, 1st Session, July 27, 28, 29, and August 4, 5, 1971, p. 31. See also Raoul Berger, "Executive Privilege in Light of *U.S. v. Nixon,*" *Loyola University of L.A. Law Review,* vol. 9 (1975), p. 26; Opinion of Chief Justice Earl Warren in *Powell v. McCormack,* 395 U.S. 486 at 546 (1969): "That an unconstitutional action has been taken before surely does not render that action any less unconstitutional at a later date"; the opinion of Justice Felix Frankfurter in *Inland Waterways Corp. v. Young* 309 U.S. 518 at 534 (1940): "Illegality cannot attain legitimacy through practice."

[17] Thomas S. Langston and Michael E. Lind, "John Locke and the Limits of Presidential Prerogative," *Polity,* vol. 24, no. 1 (Fall 1991), p. 50.

[18] Ibid., p. 51.

tional power of prerogative can only disrupt, if not destroy, the delicate balance of powers among governmental branches.

A fourth argument against executive prerogative also is a corollary to an argument in its defense. Lincoln had restated Alexander Hamilton's maxim that the first duty of statesmanship is to ensure national self-preservation. But not all agree. Is a nation worth preserving if it is not based on certain fundamental principles as the rights of individuals and the rule of law? That issue arose during the debates over the ratification of the Constitution. The Anti-Federalist, Brutus, wrote in his sixth letter—in response to Hamilton's *Federalist 23*—that indeed, governments must first be concerned with "the preservation of internal peace and good order, and due administration of law and justice." But, he added, the people do *not* consider most important "the protection and defense of a country against external enemies. . . .We ought to furnish the world with an example of a great people, who in their civil institutions hold chiefly in view, the attainment of virtue and happiness among ourselves."[19] Thus, executive prerogative is best suited to a nation that accepts self-defense as its first duty and aspires to glory internationally. The Anti-Federalists preferred the pursuit of virtue and other less glamorous quests.

Finally, critics of executive prerogative maintain that extraordinary presidential powers can result in extraordinary abuses of authority. There are certainly enough historical examples of presidential abuses of power to validate this fear. Morton H. Halperin and Daniel N. Hoffman state that "the unchecked practice of presidential discretion—often unavoidably delegated to senior advisers—has led to abuses, mistakes, and setbacks for national unity and self-confidence, if not for national security as well."[20] A. Stephen Boyan, Jr., asserts that "an appeal to national security offers a handy reason to avoid public scrutiny of unwise or mistaken policies or of abuses of constitutional rights."[21] The most con-

---

[19] Quoted in Herbert J. Storing, ed., *The Anti-Federalist* (Chicago, 1985), pp. 146-147.

[20] Morton H. Halperin and Daniel N. Hoffman, *Top Secret: National Security and the Right to Know* (Washington, 1977), p. 32.

[21] A. Stephen Boyan, Jr., "Presidents and National Security Powers: A Judicial Perspective," a paper delivered at the annual meeting of the American Political Science Association, Washington,

spicuous case of presidential use of national security to cover-up executive branch wrongdoing was, of course, in the Nixon White House.[22] Yet, even after resigning the presidency, Nixon continued in his claim that the president could take any action that he considered necessary—including such activities approved under the Huston Plan as wiretappings, burglaries, mail openings, infiltration against antiwar groups—if *he* perceived a national security threat. In a televised interview on May 19, 1977, with David Frost, Nixon declared that "when a President does it, that means that it is not illegal." Nixon went so far as to compare the country's situation during Vietnam to the crisis that Lincoln faced during the Civil War.[23] The case of the Nixon presidency gives much ammunition to the critics of executive prerogative who argue that such authority, once granted, can lead to absurd claims of presidential power and, hence, abuses of the office of chief executive.

Arthur S. Miller argued that, in the wake of Watergate, presidents could no longer get away with taking unilateral action in "perceived national emergencies." He believed the problem to be grave enough to justify "a new theory, perhaps published as a new set of *Federalist Papers* . . .that will simultaneously enable the urgent tasks of government to be accomplished with a concomitant adequate system of accountability for the exercise of power."[24]

Miller is correct to maintain that government needs to be able to respond to emergencies and be accountable. But there is no need for fundamental reform or a new set of *Federalist Papers* to achieve that necessary end. Lincolnian prerogative is necessary, proper, and certainly conducive to a republican regime's quest for ordered liberty. These ends can be—and historically have been—achieved within the framework of

---

D.C., September 1-4, 1988.

[22] Mark J. Rozell, "President Nixon's Conception of Executive Privilege: Defining the Scope and Limits of Executive Branch Secrecy," *Presidential Studies Quarterly,*" vol. 22, no. 2 (Spring 1992), pp. 323-335.

[23] "Nixon: A President May Violate the Law," *U.S. News and World Report,* May 30, 1977, p. 323.

[24] Arthur S. Miller, *Presidential Power* (St. Paul, 1977), p. 323.

the separation of powers system articulated by the only set of *Federalist Papers* this country ever will need.

In Defense of Lincolnian Prerogative

The Lincolnian notion of prerogative—that the executive has a higher duty under extraordinary circumstances than strict observance of the law—finds ample support in modern political thought, the American founding, historic precedent, and constitutional law.

Modern Political Thought

The American Constitutional Framers learned a great deal about politics and governance from the earlier leading European thinkers. The two most influential thinkers of modern constitutionalism—John Locke and Baron de Montesquieu—sought to make possible the creation of stable regimes while moderating the harsh prescriptions of such earlier thinkers as Niccolo Machiavelli and Thomas Hobbes. Whereas Machiavelli and Hobbes imagined situations in which citizens often had to sacrifice their liberties for the preservation of the regime, Locke and Montesquieu sought to create regimes characterized by both strength and liberty. To achieve these two ends simultaneously required the establishment of a system of institutionally separated governmental powers. This proposal for a separation of powers most influenced the American Constitutional Framers and enabled them to create a regime characterized by ordered liberty—one in which prerogative is recognized. An examination of Locke's and Montesquieu's theories of governance clarifies their support of prerogative.

John Locke's *Second Treatise of Government* offers a three-fold distinction of governmental powers: the legislative, the executive, and the "federative."[25] Whereas on the surface Locke's emphasis on legislative supremacy seems unequivocal, he invests considerable power in the executive. For example, the "federative power"—the power to make

---

[25] John Locke, *Second Treatise of Government,* sections 143-148.

war, peace, treaties, and alliances—is placed solely in the executive realm.[26]

Locke's chapter entitled "Of Prerogative" is perhaps the most revealing. In times of emergency, when the legislature is not in session or where the laws are silent, the executive is given "the power of doing public good without a rule."[27] For Locke, the "supreme law" of the land is the preservation of society. Only the executive can be empowered to act with discretion and "dispatch" in times of emergency. While the legislative branch has supreme law-making powers during normal times, the executive is allowed, even expected, to take extraordinary actions in times of emergency.

Locke's predecessors, Machiavelli and Hobbes, assumed that civil strife was the norm and peaceful times the exception. They thereby provided their executives with continuous and overbearing powers. Locke differs in that he takes civil strife and warfare to be exceptional states of affairs. Locke therefore shows how to maintain a strong executive, capable of acting energetically and effectively during extraordinary times, while moderating and checking the executive during normal times. As Harvey Mansfield observes:

> the end is the preservation of men, not of the laws, and to this end the executive must be very powerful, if necessary against the laws of the legislature. . .to use a Machiavellian distinction, there is an *ordinary sovereign,* the legislature which makes standing rules, and an *extraordinary sovereign,* the executive who stands perpetually ready to go beyond or against the rules.[28]

Thomas L. Pangle points out that Locke recognized the potential for the prerogative power to be used improperly and thereby threaten individual liberty. Yet, as Pangle adds, the only alternative—not conferring sufficient power upon the executive to protect society—is worse.

---

[26] Ibid., sections 146-148.

[27] Ibid., section 166.

[28] Harvey Mansfield, "The Modern Doctrine of Executive Power," *Presidential Studies Quarterly,* vol. 17, no. 2 (Spring 1987), p. 247.

> The problem is not one that can be entirely circumvented by the right sort of constitutional framework. If a constitution fails to designate an executive endowed with full prerogative, a day will surely come when that prerogative will be seized, by unconstitutional force, or ceded, by anticonstitutional clamor—and these sad expedients will be reasonable, because any constitution that fails to provide for such prerogative is a constitution that has abdicated its responsibility to provide the powers needed by a government prepared to meet the crises that can rationally be expected.[29]

The Langston and Lind interpretation of Locke—that the legislative is supreme and cannot delegate its own or extra-constitutional powers to the executive—misses the point that under any constitutional system, there are realms of undefined authority and ambiguity in which someone must be empowered to act. Locke did not want the legislative giving up its authority, but he clearly did advocate providing the executive the power to act with force and discretion in such extraordinary circumstances as emergencies or when the legislature is out of session or unable to meet. Evidence that the American Constitutional Framers provided the executive a discretionary authority to act beyond the realm of specified authority is the relative ambiguity of the executive articles of the Constitution in comparison to the legislative articles.

Montesquieu also was concerned about the problem of reconciling freedom and coercion. Montesquieu developed more clearly than Locke the proposition that power can only be checked by countervailing power. The liberty of the citizenry, he believed, can best be protected by preventing any one power from holding the authority to formulate and to execute the laws. Montesquieu devised his governmental triad—legislative, executive, and judicial powers—as a means of preventing any one arm of the government from becoming tyrannical.[30] Montesquieu wrote:

---

[29] Thomas L. Pangle, "Executive Energy and Popular Spirit in Lockean Constitutionalism," *Presidential Studies Quarterly,* vol. 17, no. 2 (Spring 1987), p. 261.

[30] Baron de Montesquieu, *The Spirit of the Laws,* Book II.

> . . . constant experience shows us that every man invested with power is apt to abuse it, and to carry his authority as far as it will go. . . .To prevent this abuse, it is necessary from the very nature of things that power should be a check to power.[31]

Although Montesquieu advocated a separation of powers system as a means of enhancing individual liberty, he did not advocate weak government. Montesquieu's executive —the "monarch"—is empowered to act with the degree of discretion necessary in times of emergency, even if the executive's actions are not specifically granted by the legislature. Montesquieu therefore allowed for a strong executive, independent of direct pressure from the "popular will," capable of acting with force and discretion.[32]

The American Founding

Taking their cues from Locke, Montesquieu, and other theorists as well, the American Framers also sought to devise a regime characterized by both liberty and power. The concept of checks and balances and the doctrine of separation of powers were devices intended to enhance liberty while maintaining "energy" in the executive.[33]

The American Framers recognized the necessity of providing the executive awesome powers during times of war. It is a paradox of republican government that such vast powers be at the hands of the executive, but, as Alexander Hamilton recognized, "the first duty of any nation is self-preservation."[34]

The Framers, in fact, were willing to provide the largest grant of discretionary power to the chief executive in the foreign affairs realm. Hamilton's *Federalist 70* is to the point.

---

[31] Ibid.

[32] Jeffrey Poelvoorde, "The Necessity of Executive Privilege," a paper delivered at the annual meeting of the American Political Science Association, Chicago, August 1983.

[33] Paul Peterson, "The Constitution and the Separation of Powers," in Gary McDowell, ed., *Taking the Constitutional Seriously* (Dubuque, 1981), p. 205.

[34] Hans J. Morgenthau, *In Defense of the National Interest* (Washington, 1982).

> Decision, activity, secrecy and dispatch will generally characterize
> the proceedings of one man in a much more eminent degree than
> the proceedings of any great number; and in proportion as the
> number is increased, these qualities will be diminished.

Hamilton's *Federalist 23* supports the view that under the Constitution certain powers to provide for the common defense—raising armies, building and equipping fleets, directing military operations—"ought to exist without limitation" because it is impossible to define in advance all threats or to determine the authority needed to meet them.

> The circumstances that endanger the safety of nations are infinite,
> and for this reason no constitutional shackles can wisely be im-
> posed on the power to which the care of it is committed. . . .[T]he
> *means* ought to be proportioned to the *end*; the persons, from
> whose agency the attainment of any *end* is expected, ought to
> possess the *means* by which it is to be attained.

In *Federalist 64* John Jay corroborated the view that "secrecy" and "dispatch" are inherent in the executive. Jay argued that under the proposed Constitution the president would be able to claim discretionary authority to withhold information during treaty negotiations "to manage the business of intelligence in such a manner as prudence may suggest. So often and so essentially have we heretofore suffered from the want of secrecy and dispatch, that the Constitution would have been inexcusably defective if no attention had been paid to those objects." Writing under the pseudonym "Pacificus," Hamilton defended President Washington's prerogative to proclaim American neutrality in the war between France and Great Britain. To Hamilton, the limits on presidential power in foreign affairs and during war were not found primarily in the Constitution, but in "the principles of free government." Except for declaring war, he wrote that "it belongs to the 'executive power' to do whatever else the law of nations, cooperating with the treaties of the country, enjoin in the intercourse of the United States with foreign powers."[35]

---

[35] Quoted in Robert S. Hirschfield, ed., *The Power of the Presidency: Concepts and Controversy,* (New York, 1982), pp. 53, 58.

Although James Madison disagreed with Hamilton's defense of the proclamation of neutrality, the chief constitutional architect wrote in *Federalist 37* that:

> Energy in government is essential to the security against external and internal danger, and to that prompt and salutary execution of the laws, which enter into the very definition of good government.

Even more germane is Madison's *Federalist 41* in which the argument advanced is that a nation must do whatever it has to for self preservation and that no constitutional or statutory provision can override that necessity:

> If a federal Constitution could chain the ambition or set bounds to the exertions of all other nations, then indeed might it prudently chain the discretion of its own government, and set bounds to the exertions for its own safety. . . .The means of security can only be regulated by the means and the danger of attack. They will, in fact, be ever determined by these rules, and by no others.

Harold Hongju Koh has pointed out that of the first thirty-six *Federalist Papers*, twenty-five of them "concerned national *in*security."[36] After two introductory papers, numbers three through eight concern foreign policy, foreign threats, and the dangers of war. The inability of the Articles of Confederation to preserve the Union are featured in numbers fifteen through twenty-two. The following papers, twenty-three through thirty-six, concerned foreign dangers, war, federal defense and fiscal powers. In all, the *Federalist Papers* make clear that the Framers were primarily concerned with creating a stable republican system characterized by strength and liberty. Strong government—executive power—not only ensures self-preservation, it enables liberty to flourish. As Edward S. Corwin had written, "the framers had in mind [their] idea of a divided initiative in the matter of legislation and a broad range of autonomous executive power or 'prerogative.'" Furthermore, the Fra-

---

[36] Harold Hongju Koh, *The National Security Constitution: Sharing Power After the Iran-Contra Affair* (New Haven, 1990), p. 74.

mers conferred "all the prerogatives of monarchy in connection with war-making except only the power to declare war and the power to create armed forces."[37]

Louis Henkin points out that the explicit constitutional powers vested in the president "are few and seem modest. . . .What the Constitution says and does not say, then, can not have determined what the President can and can not do."[38] Henkin adds:

> Much of what the President has attained may indeed lie in or between the lines of the Constitution, and all of it has been shaped by what is there. . . .residents need not and do not plead their powers with precision, or match particular act to particular power.[39]

To develop his point that presidential power does indeed stretch beyond the very narrow, specific grants of authority specified in the Constitution, Henkin quotes the former chief justice John Marshall: "The President is the sole organ of the nation in its external relations, and its sole representative with foreign nations." Henkin's analysis of Marshall's assertion is germane to the presidential prerogative controversy:

> It is not apparent that either "foreign affairs power" or "sole organ" aspires to legal precision or that they imply different measures of constitutional authority; both have come to describe a constitutional "power," supplementing if not subsuming those specified, supporting a variety of Presidential actions not expressly authorized by the Constitution.[40]

---

[37] Edward S. Corwin, *The President: Office and Powers, 1787-1948* (New York, 1948), pp. 15-16; Edward S. Corwin, *Presidential Power and the Constitution: Essays,* Richard Loss, ed., (Ithaca, 1976), p. 23.

[38] Louis Henkin, *Foreign Affairs and the Constitution* (Mineola, 1972), p. 37.

[39] Ibid., pp. 38, 45.

[40] Ibid., p. 45.

Historic Precedent and Constitutional Law

In the debate over President Washington's proclamation of neutrality, Madison, writing under the pseudonym "Helvidius," accused Hamilton, writing as "Pacificus," of having claimed for the executive the prerogatives of the British Crown. Although Madison believed that Hamilton vested too much power in the executive, Robert Scigliano writes that "Hamilton's conception has largely won out in the practice of American government."[41]

The argument that an illegitimate power is not rendered legal by repetition is unpersuasive. First, a proper reading of Locke, Montesquieu, the *Federalist Papers*, and the Constitution, makes clear that the American chief executive does have the power of prerogative. Second, although precedent does not alone establish a practice as legitimate, it does result in a presumption of validity, as many decisionmakers for years have accepted that practice as proper. Third, our constitutional law recognizes precedent as an important standard of validity. Presumably, if the exercise of prerogative were so constitutionally offensive, there would be a substantial body of legal opinion to render the practice suspect. Instead, the courts consistently have either upheld executive claims of prerogative or proclaimed that controversies over executive branch power were "political questions."

Constitutional justification for prerogative is derived from the undefined, nonenumerated reservoir of powers contained in Article II. The legislative authority is limited to the powers enumerated in Article I. But Article II provides a general grant of "executive power." The commander in chief clause is left without any enumeration of powers. The "take care" clause lacks specificity, again allowing the president a discretion to act to ensure that the whole fabric of the laws, the Constitution, is secured. The president too takes an oath to execute his office, not the laws.

Since the presidency of George Washington, numerous chief executives have acted according to a broad definition of executive power.

---

[41] Robert Scigliano, "The President's 'Prerogative Power'" in Thomas E. Cronin, ed., *Inventing the American Presidency* (Lawrence, 1989), p. 247.

Washington explained to Madison that he understood well that, being first, their actions established enduring precedents.[42] In his actions as president, Washington demonstrated that the executive power is one properly characterized by broad ranging responsibilities, energy, and efficiency.[43] Undoubtedly, history has treated most favorably presidents who were willing to act decisively during perilous times rather than cautiously according to a narrow, legalistic interpretation of what the Constitution would allow. Hence, as John F. Kennedy sagely put it, the White House has a "Lincoln Room" but no "Buchanan Room."[44]

During the twentieth century's two world wars, extra-constitutional prerogative powers were appropriated by chief executives. President Woodrow Wilson requested and received from Congress legislation conferring vast powers on the chief executive to conduct the war. The Overman Act gave Wilson nearly dictatorial powers in matters pertaining to the functions, responsibilities, and powers of administrative agencies and government personnel so that he could conduct the war as he saw fit.[45] Wilson benefited from widespread public support for his actions, and he followed in Lincoln's footsteps by seeking and receiving from Congress explicit authority to adopt extraordinary wartime measures.

Given an increasingly dangerous international situation in 1940, President Franklin Roosevelt began overriding the congressional lawmaking process. Through the use of the executive agreement—which does not require congressional consent—President Roosevelt effectively bypassed the isolationist majority in Congress on several occasions. Roosevelt concluded an alliance with Great Britain in 1940, ignoring the Senate treaty-making power, as well as congressional neutrality laws. As Richard Pious argues, Roosevelt "was wise to bypass Congress."[46] In

[42] Glenn A. Phelps, "George Washington and the Founding of the Presidency," *Presidential Studies Quarterly,* vol. 17, no. 2 (Spring 1987), p. 350.

[43] Ibid., pp. 350-354.

[44] John Kennedy, Speech to National Press Club, January 14, 1960, as quoted in John P. Roche and Leonard W. Levy, eds., *The Presidency* (New York, 1964), p. 35.

[45] Wilfred E. Binkley, *The Man in the White House* (New York, 1972), p. 196.

[46] Richard Pious, *The American Presidency,* p. 55.

the end, executive prerogative was vindicated and Congress' performance discredited. Three months prior to Pearl Harbor, Congress nearly
repealed the Selective Service Act. Funds for the construction of vital
naval facilities were blocked in Congress. Neutrality laws were not even
repealed until the end of 1941. Pious concludes that "Congress demonstrated no foresight, courage, or common sense."[47] Congress' response
to our nation's gravest crisis proved to be wholly inadequate. A major
defense of the presidential prerogative power rests on the proposition
that Congress often has failed to discharge its national security duties
with wisdom and foresight.

Roosevelt also claimed a prerogative power to take actions he
deemed necessary to overcome the domestic economic crisis. In his
1942 Labor Day address to Congress, Roosevelt demanded congressional repeal of the Emergency Price Control Act. He threatened to act
alone if Congress did not do as he wished:

> The responsibilities of the President in wartime to protect the Na-
> tion are very grave. This total war, with our fighting fronts all over
> the world, makes the use of executive power far more essential than
> in any previous war. If we were invaded, the people of this country
> would expect the President to use any and all means to repel the
> invader. . . .In the event that the Congress should fail to act ade-
> quately I shall accept the responsibility and I will act. . . .I have
> given the most thoughtful consideration to meeting this issue with-
> out further reference to Congress. I have determined in this vital
> matter to consult with Congress. . . .The American people can be
> sure that I shall not hesitate to use every power vested in me to
> defeat our enemies in any part of the world where our safety de-
> mands such defeat. When the war is won, the powers under which I
> act automatically revert to the people to whom they belong.[48]

For Roosevelt, then, the president has extraordinary responsibilities
during wartime and extraordinary powers as well to carry out these
duties. His prerogative powers derive not only from the "Commander-

---

[47] Ibid.

[48] Quoted in Hirschfield, *The Power of the Presidency,* pp. 112-113.

in-Chief" role, but also from the people. When the emergency is over, the sovereign powers revert back "to the people to whom they belong."

There is a substantial body of constitutional law recognizing presidential emergency powers, as they are implied in the Constitution. Leading Supreme Court cases confer extraordinary presidential powers to protect the nation's security;[49] to maintain secrecy and confidentiality;[50] and even to suspend constitutionally guaranteed liberties during wartime.[51] Yet critics of prerogative powers remain unconvinced. They maintain that presidents have usurped authority, abused powers, and undermined the delicate balance of powers among the governmental branches. Some of these critics want to chain presidential discretion through the use of specific statutory definitions of the chief executive's warmaking and emergency powers.[52] Through such innovations as the War Powers Act, some restrictions already have been enacted.

There is no need for any further statutory definition of presidential emergency powers. The president has a prerogative to act as Lincoln did, in times of emergency, and to do so unfettered by any specific statutory restraints. A proper understanding of the constitutional Framers' notion of the separation of powers provides all the necessary restraints against presidential excesses and also ensures the chief executive the latitude and discretion needed to act in emergencies.

Resolving the Controversy

Critics of executive prerogative are correct to argue that such a power can be—and has been—abused. But the power to do good is

---

[49] *Martin v. Mott,* 12 Wheat 19 (1827); *The Prize Cases,* 2 Black 635 (1863); *Oetjen v. Central Leather Co.,* 246 U.S. 297 (1918); *U.S. v. Curtiss-Wright Corp.,* 299 U.S. 304 (1936); *Zemel v. Rusk,* 381 U.S. 1 (1965); *First National Bank v. Banco Nacional de Cuba,* 406 U.S. 759 (1972); *Haig v. Agee,* 453 U.S. 291 (1981.)

[50] *Chicago and Southern Airlines v. Waterman Steamship Co.,* 333 U.S. 103 (1948); *U.S. v. Reynolds,* 345 U.S. 1 (1952); *U.S. v. Nixon,* 418 U.S. 683 (1974); *Department of the Navy v. Egan,* 484 U.S. 518 (1988).

[51] *U.S. v. Macintosh,* 283 U.S. 605 (1931).

[52] Halperin and Hoffman, *Top Secret: National Security and the Right to Know*; John Orman, *Presidential Secrecy and Deception: Beyond the Power to Persuade* (Westport, 1980).

always the power to do evil as well. Stripping away powers to avoid their abuse is a simplistic, dangerous resolution to the executive prerogative controversy. Even in light of the leadership abuses of King George III, the American Constitutional Framers—having learned their lessons under the failed Articles of Confederation—rejected such a resolution. Their doctrine of the separation of powers provided a timeless remedy to the problem of potential abuses of executive power.[53]

In the case of Lincoln, the coordinate governmental branches legitimized the president's actions. They did not have to. If Congress had decided that Lincoln's unilateral measures went too far, it could have withheld support for those measures by not approving them, not appropriating any funds for them, and, eventually, by impeaching the president, if he persisted in his course of action. The Supreme Court, though lacking an enforcement mechanism—as Chief Justice Taney experienced when he feebly ordered the issuance of a writ of habeas corpus—could have interpreted the president's wartime authority much more narrowly than it did in the *Prize Cases* and then struck down the president's measures as unconstitutional.

The key point is that under the doctrine of separation of powers, there are sufficient and proper limitations on prerogative powers. When presidents clearly overstep their authority—e.g., Truman and the seizure of the steel mills, Nixon's use of executive privilege—Congress or the courts, or both, can effectively challenge the chief executive's actions.

Unfortunately, the lessons of Lincoln and the Civil War have given way to the lessons of Nixon and Watergate. For the former, a strong presidency and the use of prerogative powers are vital to the security and well-being of the country. For the latter, the presidency is imperial, dangerous, and ought to be constrained by narrow statutory definitions of authority. As Michael Foley writes:

> The Watergate crisis succeeded in opening up the question of executive power to intensive analysis and critical evaluation with a brutal insurgency and dangerously inquisitive appetite for precision

---

[53] See the trenchant analysis of James W. Ceaser, "In Defense of Separation of Powers," in Robert A. Goldwin and Art Kaufman, eds., *Separation of Powers—Does It Still Work?* (Washington, 1986), pp. 168-193.

which were quite alien to the conventional manner of accommodating the presidency within the constitution's sphere of legitimacy.[54]

Lincoln's legacy for years has been revered by presidential historians. Hopefully, sometime soon—and hopefully before compelled by necessity—contemporary legal and presidential scholars, as well as congressionalists, will properly honor that legacy by calling for a much needed return to an earlier understanding of executive powers and constitutionalism.

[54] Michael Foley, *The Silence of Constitutions* (London, 1989), p. 41.

The first photograph of Lincoln with a full beard, taken by C. S. German in Spring-field, Illinois on January 13, 1861. (The Frank and Virginia Williams Collection of Lincolniana)

L incoln's visions, dreams, and premonitions occupied a crucial role in his life, but especially during his tenure as President of the United States during the Civil War. As a natural extension of his character, they formed that mysterious and intimate connection to his psyche which may only be gestured toward in historical restrospect.

John Stuart Erwin

John Erwin attended the University of Indianapolis, graduating cum laude with a B.A. in religion and English in 1977. He earned a graduate degree with honors from Methodist Theological School in Ohio in 1980, a M.A. degree from Indiana University in 1982, and the Ph.D. from Indiana University in 1987. His areas of concentration are United States history and American Studies. Dr. Erwin previously taught at Indiana University, Olney Central College, and was Division Chair of Social Sciences at Illinois Valley Community College. Currently, he serves as the Dean of Instruction at Iowa Valley Community College in Marshalltown, Iowa.

Abraham Lincoln's
Visions, Dreams, and Premonitions

The irrational and unconscious played an important role in Abraham Lincoln's life. Dreams, visions, and premonitions frequently found expression in the president's experience. Obviously, many such episodes cannot now be revealed about Lincoln because of the passage of time and the very intimate nature of such phenomena, but some of these occurrences remain as essential events in the Lincoln legacy, even when they prove to be difficult to analyze as aspects of his character. Ward Hill Lamon, a long-time friend and confidant of Lincoln's called this "the strangest feature of his character."[1] More recently, a biographer of Lincoln has placed his dreams and premonitions in the context of a response to wartime stress and fatigue, believing them to be a natural outgrowth of those pressures peculiar to the office of president in crisis. Lincoln's belief in the reality of dreams was so important he once sent a

---

[1] Ward Hill Lamon, *Recollections of Abraham Lincoln 1847-1865*, edited by Dorothy Lamon (Chicago, 1895), p. 109. Other contemporary scholars have recognized the important role of dreams for Lincoln. See, Thomas F. Schwartz's unpublished essay, "Lincoln and the Limits of Reason," (1992), pp. 11-12; and James A. Stevenson, "Abraham Lincoln's Affinity for MacBeth," *The Midwest Quarterly*, vol. 31, no. 2, (Winter, 1990), pp. 170-278.

message to Mary Todd to warn her that he had a dream in which Tad, their ten-year-old son, was threatened: "Think you had better put 'Tad's pistol away. I had an ugly dream about him."[2]

Neither of these interpretations of Lincoln's dreams, visions, and premonitions as either unnatural or natural satisfactorily explains the existence of these phenomena in his life. An attempt to place these experiences into the totality of his life as well as offer contemporary dream theory the opportunity to form an interpretational backdrop will allow a more complete analysis of these episodes. To accomplish this task, Sigmund Freud's and Carl Jung's dream interpretation theories will be interwoven into the visions, dreams, and premonitions of Lincoln's life.

Lincoln and Freud

From a very early period in his life, Lincoln believed himself destined to a high purpose.[3] Not accenting authority or power in this mission, he instead focused upon service. Freud bases much of his dream interpretation theory upon wish-fulfillment, the idea that a dream expresses one's heartfelt desires.[4] One aspect of this early childhood sense of high calling is magnanimous and self-effacing as Lincoln contemplated the benefits he would bestow upon others. There also was a gloomy shadow which hung over his grand aspiration throughout his young adult life and into his middle years. "He saw, or thought he saw, a vision of glory and blood, himself the central figure in a scene which his fancy transformed from giddy enchantment to the most appalling trag-

---

[2] Stephen B. Oates, *With Malice Toward None: The Life of Abraham Lincoln* (New York, 1977), pp. 269-270; Roy P. Basler, ed., *The Collected Works of Abraham Lincoln*, 8 vols. (New Brunswick, 1953), vol. 6, p. 256.

[3] Lamon, *Recollections of Abraham Lincoln*, p. 110; Henry B. Rankin, *Personal Recollections of Abraham Lincoln* (New York, 1916), p. 314.

[4] Sigmund Freud, *The Interpretation of Dreams*, transcribed and edited by James Strachey (New York, 1965), p. 168.

edy."[5] The tragedy in this personal scenario was Lincoln's belief that he would fall from his lofty station because of his death.

The morbidity and melancholia frequently mentioned as observed in Lincoln's demeanor may be attributed not only to his noble and tragic mission vision, but also to the reminders of his own mortality he faced through the loss of loved ones. His mother died when he was nine years old. The cabin where the Lincolns resided was thirty-five miles from the nearest doctor. This isolation from medical care hastened her death but also allowed for a particularly close relationship between mother and son to develop during the few years which preceded her death. In addition to the loss of his mother, Lincoln also experienced the death of two sons.[6]

Upon returning to his law practice after his term in Congress, Lincoln concentrated his efforts on various legal affairs. In December of 1849, Eddie, Lincoln's second son, became ill. For several weeks Lincoln and Mary Todd nursed the boy night and day, but on February 1, 1850, their four-year-old son died. Lincoln suffered the double burden of having to cope with his grief over the death of Eddie and the response of his wife Mary, who stayed in the bedroom and wept. Ultimately, Lincoln immersed himself in his work and exercised patience with Mary who, after several months, began to take the reins of the family once more.[7]

Lincoln suffered the loss of a second and favorite son, Willie, during the first term of his presidency. In February 1862, the eleven-year-old blue-eyed, precocious youngster had taken ill along with his younger brother Tad. The Lincolns were reassured by a physician that it was just a fever and they had nothing to fear. Tad gradually improved, but Willie developed an intense fever as his parents kept a nightly vigil over his bedside. One close friend of the president wrote in his diary, "The Presi-

---

[5] Lamon, *Recollections of Abraham Lincoln*, p. 110; Lloyd Lewis, *Myths After Lincoln* (New York, 1957).

[6] William H. Herndon, *Herndon's Life of Lincoln*, edited by Paul Angle (New York, 1961); Richard N. Current, *The Lincoln Nobody Knows* (New York, 1958); See also, Elton Trueblood, *Abraham Lincoln, Theologian of American Anguish* (New York, 1973).

[7] Oates, *With Malice Toward None*, pp. 69, 101.

dent is nearly worn out with grief and watching."[8] Willie died at 5:00 p.m. on February 20.

Mary did not cope any better with Willie's death than with Eddie's passing. It took over five months of constant attention by companions, coupled with loving patience by her husband, before Mary Todd would regain her emotional equilibrium. For Lincoln, the loss of a second son was almost more than he could bear. "My poor boy," he whispered, "he was too good for this earth. . .we loved him so."[9]

Longer lasting than other griefs Lincoln bore, he dreamed that Willie was still alive, playing in the leaves on the White House lawn, calling to him.[10] Freud labels this kind of dream a "typical dream" because it is very common, after a loved one has died, for people to dream that they are alive.[11] Dreams, as a wish-fulfillment, could not display anything more obvious than the deepest yearnings of life for someone who is dead, and who was especially loved. Freud readily admits that dreams of this type cause the dream interpreter problems in interpretation due to the "particularly strongly marked emotional ambivalence which dominates the dreamer's relation to the dead person."[12] In the case of Lincoln and his son Willie, however, no ambivalence resides in Lincoln's dream: he clearly wished for his son not to have died. The recurrence of the dream is evidence of the depth of anxiety he suffered over the loss of the young boy.

Freud has remarked upon the frequency with which dead relatives appear in dreams and associate with the dreamer as though they were alive. He attributes this experience to often thinking, "If my son were still alive, what would he say to this?" Freud concludes that, "Dreams are unable to express an 'if' of this kind except by representing the person concerned as present in some particular situation."[13] Willie play-

---

[8] Ibid., p. 314.

[9] Ibid.

[10] Ibid., p. 317.

[11] Freud, *The Interpretation of Dreams*, pp. 301, 466.

[12] Ibid., p. 466.

[13] Ibid., p. 465.

ing on the White House lawn in the leaves must have been a consoling dream to Lincoln that all was well with his son, beyond the obvious wish for his son to once more be alive.

Lincoln and Jung

Contrary to Freud, noted Swiss psychiatrist Carl Jung believed that the dream is "a spontaneous self-portrayal, in symbolic form, of the actual situation in the unconscious."[14] While Jung's position does not eliminate the possibility of a dream being a wish-fulfillment, as Freud contends, it does however leave open the prospect of broader interpretation of dreams. For example, one may interpret dreams as something other than direct, outward, concrete realities and perceive them as images or symbols. In the case of people who are dreamed about, it means that the person represents more than simply the recognizable individual. Freud makes the distinction between latent and manifest content in dreams. Manifest content is that which is recognizable and latent content is that material which lies behind literal ideas or people in the dream.[15] Jung suggests that the people we see in our dreams may also represent aspects of ourselves. For example, in Lincoln's dream of his son Willie playing in the leaves on the White House lawn, he may be remembering through the image of his son his own carefree days of youth. It is very natural for one who is under extraordinary stress to cope with that pressure by escaping into an imagination of a place or time when things were less stress-filled. By the time of Willie's death, it was generally accepted that the Civil War would be a prolonged conflict, a belief in marked contrast to early Union hopes of a quick victory.

Besides the obvious wartime pressures of the office of president—prompting Lincoln to dream of his son Willie and vicariously enjoy the playtime in the leaves on the lawn—he also had frequently played, teased, and jousted with his sons, and found particular pleasure

---

[14] Carl Jung, *The Structure and Dynamics of the Psyche, Collected Works*, 20 vols. (New York, 1960), vol. 8, p. 263.

[15] Freud, *The Interpretation of Dreams*, pp. 44-55.

in those moments with his middle son. One biographer notes that as the war intensified, Lincoln found his sons to be an antidote to the anxieties and depressions of the presidential office. "He treasured their fleeting moments together, when he could forget about McClellan, forget about feuding generals and irate politicians, and could relax with his sons in their world, sharing in their fun and reading them stories with his spectacles on. He loved to recount the antics of his 'two little codgers' and bragged about them to anyone who would listen."[16]

Lincoln's dream of Willie not only objectively signaled the depth of his mourning for the loss of his son, but also subjectively represented the loss of relaxation as a tension-reducing device during the tremendous pressures of wartime. He often jostled and teased with his sons in the evening and now that diversion was lost as a stress reducing activity.[17]

Besides dreams, Lincoln occasionally experienced episodes which he viewed as signs. The sign deliberately signaled futuristic occurrences. The premonitory nature of these signs is illustrated by his renomination at Baltimore in 1864. The War Department and Lincoln kept continuous telegraphic communication. With General Ulysses S. Grant's forces locked in a siege with Robert E. Lee's Army of Northern Virginia just outside of Richmond and Petersburg, Lincoln was oblivious to anything except for the direct news of the war's activities. After a quick luncheon back at the White House, he rushed over to the War Department, where the first dispatch shown to him stated the nomination of Andrew Johnson for vice-president. "This is strange," he said, "I thought it was usual to nominate the candidate for president first." The messenger was amazed. "Mr President, have you not heard of your own renomination? It was telegraphed to you at the White House two hours ago."[18]

Lincoln had not seen the message and had not asked any questions about it. Upon reflecting on this experience, Ward Lamon said that Lincoln was reminded of a mysterious event which took place after his

[16] Oates, *With Malice Toward None*, p. 311.

[17] Dan Gollub, "A Complementary Approach to Freudian and Jungian Dream Interpretation," *Psychology* (1986), pp. 62-71. Also see, James A. Hall, *Jungian Dream Interpretation* (Toronto, 1983) pp. 23ff.

[18] Lamon, *Recollections of Abraham Lincoln 1847-1865*, p. 111.

election in 1860. While reclining in his room at Springfield he saw a double image of himself in a mirror. On one side was Lincoln's face "reflecting the full glow of health and hopeful life." In the same mirror and at the same time, in addition to this healthful image, was an extremely pale image of himself.[19] Sometimes Lincoln would look in the mirror to see if the double image appeared again before him. The images reappeared and then vanished. In conversation with Lamon, Lincoln could not rationalize this phenomenon and yet several events resulted. First, he had attempted to reproduce this experience of the double reflection at the White House, but without success. Second, the double image had given him cause to worry. Third, the phenomenon had a meaning which was clear to Lincoln. To him, the image was a sign. The healthful, positive image foretold of a safe passage through his first presidential term; the ghostly one, that he would die before the end of his second term in office.[20]

The reason Lincoln consciously forgot the dispatch with news of his renomination for the presidency must take account of the unconscious influence the 1860 double-image vision had on him. He firmly believed in the certainty of his re-election and with the same conviction, his pending death before the end of his second term.[21]

Faced with the question of how he could function as president during a civil war with this "portentous horror" looming before him, Lamon

---

[19] Ibid., pp. 111, 112.

[20] Ibid., p. 112.

[21] Biographers differ on this point. Lamon represents those who believe that Lincoln had some intuition of his reelection. Oates, et. al. accent Lincoln's uncertainty about his reelection in 1864. Crucial to the thesis presented in this chapter is Lincoln's double-image vision in which he sees himself as a two-term president. Historian Don E. Fehrenbacher, in a paper originally presented at a Brown University symposium on Lincoln in June 1984 and published in John L. Thomas, ed., *Abraham Lincoln and the American Political Tradition* (Amherst, 1986), indicates the difficulty this particular double-image phenomenon presents for Lincoln scholars. He traces the text and context of the story citing, Noah Brooks, *Washington in Lincoln's Time* (New York, 1958), Lamon, *Recollections of Abraham Lincoln*, and artist Francis Carpenter's *Six Months at the White House With Abraham Lincoln*, (New York, 1866), as they relate to this incident. After explaining the differences between these three writers, Fehrenbacher concludes his historiographical exploration by writing: "Nevertheless, we are left with strong evidence that Lincoln did see the double image in 1860, that the incident made a considerable impression on his mind, that he spoke of it more than once in 1864, and that at least some part of the substance of his account can be summarized with some confidence." Thomas Schwartz is recognized for assisting the author on this point in Lincoln scholarship.

concluded that it was Lincoln's indomitable sense of humor, his sense of duty to the country, and most importantly his fatalism, i.e., "his belief that 'the inevitable' is right," that led him through those years.[22] Lincoln, from a very early age, considered dreams and visions as possibly premonitory. Carl Sandburg points out the importance of dreams to young Abe Lincoln's father, who once told about a dream wherein he saw a path leading to a strange house. Once inside the house, he observed the walls, the chairs, the table, and the fireplace. A woman was sitting at the fireside paring an apple. As he gazed upon her, her features became clear. She was the woman who became his wife.[23]

Tom Lincoln's dream occurred night after night until he finally went to the path he identified in his dream and walked directly to the house and entered it to find a woman sitting by the fireside paring an apple, just as he had seen it in his dream. The rest of the dream came to pass. The dream was told to Abe by his father and he was encouraged by Tom to find meaning in his dreams. This early inculcation into dream interpretation Sandburg attributed to the superstition of the frontier people—a kind of folk religion. But it seems more likely that the predestinarian Baptist faith the Lincoln family was known to follow would have accounted just as readily for the reliance upon dreams as a source of direction. The Old and New Testaments are replete with examples illustrating the role of dreams as a source of divine revelation.[24] Lincoln's Baptist family background, particularly his own thorough reading and extensive use of the Bible, formed his dream interpretations as much or more than the folk superstition of the pioneer Midwest.

For example, the best known dream incident for Lincoln was the disturbing premonitory dream he had prior to his assassination. Talking with a group of friends just prior to that event, he related how he had an upsetting dream wherein he saw his body lying in state in the White House. After the dream, Lincoln turned to the Bible and randomly opened it. His eyes focused upon the twenty-eighth chapter of Genesis,

---

[22] Lamon, *Recollections of Abraham Lincoln*, p. 113.

[23] Carl Sandburg, *Abraham Lincoln, The Prairie Years* (New York, 1926), pp. 65-66.

[24] Morton T. Kelsey, *Dreams: The Dark Speech of the Spirit* (New York, 1968) pp. 79ff.

which describes Jacob's dream. He said, "I turned to other passages and seemed to encounter a dream or vision. . . .I kept on turning the leaves of the old book, and everywhere my eyes fell upon passages recording matters strangely in keeping with my own thoughts—supernatural visitations, dreams, visions, and so forth."[25]

Lincoln noted the exceptional nature of this dream when he commented to his friends gathered that evening, "If we believe the Bible, we must accept the fact that in the old days God and His angels came to men in their sleep and made themselves known in dreams. Nowadays dreams are regarded as very foolish, and are seldom told, except by old women and by young men and maidens in love."[26] Obviously aware of the skepticism his dream interpretation would receive by the general public or office holders, Lincoln related it only to his wife and a few intimate friends. He must have struck a serious posture as he remarked about the Bible and dreams because as he finished, Mary Todd asked him, "Why, you look dreadfully solemn; do you believe in dreams?" Lincoln responded, "I can't say that I do; but I had one the other night which has haunted me ever since." He then tried to drop the subject but emphasized the powerful impact the dream had upon him by saying, "I have done wrong to mention the subject at all; but somehow the thing has got possession of me, and, like Banquo's ghost, it will not down."[27]

Lincoln revealed much about his dream and its interpretation with the words, "like Banquo's ghost." John Wilkes Booth, Lincoln's assassin, was a well-known Shakespearean actor who acted in the play *Mac-Beth*, in which Banquo is a departed Scottish general. John T. Ford, the owner and manager of Ford's Theater, where Lincoln was assassinated, once remarked on Booth's acting with specific reference to his gymnastic jumps on stage that "Booth would not content himself with the usual

---

[25] Kelsey, *Recollections of Abraham Lincoln*, p. 79; Lewis, *Recollections of Abraham Lincoln*, p. 294; Lamon, *Recollections of Abraham Lincoln*, p. 113; also see William J. Wolf, *Lincoln's Religion* (Philadelphia, 1970), p. 29.

[26] Wolf, *Lincoln's Religion*, p. 29.

[27] Lamon, *Recollections of Abraham Lincoln*, p. 114.

steps to reach the stage, but had a ledge of rocks some ten or twelve feet high erected, down which he sprang on the stage."[28]

Jung's "Synchronicity" Hypothesis

The coincidence of this string of events begs for interpretation: at the very time Lincoln experiences a haunting dream—which in retrospect is viewed by intimates like Lamon as a premonitory dream—he makes a reference to a character from a Shakespearean play, and then is subsequently assassinated by a Shakespearean actor who plays the lead role in that drama. On the meaningful cross-connection of events, Carl Jung postulates that something other than mere chance is at work. Jung calls the simultaneity of the causally unconnected "synchronicity."[29] After citing several examples in his essay, "Synchronicity: An Acausal Connecting Principle," Jung postulates that "there seems to be an a priori, causally inexplicable knowledge of a situation which at the time is unknowable."[30]

Jung believed that there were two aspects to synchronicity. First, an unconscious image enters into consciousness either directly (literally or indirectly, suggested or symbolized), in the form of an idea, dream, or premonition. Second, an objective event coincides with this content.[31] Lincoln, of course, never lived to testify to the premonitory nature of his dream, but Lamon, his close associate and bodyguard, did. Lamon, charged with the personal protection of Lincoln, carefully recorded the details of the dream as the president spoke to Mary Todd. "About ten days ago," he said,

> I retired very late. I had been up waiting for important dispatches from the front. I could not have been long in bed when I fell into a

[28] Carl Sandburg, *Abraham Lincoln, The War Years*, vol. 4. (New York, 1939) p. 313. This observation by Ford was made upon witnessing Booth play the lead part in *MacBeth* in the scene in which he entered the den of witches.

[29] Jung, *Collected Works*, 20 vols. (Bollingen Foundation, 1960), vol. 8, p. 418ff.

[30] Ibid., p. 447.

[31] Ibid.

slumber, for I was weary. I soon began to dream. There seemed to be a death-like stillness about me. Then I heard subdued sobs, as if a number of people were weeping. I thought I left my bed and wandered downstairs. There the silence was broken by the same pitiful sobbing, but the mourners were invisible. I went from room to room; no living person was in sight, but the same mournful sounds of distress met me as I passed along. It was light in all the rooms; every object was familiar to me; but where were all the people who were grieving as if their hearts would break? I was puzzled and alarmed. What could be the meaning of all of this? Determined to find the cause of a state of things so mysterious and so shocking, I kept on until I arrived at the East Room, which I entered. There I met with a sickening surprise. Before me was a catafalque, on which rested a corpse wrapped in funeral vestments. Around it were stationed soldiers who were acting as guards; and there was a throng of people, some gazing mournfully upon the corpse, whose face was covered, others weeping pitifully. 'Who is dead in the White House?' I demanded of one of the soldiers. 'The President,' was his answer; 'he was killed by an assassin!' Then came a loud burst of grief from the crowd, which awoke me from my dream. I slept no more that night; although it was only a dream, I have been strangely annoyed by it ever since."[32]

This dream sequence so disturbed Lincoln that he referred to it later with Hill Lamon by closing with a quotation from *Hamlet*, "To sleep; perchance to dream! aye, there's the rub!" In typical fashion, he tried to place the death dream in a humorous light. He told Lamon that "your apprehension of harm to me from some hidden enemy is downright foolishness."[33] He then indicated to Lamon that the dead figure in the dream was someone other than himself which reminded him of an old farmer in Illinois whose family became sick from eating greens. A poisonous herb brought some family members dangerously close to dying. "There was a half-witted boy in the family called Jake; and always afterward when they had greens the old man would say, 'Now, afore we

---

[32] Lamon, *Recollections*, pp. 115-116.

[33] Ibid.

risk these greens, let's try 'em on Jake. If he stands 'em, we're all right.'"[34]

Lincoln ended his parable by saying that it was the same with him as the family who feared eating poisonous greens. "As long as this imaginary assassin continues to exercise himself on others," Lincoln remonstrated, "I can stand it." His mood shifted to a more serious note and he concluded his conversation with Lamon by saying, "I think the Lord in his own good time and way will work this out all right. God knows what is best."[35]

Other Explanations

There exists a widespread belief that dreams may foretell the future, yet experimental data is more difficult to find. Writers Montague Ullman, Stanley Krippner, and Alan Vaughn, in their *Dream Telepathy*, reveal in their laboratory studies that one of the largest dream categories reported was precognitive dreams.[36] Lest one is inclined to view Lincoln's dream as mere chance, the above-mentioned research indicates that precognitive dreams are not rare, but are occurrences which happen with more frequency than usually acknowledged.

Carl Jung observed the link between telepathic dreams and "a powerfully affective event" such as death, and he believed that this helped explain the premonition of it "or its perception at a distance or at least make it more intelligible."[37] Most telepathic dreams Jung analyzed were of this type. Citing the work of a probability researcher, Jung stated that the specialist found a probability of more than 1 in 4,000,000 for telepathic precognitions of death, which meant that the interpretation of

[34] Ibid., p. 117.

[35] Ibid.

[36] Montague Ullman, Stanley Krippner, and Alan Vaughn, *Dream Telepathy* (New York, 1973); Montague Ullman, "An Experimental Approach to Dreams and Telepathy," in *Archives of General Psychiatry* vol. 14 (1966) pp. 605-613; and Hall, *Jungian Dream Interpretation*, pp. 92-95. See also, Louise Rhine, *Hidden Channels of the Mind* (New York, 1961), and her "Psychological Processes in ESP Experiences I. Waking Experiences, II. Dreams," *Journal of Parapsychology*, vol. 26 (1962) pp. 88-111, 171-199; and Hall, *Jungian Dream Interpretation*, p. 119.

[37] Jung, *Collected Works*, p. 162.

such a warning due to chance was four million times more unlikely than explaining it as a telepathic or acausal, meaningful coincidence.[38]

Not all dream theorists agree with Jung. Sigmund Freud vigorously defended the rationalist position in his seminal work, *The Interpretation of Dreams* by including in Appendix A, "A Premonitory Dream Fulfilled."[39] Therein, Freud states his position on the origin of premonitory dreams. After relating the premonitory dream experience of one of his patients, Frau B., Freud concluded that "the creation of a dream after the event, which alone makes prophetic dreams possible, is nothing other than a form of censoring, thanks to which the dream is able to make its way through into consciousness."[40]

This may be an adequate analysis of Frau B.'s experience because she only remembered the dream about meeting a Dr. K. after the fact. Freud postulates that this is the only manner in which there can be foreknowledge. Information about the future only occurs based upon the present and past. Freud believed that premonitory dreams became another form of wish-fulfillment.[41]

The fact that Lincoln knew about numerous threats upon his life prior to his dream lends credibility to Freud's theory.[42] As his personal bodyguard, Lamon warned Lincoln time and again about the dangers of traveling unprotected in public as president during wartime.[43] Lincoln also received numerous death-threat notices, of which several have been preserved.

Yet for all of the foreknowledge Lincoln had about the possibility of his own death, foreknowing the actuality of his assassination in a dream is another matter. Freud did not deal with the premonitory death-dream among his analysands except when it dealt with a friend or relative (as opposed to when such a dream referred to the death of the self in

[38] Ibid., p. 430.

[39] Freud, *The Interpretation of Dreams*, pp. 661-665.

[40] Ibid., p. 664.

[41] Ibid., pp. 659-660.

[42] Sandburg, *The War Years*, p. 310ff.

[43] Lewis, *Myths After Lincoln*, pp. 293, 294.

reality).[44] True telepathy was not possible in Freud's system of dream interpretation. Jung, on the other hand, makes allowance for meaningful coincidences in his theory of synchronicity and believes that certain conditions may transpire in which space and time are transcended and an individual may have access to events or information which are, in a waking, conscious state, futuristic.

Another premonitory dream which for Lincoln repeated itself frequently happened the night before a Union victory. In this dream, Lincoln witnessed a ship rapidly sailing away, badly damaged. In hot pursuit, Union vessels closed in upon the ship and obtained victory. In a parallel dream, he saw the end of a battle on land, the enemy routed, and the Union forces in possession of important ground. Lincoln had this dream before the battles of Antietam and Gettysburg and other major land engagements during the war. The night before his assassination Lincoln dreamed once more of the victorious land battle. On the morning of April 14, 1865, Lincoln held a cabinet meeting attended by General Grant. Lincoln asked Grant if he had any news from Maj. Gen. William T. Sherman, who faced Confederate Gen. Joseph E. Johnston in North Carolina. Grant replied that he did not have news yet, but he expected to receive at any moment word of Johnston's surrender. Lincoln said with great assurance, "We shall hear very soon, and the news will be important." When asked by Grant why he believed this with such conviction, Lincoln responded, "I had a dream last night; and ever since the war began I have had the same dream just before every event of great national importance. It portends some important event that will happen very soon."[45]

Lincoln did not find his dream exceptional. Instead, before his cabinet and leading general, he simply stated its impression and influence upon him as a natural experience. The lone ship sailing and the victorious land battle dreams elicited from Lincoln a satisfying response because of his positive experience with the subsequent events. Jung would interpret these dreams as telepathic, while Freud would view them as

---

[44] Sandburg, *Abraham Lincoln*, pp. 322-323; Freud, *The Interpretation of Dreams*, pp. 97, 282-301, 659.

[45] Lamon, *Recollections of Abraham Lincoln*, p. 118.

wish-fulfillments. Both may be right. His wish, both consciously and unconsciously, would be for success on the battlefield for the Union. If Lincoln had told about the dream after the battlefield victories, then Freud's theory seems a likely interpretation; but that wasn't the case. Lincoln told others his dream prior to the news of victory from the battlefield. A meaningful coincidence between his recurring dream and the successful battles existed throughout the duration of the war, which explains his confidence in receiving good news from the war dispatches the next day after his dream.

Conclusions

Lincoln's visions, dreams, and premonitions occupied a crucial role in his life, but especially during his tenure as president of the United States during the Civil War. As a natural extension of his character, they formed that mysterious and intimate connection to his psyche which may only be gestured toward in historical retrospect. Just as the nation was split by war, so was Lincoln's very being divided by his rational conscious self and his irrational unconscious experiences—a division difficult to fathom.

Lincoln gave us a glimpse into this enigma of the personality when he quoted often from Byron's poem "Dream":

> Sleep hath its own world,
> A boundary between the things misnamed
> Death and existence: Sleep hath its own world
> And a wide realm of wild reality.
> And dreams in their development have breath,
> And tears and tortures, and the touch of joy;
> They leave a weight upon our waking thoughts,
> They take a weight from our waking toils,
> They do divide our being.[46]

Jung's synchronicity theory still leaves questions unanswered. How does the unconscious image arise, and how the coincidence? Lincoln

---

[46] Ibid., p. 121.

gave no explanation. He simply trusted his dream experience either from the basis of the repetition of the meaningful coincidences or a predisposition toward reliance upon the efficacy of dreams, visions, and premonitions reflected in his Midwestern, pioneer background or his biblical faith.

This daguerreotype is the first known photograph of Lincoln, taken by N. H. Shepherd of Springfield, Illinois. At the time of the photo, Lincoln was the Congressman-elect from Illinois. (The Frank and Virginia Williams Collection of Lincolniana)

S aints by their nature, according to one scholar, "are not very good at political calculation." Lincoln was no saint; neither was he a prophet. He did think, at times, theologically, but he was not a theologian—although he has been pictured as such.

Stephen K. Shaw

Stephen Shaw is an associate professor of political science at Northwest Nazarene College, where he also serves as chair of the department. A native of Shreveport, Louisiana, he holds a B.A. from Southern Nazarene University and both a M.A. and Ph.D. with honors in political science from the University of Oklahoma. His special interest is constitutional law. He is the author of *The Ninth Amendment* (Garland, 1990), and has contributed articles to professional journals and books.

Abraham Lincoln and Civil Religion:
The President and the Prophetic Stance

In the beginning, and to some extent ever since, Americans have interpreted their history as having religious meaning. They saw themselves as being a "people" in the classical and biblical sense of the word. They hoped they were a people of God. They often found themselves to be a people of the devil. American history, like the history of any people, has within it archetypal patterns that reflect the general condition of human beings as pilgrims and wanderers on this earth. Founded in an experience of transcendent order, the new settlements habitually slipped away from their high calling and fell into idolatry, as the children of Israel had done before them. Time and again there have arisen prophets to recall this people to its original task, its errand into the wilderness. Significant accomplishments in building a just society have alternated with corruption and despair in America, as in other lands, because the struggle to institutionalize humane values is endless on this earth. But at times the issue grows acute. A period of history hangs in the balance. A people finds that it must decide whether its immediate future will be better or worse, and sometimes whether it will have a future at all.[1]

---

[1] Robert N. Bellah, *The Broken Covenant* (New York, 1975), p. 2.

Politics in the United States has always had a religious dimension to it. "From its Founding," according to one scholar, "the American republic has provided a proving ground for the relating of religion to politics."[2] From the 17th century to the present, this "proving ground" has witnessed both the loftiest and lowest elements in a political community's efforts to understand itself and to establish a basis, something beyond crass self-interest, for its continued existence. Determining just how religion and religious commitments are to relate to the functioning of government and politics in the United States, however, has proven to be no easy task, particularly given the inherent tension that exists between the ideal and the actual due to the fact that the country itself was established "so centrally on utopian millennial expectations."[3] Nonetheless, "Americans have characteristically understood from the outset of national life that within their culture, some form of public religion. . .has served as a basic religious medium in the culture and as such has been enormously significant in the society."[4]

This public religion, or "public religious dimension is expressed in a set of beliefs, symbols, and rituals" that the sociologist Robert Bellah described as "the American civil religion."[5] Initially conceived as either a religion or a religious dimension, civil religion was later defined as "that religious dimension, found. . .in the life of every people, through which it interprets its historical experience in the light of transcendent reality."[6]

While not every student of this religious component of our nation's political history has preferred the term "civil religion,"[7] this particular entity is commonly interpreted as referring to "the widespread acceptance by a people of perceived religio-political traits regarding their

---

[2] Kenneth W. Thompson, "The Religious Transformation of Politics," *The Review of Politics,* vol. 50 (Fall, 1988), p. 547.

[3] Bellah, *Broken Convenant,* p. ix.

[4] John F. Wilson, *Public Religion in American Culture* (Philadelphia, 1979), p. 19.

[5] Robert N. Bellah, "Civil Religion in America," *Daedalus,* vol. 96 (Winter 1967), p. 4.

[6] Bellah, *Broken Covenant,* p. 3.

[7] Wilson, *Public Religion,* p. 33.

nation's history and destiny."[8] Central to American civil religion, for instance, has been "the conviction that the American people are God's New Israel, his newly chosen people."[9] This belief of chosenness, this American Israel theme, "has become so pervasive a motif in the national life that the word 'belief' does not really capture the dynamic role that it has played for the American people. It has long since passed into 'the realm of motivational myths.'"[10]

This conviction and image of chosenness, evident throughout our national political history, is ambiguous and complex (as is the case with much of American civil religion) and "accounts for much of the best in America as well as the worst."[11] On the one hand, American civil religion, which encompasses this particular belief or myth of being favored by the Almighty, is viewed as "indispensable."[12] On the other hand, this religious dimension of our political regime can and has fostered messianic illusions, idolatrous national worship, and ultimately "arrogant self-righteous ness."[13] According to Bellah and Hammond:

> It may be a sobering thought, but most of what is good and most of what is bad in our history is rooted in our public theology. Every movement to make America more fully realize its professed values has grown out of some form of public theology. . .But so has every

---

[8] Richard V. Pierard and Robert D. Linder, *Civil Religion and the Presidency* (Grand Rapids, 1988), pp. 22-23. "It relates their society to the realm of ultimate meaning, enables them to look at their political community in a special sense, and provides the vision which ties the nation together as an integrated whole. . .Civil religion is unique in that it has reference to power within the state, but because it focuses on ultimate conditions, it surpasses and is independent of that power."

[9] Conrad Cherry, *God's New Israel* (Englewood Cliffs, 1971), p. 21. "Beheld from the angle of governing myths and symbols, the history of the American civil religion is a history of the conviction that the American people are God's New Israel, his newly chosen people. The belief that America has been elected by God for a special destiny in the world is the focus of American sacred ceremonies, the inaugural addresses of our presidents, the sacred scriptures of the civil religion." Wilson, *Public Religion,* p. 33. [T]he basic theme is one of chosenness. America has been selected for its covenant, or mission. In this respect the form of the myth is also ineradicably Hebraic, for ancient Israel provides the dominant model for a community bearing this burden of historical destiny.

[10] Cherry, *God's New Israel,* p. 21; Wilson, *Public Religion,* p. 40.

[11] Bellah, *Broken Covenant,* p. 39.

[12] Robert N. Bellah and Phillip Hammond, *Varieties of Civil Religion* (New York, 1980), p. 12.

[13] Cherry, *God's New Israel,* p. 23.

> expansionist war and every form of oppression of racial minorities and immigrant groups.[14]

In other words, American civil religion is not unalloyed; neither is it unimportant.

This religious dimension to political life in the United States, and here the preferred term is civil religion, has usually had one vital theologian at its center: the president.[15] In spite of the uneven record of American civil religion, however, "we did produce at a critical juncture in our history at least one great civil theologian, Abraham Lincoln."[16] According to one scholar, the 16th president is "perhaps our only" civil theologian and "certainly represents civil religion at its best." [17] In the view of Kenneth Thompson,

> No American President has achieved greater clarity in laying down the underlying political and moral principles on which his policies and actions were based. We look back to his political rhetoric and policy statements for the model of the leader speaking in his time and for the ages. . .He stands alone among American Presidents who thought clearly about political ethics.[18]

Lincoln's Prophetic Stance

Abraham Lincoln, in the words of Martin Marty, an American historian of religion, "stands at the spiritual center of American history and increasingly is seen as the theological thinker whose reflections are most

---

[14] Bellah and Hammond, *Varieties of Civil Religion,* p. 15.

[15] Michael Novak, *Choosing Our King,* p. xv: "Americans treat America as a religion. . .The president is the one pontiff bridging all." Pierard and Linder, *Civil Religion,* p. 25: "The president's role in the expression of such a faith should be rather obvious. He is in effect the 'pontifex maximus' of American civil religion—principal prophet, high priest, first preacher, and chief pastor of the American nation."

[16] Bellah and Hammond, *Varieties of Civil Religion*, p. 12.

[17] Ibid., p. 15; Bellah, "Civil Religion in America," p. 12.

[18] Kenneth W. Thompson, ed., *Essays on Lincoln's Faith and Politics* (Lanham, 1983), p. ix.

apt and most profound."[19] These reflections, almost exclusively rendered in an explicitly public, political venue—most notably during the demanding days of the Civil War—reveal a mature, serious religious and political faith that, according to the late American theologian Reinhold Niebuhr, "was primarily informed by a sense of providence,"[20] as demonstrated by his insightful phrase in the Second Inaugural Address, "The Almighty has His own purposes."[21]

This "sense of providence" is at the center of Lincoln's religious faith and his conception of political religion and political ethics, particularly with respect to his efforts to govern the nation, to provide presidential leadership during the Civil War, and, perhaps most of all, in his attempts to make sense of that bloody, divisive conflict. As interpreted by Neibuhr, and of especial importance for this analysis of Lincoln, "the chief evidence of the purity and profundity of Lincoln's sense of providence lies in his ability. . .to avoid the error of identifying providence with the cause to which the agent is committed."[22] Recognizing this unique and impressive (even moving) Lincolnian ability is essential to understanding his use of and role in the American civil religion.

Martin Marty has distinguished between "prophetic" and "priestly" civil religion.[23] The prophetic role means that the individual in question, in this case the president of the United States, is fully cognizant of and acts on the fact that the nation is both shaped by God and is judged by God. In prophetic civil religion, "the president seeks to conform the nation's actions to the will of the Almighty, thus countering idolatrous religious nationalism and calling the nation to repent of its corporate political sins."[24] The prophetic strain of American civil religion, accord-

---

[19] Martin E. Marty, *Pilgrims in Their Own Land* (Boston, 1984), p. 220.

[20] Reinhold Niebuhr, "The Religion of Abraham Lincoln," in Allan Nevins, ed., *Lincoln and the Gettysburg Address* (Urbana, 1964), p. 73.

[21] Don E. Fehrenbacher, ed., *Speeches and Writings*, 2 vols., (New York, 1989), vol. 2, p. 687.

[22] Niebuhr, "The Religion of Abraham Lincoln," p. 74.

[23] Martin E. Marty, "Two Kinds of Civil Religion," in Russell E. Richey and Donald G. Jones, eds., *American Civil Religion* (New York, 1974), p. 145.

[24] Pierard and Linder, *Civil Religion,* p. 24.

ing to Marty, "will tend to be dialectical about civil religion, but with a predisposition toward the judgmental."[25] Not all presidents have performed this prophetic role; in fact, it is more the deviation than the archetypical presidential pattern in American civil religion.[26] Much more common is the priestly variety of civil religion, which "will normally be celebrative, affirmative, culture-building."[27]

Most presidents, in other words, have sought to comfort the afflicted rather than afflict the comfortable, as President Lincoln himself did at times, such as in the Second Inaugural Address.[28] Most occupants of the Oval Office, including Lincoln, have exhibited a combination of the prophetic and the priestly. Normally, however, one strain exerts more influence than its counterpart. In the case of Abraham Lincoln, the prophetic took precedence over the priestly, even before he established residence at the White House.[29] "Lincoln's moral imagination worked in and through a kind of configuration of the symbols of the Old and New Testaments. It is, for example, impossible to grasp fully what Lincoln believed he was doing in his debates with Douglas throughout the period of 1854-60 without seeing it as a performance of a prophetic role in the Old Testament sense." Abraham Lincoln stands squarely within the prophetic version of American civil religion.[30] On this point of interpretation, almost all scholars concur.[31]

Lincoln adopted what can most accurately be called a prophetic stance, but he was not a prophet. He sought to know and do the will of God while conceding the extreme difficulty of doing so: "Certainly there

[25] Marty, "Two Kinds of Civil Religion," p. 145.

[26] Richard J. Neuhaus, "To Be at Home," in Leroy S. Rounder, ed., *Civil Religion and Political Theology* (Notre Dame, 1986).

[27] Marty, "Two Kinds of Civil Religion," p. 145.

[28] Pierard and Linder, *Civil Religion and the Presidency,* p. 26.

[29] Harry V. Jaffa, *Crisis of the House Divided* (Chicago, 1959), p. 226.

[30] See generally, Marty, "Two Kinds of Civil Religion," *Pilgrims in Their Own Land;* William J. Wolf, *Lincoln's Religion* (Philadelphia, 1970); Elton Trueblood, *Abraham Lincoln: Theologian of American Anguish* (New York, 1973).

[31] See, for example, Melvin B. Eddy, Jr., Abraham Lincoln and American Civil Religion: A Reinterpretation," *Church History,* vol. 44 (June, 1975), pp. 229-241.

is no contending against the Will of God; but still there is some difficulty in ascertaining, and applying it, to particular cases."[32] According to Pierard and Linder, Lincoln "adopted a prophetic stance by alerting the chosen people to the judgments of the Almighty, and he steered the public faith away from an idolatrous priestly civil religion which made the nation itself transcendent."[33] But Lincoln did not see himself as a messenger from God, pronouncing the necessary judgment of God upon an evil, immoral and fallen people. Rather, as he expressed the matter on several occasions, the president saw himself as "a humble instrument in the hands of the Almighty."[34]

Lincoln wrote the following to Mrs. Eliza Gurney, widow of Joseph J. Gurney, an English Quaker:

> We are indeed going through a great trial—a fiery trial. In the very responsible position in which I happen to be placed, being a humble instrument in the hands of our Heavenly Father, as I am, and as we all are, to work out his great purposes, I have desired that all my works and acts may be according to his will, and that it might be so, I have sought his aid—but if after endeavoring to do my best in the light which he affords me, I find my efforts fail, I must believe that for some purpose unknown to me, He wills it otherwise. If I had had my way, this war would never have been commenced; if I had been allowed my way, this war would have been ended before this, but we find it still continues; and we must believe that He permits it for some purpose of his own, mysterious and unknown to us; and though with our limited understandings we may not be able to comprehend it, yet we cannot but believe, that he who made the world still governs it.[35]

Two years later, President Lincoln communicated a similar if not identical perspective to the same individual:

---

[32] Fehrenbacher, ed., *Lincoln, Speeches and Writings,* vol. 1, p. 685.

[33] Pierard and Linder, *Civil Religion and the Presidency,* p. 105.

[34] Fehrenbacher, ed., *Speeches and Writings,* vol. 2, p. 209.

[35] Roy P. Basler, ed., *The Collected Works of Abraham Lincoln,* 8 vols. (New Brunswick, 1953), vol. 5, p. 478.

> The purposes of the Almighty are perfect, and must prevail, though
> we erring mortals may fail to accurately perceive them in advance.
> We hoped for a happy termination of this terrible war long before
> this, but God knows best, and has ruled otherwise. We shall yet
> acknowledge His wisdom and our own error therein. Meanwhile
> we must work earnestly in the best light He gives us, trusting that
> so working still conduces to the great ends He ordains. Surely He
> intends some great good to follow this mighty convulsion, which
> no mortal could make, and no mortal could stay.[36]

These are not the words and thoughts of a prophet delivering the express (and understood) message of God. Instead, what is found here is what one scholar has described as "the prophetic stance," or prophetic attitude, which "is not one of anxiety and desperation. The very term *prophetic* signalizes confidence in the future. To stand prophetically is to rely, in one's own weakness, on the strength of God."[37]

In Lincoln's prophetic civil religion, we find the pious and the skeptical, the trusting and the hesitant. He possessed an unshakable faith in and unwavering commitment to the Union and the principles, the creed, on which it was based.[38] He "regarded the nation with a sense of religious mysticism, and believed the nation to be, as he said in his Annual Message to Congress in late 1862, "the last, best, hope on earth." He spoke, on more than one occasion, to the fact that in his opinion, the nation—"this favored land"—had not yet been forsaken by God. As he said at Trenton, New Jersey, on his way to Washington, D.C., Americans were the Almighty's "almost chosen people."[39]

Yet, he was equally convinced that God's purposes and the purposes of man were not necessarily identical, perhaps seldom were they in any form approximating nearly-perfect alignment. The designs of Provi-

---

[36] Fehrenbacher, *Speeches and Writings,* vol. 2, p. 627.

[37] Glenn Tinder, *The Political Meaning of Christianity* (New York, 1991), p. 9.

[38] Fehrenbacher, ed., *Speeches and Writings,* vol. 2, p. 209. See, for example, Lincoln's 1861 speech at Independence Hall in Philadelphia, where he proclaims he "would rather be assassinated on this spot than to surrender" the principle of equality contained in the Declaration of Independence.

[39] Marty, "Two Kinds of Civil Religion," p. 148; Fehrenbacher, *Speeches and Writings,* 2, pp. 205, 209, 223, 415.

dence were more mysterious than manifest, as he wrote to Mrs. Gurney in 1862. According to one scholar, Lincoln knew that "the drama of history is shot through with moral meaning; but the meaning is never exact. Sin and punishment, virtue and reward are never precisely proportioned."[40]

Lincoln fully believed in national destiny. In the words of Niebuhr, his faith "is identical with that of the Hebrew prophets, who first conceived the idea of a meaningful history."[41] This idea of a meaningful, and ultimately fathomable, history for the United States, or "a prophetic sense of American destiny," is clearly evident in Lincoln's thoughts and actions.[42] Lincoln, however, was skeptical of knowing with complete certainty the will of God in political affairs. Moreover, he was equally dubious of the claims of others to the possession of such desired yet elusive intelligence:

> I am approached with the most opposite opinions and advice, and that by religious men, who are equally certain that they represent the Divine will. I am sure that either the one or the other class is mistaken in that belief, and perhaps in some respects both. I hope it will not be irreverent for me to say that if it is probable that God would reveal His will to others, on a point so connected with my duty, it might be supposed He would reveal it directly to me; for, unless I am more deceived in myself than I often am, it is my earnest desire to know the will of Providence in this matter. *And if I can learn what it is I will do it!* These are not, however, the days of miracles, and I suppose it will be granted that I am not to expect a direct revelation. I must study the plain physical facts of the case, ascertain what is possible and learn what appears to be wise and right. The subject is difficult, and good men do not agree.[43]

During the same time period, Lincoln wrote the so-called "Meditation on the Divine Will," in which he expressed an attempt to grapple

[40] Niebuhr, "The Religion of Abraham Lincoln," p. 74.

[41] Ibid., p. 75.

[42] Tinder, *The Political Meaning*, p. 147.

[43] Fehrenbacher, *Speeches and Writings*, 2, p. 361.

with political reality from a similar vantage point, beginning with the declarative: "The will of God prevails."[44]

> In great contests each party claims to act in accordance with the will of God. Both *may* be, and one *must* be wrong. God cannot be for and against the same thing at the same time. In the present civil war it is quite possible that God's purpose is something different from the purpose of either party—and yet the human instrumentalities, working just as they do, are of the best adaptation to effect His purpose. I am almost ready to say this is probably true—that God wills this contest, and wills that it shall not end yet. By his mere quiet power, on the minds of the now contestants, He could have either saved or destroyed the Union without a human contest. Yet the contest began. And having begun He could give the final victory to either   side any day. Yet the contest proceeds.[45]

Similarly, Lincoln's Second Inaugural Address, depicted by one scholar as "categorically unique in the attempt it represents to explicate a religious framework of national destiny," movingly symbolizes his prophetic civil religion ."[46]

> Neither party expected for the war, the magnitude, or the duration, which it has already attained. Neither anticipated that the *cause* of the conflict might cease with, or even before, the conflict itself should cease. Each looked for an easier triumph, and a result less fundamental and astounding. Both read the same Bible, and pray to the same God; and each invokes His aid against the other. It may seem strange that any men should dare to ask a just God's assistance in wringing their bread from the sweat of other men's faces; but let us judge not that we be not judged. The prayers of both

---

[44] Ibid., p. 369.

[45] Ibid., p. 359.

[46] Wilson, *Public Religion,* p. 50; Wolf, *Lincoln's Religion,* p. 136: "The Second Inaugural Address was to be the climactic expression of this biblical faith. It reads like a supplement to the bible"; Trueblood, *Abraham Lincoln,* p. 5: "His Second Inaugural, which has been widely acclaimed as the noblest state paper of the nineteenth century, is also recognized by those who study it carefully as a theological classic." Bellah, *The Broken Covenant,* pp. 53-54: "It is in Lincoln's Second Inaugural Address that we find perhaps the greatest expression of the theme of covenant and judgment in the entire course of American history."

could not be answered, that of neither has been answered fully. The Almighty has His own purposes.[47]

The Second Inaugural, perhaps best understood "as an expression of Lincoln's living faith," exhibits Lincoln's prophetic stance as unequivocally as anything he wrote or uttered.[48] Here we find the president confronting the dilemmas of faith and the responsibilities of office. Here we find Lincoln doubtful of knowing the will of God yet attempting—albeit with his own imperfections and limitations—to know it and follow it as much as possible. He was acutely aware of his doubt and his faith, yet paralyzed by neither. As one attempting to be faithful to the will of God in his life and the life of the nation, Lincoln could easily point out, as he did in the Second Inaugural, the differences between the plans of God and those of humans. He also could easily recognize the consequences of doing so: "I expect the [Inaugural address] to wear as well as—perhaps better than—anything I have produced," he wrote to Thurlow Weed, "but I believe it is not immediately popular. Men are not flattered by being shown that there has been a difference of purpose between the Almighty and them. To deny it, however, in this case, is to deny that there is a God governing the world."[49]

In spite of seeking the inscrutable will of God, and in spite of being politically unpopular as well, Lincoln recognized the duty incumbent upon a politician to act and upon a statesman to think of the future in terms other than mere political interest. He was prophetic yet prudent, idealistic perhaps, but not utopian. As he said in his 1862 message to Congress, "Fellow-citizens, *we* cannot escape history. . . .The fiery trial through which we pass, will light us down, in honor or dishonor, to the latest generation. . . .We—even *we here*—hold the power, and bear the responsibility."[50] While this force, this history, meaningful and mysterious, providentially directed, could not be fully grasped, nei-

[47] Fehrenbacher, *Speeches and Writings,* 2, pp. 686-687.

[48] David Hein, "Lincoln's Theology," in Kenneth W. Thompson, ed., *Essays on Lincoln's Faith and Politics* (Lanham, 1983), p. 131,

[49] Fehrenbacher, *Speeches and Writings,* 2, p. 689.

[50] Ibid., p. 415.

ther could it be evaded. In the words of one scholar, "Lincoln had described Providence's scroll unfolding toward an indeterminate end that no human being could fathom but which was a reality nonetheless. Some aspects of spiritual truth remained forever in the higher order of a *mysterium tremendum* where they constituted objective truth."[51]

Lincoln possessed faith in God, in spite of the difficulty, if not near-impossibility, of ascertaining and applying God's will. "And while it has not pleased the Almighty to bless us with a return of peace, we can but press on, guided by the best light He gives us, trusting that in His own good time, and wise way, all will yet be well."[52] He also possessed faith in the American political system and its credal foundation, in spite of the wide and seemingly impassable gulf between ideal and reality. His fear was that both faiths, the religious and the political, would atrophy, even perish, if the principles and ideals on which those faiths were established were forgotten or ignored. As he stated, in quoting Jefferson, "I tremble for my country when I remember that God is just."[53]

The American political system had declared early on, according to Lincoln, that it stood for something different, that it represented "something more than common," as the president-elect declared at Trenton in 1861.[54] An ideal, universal in scope, had been put forth, a *proposition* in the words of the Gettysburg Address.[55] The truth of and national commitment to "the original idea for which that struggle " to establish and maintain a republic was made was constantly being tested.

> As your Father in Heaven is perfect, be ye also perfect. He set that
> up as a standard, and he who did most towards reaching that stand-
> ard, attained the highest degree of moral perfection. So I say in

---

[51] See Lincoln's Second Inaugural, where he explores or supposes the possibility of the war being some form of divine punishment. Even if that were the case, in Lincoln's eyes "so still it must be said 'the judgments of the Lord, are true and righteous altogether.'"

[52] Ibid., p. 393.

[53] Ibid., p. 41.

[54] Ibid., p. 209.

[55] Garry Wills, *Lincoln at Gettysburg* (New York, 1992).

relation to the principle that all men are created equal, let it be as nearly reached as we can.[56]

Lincoln's Theological-Political Statesmanship

"Saints by their nature," according to one scholar, "are not very good at political calculation."[57] Lincoln was no saint; neither was he a prophet. He did think, at times, theologically, but he was not a theologian—although he has been pictured as such.[58] First and foremost he was a politician. He may have thought and acted theocentrically at various times throughout his career, especially while in the White House, but he still was a politician. Lincoln was "a man of great spiritual depth. But he was also a cunning and sagacious man of power. . .Lincoln can with some justice be characterized as both Christ-like and Machiavellian."[59]

Perhaps he is best seen, in his theological–political reflections, as a Christian realist.[60] He sought the will of God but not in an irresponsible or arrogant fashion. He was that "rare and unique human being who could be responsible in executing historic tasks without equating his interpretation of the task with the divine wisdom."[61]

According to Niebuhr, "It was Lincoln's achievement to embrace a paradox which lies at the center of the spirituality of all western culture; namely, the affirmation of a meaningful history and the religious reservation about the partiality and bias which the human actors and agents betray in the definition of meaning."[62] This achievement, as events during Lincoln's time and down to the present day prove, was (and remains) no small feat. Those political leaders who possess visions of a better

---

[56] Fehrenbacher, *Speeches and Writings,* 1, p. 458.

[57] Thompson, "The Religious Transformation," p. 552.

[58] Wolf, *Lincoln's Religion,* pp. 24-25; Trueblood, *Abraham Lincoln,* pp. 5-7.

[59] Tinder, *The Political Meaning,* p. 133.

[60] Thompson, "The Religious Transformation."

[61] Niebuhr, "The Religion of Abraham Lincoln," p. 87.

[62] Ibid., p. 77.

society and who aspire to realize that goal all too often fall prey to moral self-righteousness or some form of partisan political triumphalism. In Lincoln, we find "an example of an individual who refused to be God, and appealed to our better natures to cherish and preserve the right of each to tell the other 'that he is not God.'"[63] Given that Lincoln "was the last President of the United States who could genuinely use words,"[64] his concluding paragraph in the Second Inaugural Address best expresses his Christian statesmanship:

> With malice toward none; with charity for all; with firmness in the right, as God gives us to see the right, let us strive on to finish the work we are in; to bind up the nation's wounds; to care for him who shall have borne the battle, and for his widow, and his orphan—to do all which may achieve and cherish a just, and a lasting peace, among ourselves, and with all nations.[65]

[63] Sidney E. Mead, *The Nation With the Soul of a Church* (New York, 1975), p. 77.

[64] Robert Lowell, "On the Gettysburg Address," in Allan Nevins, ed., *Lincoln and the Gettysburg Address* (Urbana, 1964), p. 88

[65] Ferenbacher, *Lincoln, Speeches and Writings,* 2, p. 687.

Presentation photograph signed by Abraham Lincoln, shot from a photograph probably taken by Roderick M. Cole of Peoria about 1858. (The Frank and Virginia Williams Collection of Lincolniana)

Lincoln defined the policies that created the war and formuated the specific apocalyptic language that gave it meaning for a Bible-drenched culture, from the image of the fiery trial in 1862, to that of the sacrificial redefinition of the nation's purpose at Gettysburg in 1863.

Charles B. Strozier

Charles Strozier received his B.A. from Harvard in 1966, and Ph.D. from the University of Chicago in 1971. From 1971 to 1980 he was a Candidate at the Chicago Institute for Psychoanalysis. He is a professor of history at John Jay College as well as practicing psychoanalyst at the Training and Research Institute in Self Psychology in New York. He is the author of *Lincoln's Quest for Union: Public and Private Meanings* (Basic Books, 1982), which presents the psychological story of Lincoln up to 1860, and *Apocalypse: On the Psychology of Fundamentalism in America* (Beacon Press, 1994). Recently he has begun to publish a series of papers related to his study of Lincoln's leadership.

Abraham Lincoln
and the Apocalyptic at Mid-Century

This essay probes the historical beginnings of the apocalyptic in the American psyche.[1] For my research during the last five years, besides familiar historical work in libraries and dusty archives, I have attended more church services and Bible studies than I ever thought possible to cram into one lifetime, and conducted extensive psychological interviews that were taped and transcribed with individual fundamentalists in a variety of church settings (I often interviewed each person as many as four times). Despite this immersion into the fundamentalist world, I retain my sturdy agnosticism but have also deepened my respect for those whose faith leads them toward literalism and apocalypticism.

I should be clear how I use the word "apocalyptic." It is a transliteration of the Greek word *apokalypsis* meaning "to uncover or disclose," and within the Judeo-Christian tradition means the specific ways in which God reveals himself or herself to humans. Prophecy, in turn, is

---

[1] The material for this chapter is adapted from my book, *Apocalypse: On the Psychology of Fundamentalism in America* (Boston, 1994). The apocalyptic is as old as human culture and is specifically rooted in Christianity from 95 A.D. with the writing of the book of Revelation. There was much millennial anxiety before the end of the Year 1,000 (see Henri Focillon, *The Year 1,000*), as well as throughout the middle ages (see Norman Cohn, *In Pursuit of the Millennium*). The apocalyptic was, however, transformed at the level of theory in the 19th century and forged in the new American nation that emerged from the Civil War—which is my argument in this chapter.

the form of our access to that apocalypse. The last book of the Bible was also written last, in 95 A.D., after the destruction of the Temple and the Roman massacre of as many as a million Jews. God's revelation, as disclosed to John of Patmos (a revelation which I should note has always been discredited by the established Christian church though now has so much history in it that it could never be removed from the New Testament) comes in the form of a violent and destructive end of human history, some kind of parenthesis that fundamentalists read as the millennium, and the great climax of the final judgment which sorts out those who go to heaven while nonbelievers are thrown into the lake of fire.

The apocalyptic is that which relates, strictly speaking, to the specific forms of our forthcoming destruction, including the 7-year period of Tribulation with its ferocious and unfolding violence of trumpets, seals, and vials that ends with the great battle between the forces of good and evil on the plains of Armageddon in part of what is present-day Israel. But the term "apocalyptic" also has a series of looser and more secular meanings that have accrued to it over the centuries, and that, like it or not, have become part of its associative meaning. Thus the apocalyptic is also the prophetic (as that which foretells what will happen), the terrible (or any imminent disaster or final doom), the grandiose (or any wild and unrestrained predictions), and the climactic (or anything that is ultimately decisive). I would add to these curiously limited dictionary meanings that the apocalyptic as well connotes the violent, the redemptive, and the hopeful. Thus the Civil War, Hurricane Andrew, and the return of Jesus can all be quite accurately called apocalyptic.

Preliminaries to the Civil War

Revelation comes to us in stages, which I want to try and break down in relation to the Civil War. It begins with *the wait*, which is why, in literature and art, as Frank Kermode has so brilliantly shown, anything with an apocalyptic theme has trouble with its ending.[2] Francis Ford Coppola shot several endings to "Apocalypse Now," discarded the

---

[2] Frank Kermode, *The Sense Of An Ending: Studies In The Theory of Fiction* (New York, 1967).

70mm ending when he went to 35mm, and never could have imagined that the real end was perhaps the permanent distress and dislocation he brought to the small corner of the Philippines where he shot the movie.[3] At the personal level the apocalyptic wait is like clinging to a love relationship when you don't know if it will end or what you will be like when it's over. Collective death, nuclear or otherwise, is that terror projected on a cosmic screen. The wait is awful, and we don't even know what we're waiting for, a theme Samuel Beckett exploited so well in *Godot* and *Endgame*.[4]

Antebellum America, as well, seemed obsessed with its own apocalyptic anxieties. It was an era of rapid social change but, more importantly, a time when the great moral blot of slavery at last pushed people to feel radical social change was necessary. From the 1820s on, a spirit of intense revivalism and religious fervor swept the land, from Charles Grandison Finney's evangelical successes in the burned-over district of upstate New York, to the appearance of whole new religions (like Mormonism), and to the widespread presence of much specific apocalyptic prediction. William Miller, the most famous such prophet, may have had a million followers in the early 1840s, though after his failed prediction of the return of Jesus on October 22, 1844—called the Great Disappointment—his movement rapidly disintegrated.[5]

Less visibly, Antebellum America was also a time of creative transformation in theological thought. The mainstream Protestants struggled, and some denominations divided, over the issue of slavery, as well they should have. Those developments generated much noise at the time, but the most consequential theological discussion occurred during the 1830s among a small band of Plymouth Brethren led by John Nelson Darby.[6]

---

[3] Susan Sontag, *AIDS and Its Metaphors* (New York, 1988).

[4] Samuel Beckett, *Waiting for Godot: A Tradicomedy in Two Acts* (London, 1957); Harold Bloom, ed., *Endgame* (New York, 1988).

[5] Ronald L. Numbers and Jonathan M. Butler, eds., *The Disappointed: Millerism and Millenarianism in the Nineteenth Century* (Bloomington, 1987). Note also Malcolm Bull and Keith Lockhard, *Seeking a Sanctuary: Seventh-Day Adventism & the American Dream* (New York, 1989).

[6] Note especially Paul Boyer, *When Time Shall Be No More: Prophecy Belief in Modern American Culture* (Cambridge, 1992). Cp. George Marsden, *Fundamentalism and American*

All the key ideas of what we know now as "premillennial dispensation-alism," which is the ideological basis of contemporary fundamentalism, took shape in those years: the idea of the rapture, the "new" premillen-nialism that it was connected with—the idea that human history ends and Jesus returns before the millennium to rule during it, an idea which completely reversed the exuberant enthusiasms of Jonathan Edwards' post-millennialism—and the theory of dispensationalism that substituted for the kind of end-time arithmetic of William Miller a conceptualization that placed us in the last days without having to predict the actual time of the end. The only subsequent development at the level of theory that mattered was that of inerrancy in the 1880s that forged a long tradition of loose biblical literalism into dogma.[7]

Ideological change, of course, occurs in a context, and there were abundant cultural and political correlates for the new ideas about the apocalyptic emerging in isolated corners of America. *The wait* affected peoples' minds and souls, and profoundly influenced the shape of politics. The antislavery movement, for example, beginning in earnest in the 1830s, reacted with moral outrage and a mounting sense of frustration to the continued existence of slavery. At first, a strong religious fervor encouraged abolitionists to commit themselves to a variety of reform movements (especially temperance) and remain peaceful, even pacifist, in their means.[8] But after the war with Mexico and the huge land grab in 1848 seemed to open up the country to domination by a white-led South based in slavery, abolitionists bemoaned the possibility of radical but peaceful social change. They felt the struggle was being lost. Moral

---

Culture: The Shaping of Twentieth Century Evangelicalism, 1870-1925 (New York, 1980); and Timothy Weber, *Living in the Shadow of the Second Coming: American Premillennialism, 1875-1982* (Chicago, 1987).

[7] Note especially Weber, *Living in the Shadow.* Cp. Ernest Sandeen, *The Roots of Fundamentalism: British and American Millenarianism, 1800-1930* (Chicago, 1970).

[8] Lawrence Friedman, "Antebellum American Abolitionism and the Problem of Violent Means," *The Psychohistory Review,* vol. 9 (1980), pp. 26-32, however, persuasively argues that the degree of genuine pacifism that infused the abolitionists in the 1830s is open to some question. The basic question the abolitionists failed to grapple with was whether violence was acceptable if used defensively. The test case was the shooting of Elijah Lovejoy in Alton, Illinois. See also, Charles B. Strozier, *Lincoln's Quest for Union: Public and Private Meanings* (New York, 1982), p. 188.

persuasion was not working. And so the old pacifism gave way to accommodation to violence as the only way to end slavery. John Brown's attack on some proslavery settlers in 1856 at Pottawatamie, Kansas, helped reshape attitudes and prepare the ground for his raid on Harpers Ferry in 1859. When the firing on Fort Sumter was announced in the United States Senate, it was said there was a lusty cheer from an abolitionist in the balcony, which represented the long journey traveled by the spiritual children of Lyman Beecher.[9]

The terror of the apocalyptic wait pushed the culture to extremes. There was almost war in 1850, especially over the return of fugitive slaves. Some, like Lincoln, reluctantly accepted the great compromise measures of that year: "I confess," he said, "I hate to see the poor creatures hunted down. . .but I bite my lip and keep quiet." Others, however, were much more vehement in their denunciation. "Let the President drench our land of freedom in blood," said Joshua Giddings of Ohio, "but he will never make us obey *that* law."[10] Throughout the rest of the decade there was much apocalyptic rhetoric about the "irrepressible conflict" (William H. Seward), the "impending crisis" (Hinton R. Helper), more loosely of the great fight to come, and of course Lincoln's own imagery of the "House Divided" in 1858 (which resonated so widely in part because it was imagery based in three of the four gospels):[11] "It will become *all* one thing, or *all* the other," Lincoln said from the floor of the House of Representatives in Springfield, prophesying a climactic end to the great issue facing the nation. After that apocalyptic lead, he proceeded to detail what he saw as the contemporary political developments leading toward the stark choices he envisioned, namely a plot at the highest levels to nationalize slavery.[12]

As the crisis deepened in the next three years, so did the sense of inevitability, north and south, about the approaching war. Nevertheless,

---

[9] Cp. U.S. Grant to Frederick Dent, Galena, April 19, 1861, p. 956: "In all this I can but see the doom of Slavery."

[10] Geoffrey C. Ward with Ric Burns and Ken Burns, *The Civil War* (New York, 1990), p. 19.

[11] Matthew 12:22-28; Mark 3:22-26; and Luke 11:14-20.

[12] Charles B. Strozier, *Lincoln's Quest for Union,* pp. 182-187; Cp. Don Fehrenbacher, *Prelude to Greatness: Lincoln in the 1850s* (Stanford, 1962).

as Don Fehrenbacher has recently noted, it remains surprising that the South should have taken such an apocalyptic view of the perfectly legal election of Abraham Lincoln. Somehow they had come to feel that the Republican party was a "hostile, revolutionary organization bent on total destruction of the slaveholding system."[13] And so, mysteriously it has always seemed to me, the Confederate States of America squandered whatever moral authority they might have possessed in their attempt to build a new nation and fired the first shot.

The Outbreak of War

Within the apocalyptic script, once war began *the wait* was followed by a *purging through violence.* An extraordinary number of generals, most notably Thomas J. "Stonewall" Jackson, were self-defined as Christian soldiers marching onward, and only slightly more secular types, such as William T. Sherman, sounded like Old Testament prophets. In general, as historian Charles Royster notes, northern military, political, and spiritual leaders talked loosely of a policy of extermination and repopulation of the South that would have to precede any regeneration of it in a way that set no limits on the destruction necessary to accomplish such goals. And both sides, he continues, descended into "visions of purgation and redemption, into anticipation and intuition and spiritual apotheosis, into bloodshed that was not only intentional pursuit of interests of state but was also sacramental, erotic, mystical, and strangely gratifying. This process of taking the war to heart, believing that it would change everyone, worked as strongly as any other influence toward making it more inclusive and more destructive."[14]

Lincoln was not always helpful in taming such impulses. In his First Inaugural Address, he talked loosely about secession as the "essence of anarchy," and on July 4, 1861, characterized the firing on Fort Sumter as an attempt to "end free government upon the earth," which

---

[13] Don Fehrenbacher, in Ward, *The Civil War,* p. 84.

[14] Charles Royster, *Destructive War: William Tecumseh Sherman, Stonewall Jackson, and the Americans* (New York, 1991), pp. 82, 241.

became, by the end of 1862, a war to defend our fragile democracy as the "last, best hope on earth."[15] The apocalyptic, in fact, was everywhere in Lincoln's rhetoric: in military strategy ("I think to lose Kentucky is nearly the same as to lose the whole game");[16] in his transmutation of individual soldiers' mortality for the nation's immortality in the Gettysburg Address;[17] and in his characterization of the war as a "fiery trial" through which we must pass.[18] As David Hein has noted, Lincoln surely used this phrase in conscious knowledge of its biblical origins in I Peter 4:12-13, where the experience of the fiery trial is that of martyrdom, or participation in the sufferings of Christ.[19]

Americans moved easily and quickly into this imagery of a purging through violence. As James H. Moorhead has noted, for example, the Civil War was the first time (and I would add the last) in our history that there was a virtually unanimous feeling among northern ministers that the war was hastening the day of the Lord and was a "climactic test of the redeemer nation and its millennial role."[20]

By the second year of the war soldiers were singing that apocalyptic favorite, "Mine eyes have seen the glory of the coming of the Lord," who is "trampling out the vintage where the grapes of wrath are stored," not to mention the implicit theme of sacrifice in their song, "We are coming Father Abraham, We are coming, We are coming." Horace Greeley spoke from within the violence of the apocalyptic when he wrote on July 7, 1864: "Our bleeding, bankrupt, almost dying country longs for peace—shudders at the prospect of fresh conscriptions, of

---

[15] Don Fehrenbacher, ed., *Lincoln*, 2 vols. (New York, 1989), vol. 1, p. 220; ibid., p. 250, 415.

[16] Ibid., p. 269.

[17] Royster, *Destructive War*, p. 151

[18] "The fiery trial through which we pass, will light us down, in honor or dishonor, to the latest generation," Fehrenbacher, *Lincoln* 1, p. 415.

[19] David Hein, "Lincoln's Theology and Political Ethics," in Hans J. Morgenthau and David Hein, *The Mind of Abraham Lincoln*, in series, Kenneth W. Thompson, ed., *American Values Projected Abroad*, 4 vols, (Lantham, 1983), vol. 4, p. 145.

[20] James H. Moorhead, *American Apocalypse: Yankee Prostestants and the Civil War, 1860-1869* (New Haven, 1978), p. x.

further wholesale devastations, and of new rivers of human blood."[21] And the now famous Sullivan Ballou wrote to his wife of his personal apocalyptic on the eve of his death in the first great battle of the war: "But, O Sarah! if the dead can come back to this earth and flit unseen around those they loved, I shall always be near you; in the gladdest days and in the darkest nights. . .*always, always,* and if there be a soft breeze upon your cheek, it shall be my breath, as the cool air fans your throbbing temple, it shall be my spirit passing by. Sarah do not mourn me dead; think I am gone and wait for thee, for we shall meet again."[22]

Lincoln's Role

It seems to me that many thoughtful observers have been wrong in their strenuous efforts to rationalize Lincoln and take him out of this cultural apocalyptic in which he thrived and to which he gave such powerful voice. He was himself undogmatic, cautious, forgiving, ambiguous, and always sensitive to the inscrutable ways of God. One has to be impressed by the subtle irony of someone who could call Americans the "almost chosen people."[23] And yet Lincoln defined the policies that created the war and formulated the specific apocalyptic language that gave it meaning for a Bible-drenched culture, from the image of the "fiery trial" in 1862, to that of the sacrificial redefinition of the nation's purpose at Gettysburg in 1863,[24] to God's purposes in ending slavery about which he spoke in the Second Inaugural:

> If we shall suppose that American Slavery is one of those offenses which, in the providence of God, must needs come, but which, having continued through His appointed time, he now wills to remove, and that He gives to both North and South, this terrible war, as the woe due to those by whom the offense came, shall we

---

[21] James M. McPherson, "American Victory, American Defeat," in Gabor S. Boritt, ed., *Why The Confederacy Lost* (New York, 1992), p. 40.

[22] Ward, *The Civil War,* pp. 82-83.

[23] Fehrenbacher, *Lincoln,* 2, p. 209.

[24] See Garry Wills, *Lincoln at Gettysburg: The Words That Remade America* (New York, 1992).

discern therein any departure from those divine attributes which the believers in a Living God always ascribe to Him? Fondly do we hope—fervently do we pray—that this mighty scourge of war may speedily pass away. Yet, if God wills that it continue, until all the wealth piled by the bond-man's two hundred and fifty years of unrequited toil shall be sunk, and until every drop of blood drawn with the lash, shall be paid by another drawn with the sword, as was said three thousand years ago, so still it must be said "the judgments of the Lord, are true and righteous altogether."[25]

If the wait gave way to a purging through violence, the final phase of the American apocalypse was the redemption as people understood the death of Lincoln. Shot on Good Friday and dead the following morning, Lincoln immediately became, in those Easter morning sermons, a modern Jesus whose blood sacrifice fulfilled prophecy.[26] Less than a week after the assassination, Ralph Waldo Emerson underlined this theme when he noted that God had given us Lincoln to direct the country through the war.[27] And Henry Ward Beecher added that, "His life now is grafted upon the Infinite, and will be fruitful as no earthly life can be."[28] This theme of Lincoln as Jesus who died for our sins of bloody fratricide is, of course, quite familiar in the American consciousness. My point is perhaps less obvious: Lincoln's death evoked the passion of Jesus but much more powerfully fitted into the imagery of the Second Advent, of the millennium that follows the period of Tribulation; in other words, of the specifically apocalyptic as detailed in the last book of the Bible, and as more generally the redemption, or cure, or hope that one yearns to have follow any apocalyptic violence.

---

[25] Fehrenbacher, *Lincoln,* 2, p. 687.

[26] Moorhead, *American Apocalypse,* pp. 174-175.

[27] Waldo W. Braden, ed., *Building the Myth: Selected Speeches Memorializing Abraham Lincoln* (Urbana, 1990), pp. 33-34.

[28] Braden, *Building the Myth,* pp. 37-46.

Conclusion

C. Vann Woodward recently commented on the terrible Civil War we fought, "terrible in its magnitude and its persistence, terrible in its ferocity, and its sickening cost in human life," and terrible as well in its "doublethink and truespeak rhetoric" in which "lies a haunting anticipation of the Orwellian era."[29] It is not a question whether the war brought some good and perhaps had to be fought; the end of the obnoxious institution of slavery has to be judged as a positive outcome of the war. But as we struggle for justice nearly a century and a half later we have to ask what were blacks emancipated into and for? What is the nature of that millennium for which all those people, black and white, died? And what is the meaning now of having forged, but not discarded, the apocalyptic as the core experience of our nationality? "Strange (is it not?)," wrote Walt Whitman, "that battles, martyrs, blood, even assassination should so condense—perhaps only really, lastingly condense—a Nationality."[30]

[29] Ward, *The Civil War,* pp. 398-399.

[30] Ibid., p. 393.

The last portrait of Lincoln, taken by Alexander Gardner on April 10, 1865, four days before the President was shot at Ford's theater. (The Frank and Virginia Williams Collection of Lincolniana)

S adly, three fourth-
grade teachers did
not bring Abraham
Lincoln into their
social studies curricu-
lum in any way.
Another noted that
"for Presidents' Day,
nothing was done,"
but that she "did have
to put up a February
bulletin board in the
hall on which it high-
lighted February's
high points—Chinese
New Year, Black His-
tory Month, and Presi-
dents' Day."

Sherry L. Field

Sherry Field is an assistant professor of social
science education at the University of Georgia at
Athens. She teaches social studies methods and
graduate courses to elementary preservice and
inservice teachers. Born in Rusk County, Texas,
she received a B.S. Ed. from Texas Tech University in 1973, a M.Ed. in 1975 from Stephen F.
Austin University and a Ph.D. from the University of Texas at Austin in 1991. She has taught
elementary school for 13 years. Her dissertation
is entitled *Doing Their Bit For Victory: U.S. Elementary Social Studies During World War II*.
She has participated as an invited researcher in
two law-related education conferences spon-
sored by the American Bar Association.

The Legacy of Abraham Lincoln
in the Elementary Classroom

The study of great American presidents is not new to elementary school social studies pupils. One of the major features of the American history curriculum is the incorporation of content about important Americans, including significant presidents and historical figures. Content about the presidents is advanced in various ways in elementary schools, and Presidents' Day is generally acknowledged in the curriculum and celebrated in classrooms.

There can be no doubt that Abraham Lincoln is one of the most revered and celebrated American presidents. Only a few presidents have been accorded the popular attention in literature and in factual accountings from history that has been accorded Lincoln. This attention to our sixteenth president seems particularly prominent in school history. Still, recent curricular revisions have prompted new attention to subjects and issues previously ignored and less attention to some of the more traditional issues, events, and historical figures. Because of this rewriting and compression of American school history, the following questions are raised: What place does Lincoln enjoy in contemporary elementary school social studies? Is Lincoln still a prominent figure in elementary school social studies textbooks? And, finally, how do practicing elementary school teachers engage in the study of Lincoln? This chapter offers evidence about Lincoln's current status in school history. The portrayal developed is based on a content analysis of a popular social studies textbook series and the interviews and self-reports of 37 elementary school teachers in the greater Denver, Colorado area.

Findings from Elementary Social Studies Textbooks

Analysis of an elementary social studies textbook series for content relating to Abraham Lincoln seems to be an appropriate starting point to determine one aspect of readily-available material. Social studies textbook series in the United States generally follow an extension of the "expanding environments" construct; that is, they call for the following foci: Grade One—Home and Family; Grade Two—Neighborhoods; Grade Three—Communities; Grade Four—State or Regions; Grade Five—Nation (American History); and Grade Six—World. For the purposes of this study, the elementary social studies textbooks from Houghton-Mifflin were read and analyzed.[1] All direct and indirect references to Abraham Lincoln were recorded. References included mention in textual passages, photographs, charts, and captions in student textbooks, and indications to extend textual study related to Abraham Lincoln in teacher editions. For example, in some instances Lincoln was not mentioned in the student text but was indicated in the teacher edition as an extension of a given lesson. Analysis of the Houghton-Mifflin social studies series is meant to serve only as an average depiction of Lincoln references found in a typical textbook series.

Abraham Lincoln does not receive much attention in the primary grade (1-3) textbooks of the Houghton-Mifflin series. Not surprisingly, no reference to Lincoln is found in the first grade text, *I Know a Place*. In the second grade text, *Some People I Know*, Lincoln's portrait appears in the teacher's edition at the beginning of Unit 3, entitled *Living in Our Country*. Teachers are directed to teach the song "Old Abe Lincoln" as

---

[1] Beverly J. Armento, Gary B. Nash, Christopher L. Salter, and Karen K. Wixson, *Elementary Social Studies Series, Grades 1-6* (Boston, 1991).

"one way to introduce Unit 3." The words to the song, however, are neither stimulating nor informative. For example, the verse of the song suggests, "Old Abe Lincoln came out of the wilderness, out of the wilderness, out of the wilderness. Old Abe Lincoln came out of the wilderness, His truth goes marching on!"[2] Several books and resources for teacher use are suggested at the beginning of this unit, but none refer to Abraham Lincoln.[3] Lincoln appears for the first time in the children's text in the lesson, *Why Do We Celebrate Presidents' Day*? Second graders learn that "Abraham Lincoln was President when the states in the North and the states in the South fought a terrible war. The North won the war, and the United States became one country again. On Presidents' Day, Abraham Lincoln is remembered for bringing our country back together."[4] Students are asked to consider, at the end of the lesson, why George Washington and Abraham Lincoln were "important presidents."[5] At the unit's end, students are instructed to find a library book, read about either Washington or Lincoln, and "write some sentences about what you have learned."[6] Two activities are also suggested: Making a class flag and making stovepipe hats "like Abraham Lincoln wore."[7] After this second grade study, pupils do not read about Abraham Lincoln again until a lesson on "National Holidays" appears in the third grade textbook, *From Sea to Shining Sea.* Here, Lincoln's name appears on a chart of National Holidays,[8] and he is remembered in this textual reference: "We honor George Washington and Abraham Lincoln on Presidents' Day."[9]

[2] Armento, *Some People I Know,* Teacher edition, p. 99D.

[3] Ibid., pp. 100-101.

[4] Ibid., pp. 110-111.

[5] Ibid., p. 111.

[6] Ibid., p. 133.

[7] Ibid., p. 133.

[8] Armento, *From Sea to Shining Sea,* p. 221.

[9] Ibid., p. 223.

Why is Abraham Lincoln regarded so superficially in these primary textbooks and excluded from the fourth grade texts? Perhaps because neither American history nor national government is a typical focus topic for young children in the social studies. But even on the fifth grade level, with American history as the major emphasis, Abraham Lincoln is accorded only a few pages mention in *America Will Be*. Those few pages are telling in their inclusion and in their omission. Reference is first made to Abraham Lincoln in a section describing the formation of the Republican party and its divided stance on the issue of slavery. In slightly more than one paragraph, Lincoln's role and stance are posited: "He had served a term in Congress and had spoken out against slavery throughout his career. But it was not until Lincoln joined the Republicans that he became an important political figure." The paragraph concludes that Lincoln's "clever and forceful speeches—on slavery and other subjects—made him a leader of this new party"[10]

Abraham Lincoln is featured again seven pages later in an explanation of the Supreme Court decision of the Dred Scott case. A lithograph of one of the Lincoln–Douglas debates appears in the upper right quarter of the page with the caption, "Thousands of voters came to hear the debates between Abraham Lincoln and Stephen Douglas. The rest of the nation followed these debates in newspapers."[11] Lincoln's prominence as a public speaker is chronicled in textual references to the "series of seven public" Lincoln–Douglas debates. To signify Lincoln's declaration for the senate seat from Illinois, an appropriate excerpt from his nomination speech is provided for fifth grade readers: "A house divided against itself cannot stand. I believe this government cannot endure, permanently half slave and half free. I do not expect the Union to be dissolved—I do not expect the house to fall—but I do expect it will cease to be divided. It will become all one thing or all the other."[12]

Another likeness of Lincoln appears on the succeeding page of text. Here, on a campaign facsimile of an American flag, Lincoln is featured

---

[10] Armento, *America Will Be*, p. 456.

[11] Ibid., p. 463.

[12] Ibid., p. 463.

in the field of blue. Amidst the stripes of red and white are the words, "For President Abram [sic] Lincoln. For Vice President Hannibal Hamlin." The caption and text inform young readers that Lincoln was the Republican party's successful candidate for president in the 1860 election, an election which "many Southerners believed. . .would decide the future of slavery in the United States."[13] An excerpt from the Emancipation Proclamation is pictured later in the *Civil War and Freedom* lesson, with the explanation that since the "North seemed no closer to defeating the South. . .maybe he [Lincoln] could do it with laws."[14] Additionally, the Teacher Edition encourages teachers to assign a written comparison of the Emancipation Proclamation with the Thirteenth Amendment to the Constitution and the use of Aaron Copeland's *Lincoln Portrait.*[15] Reference to Lincoln is made once more in the fifth grade textbook, at the end of the text in a section called the "Minipedia." A one-half page history of the Gettysburg Address is included, and two versions of the speech are denoted at the bottom of the page.[16]

Analysis of the Houghton-Mifflin elementary social studies textbook series leads us to the conclusion that Abraham Lincoln is given scant attention—no mention in textbooks for grades one, four, or six, only a few sentences in grades two and three, and a few paragraphs in the grade five textbook. Author Gary Nash notes in the preface to each Houghton-Mifflin elementary social studies Teacher Edition that "No one would think of writing a textbook without Abraham Lincoln or Julius Caesar. So it's not that we're completely changing the old vision in which famous people were carved in marble."[17] Still, the vision of this textbook series seems to be narrow when dealing with historical figures.

---

[13] Ibid., p. 464.

[14] Ibid., p. 470.

[15] Armento, *America Will Be,* Teacher Edition, p. 470.

[16] Armento, *America Will Be,* p. 556.

[17] Armento, *Teacher Edition,* p. T14.

Lincoln in the Classroom

The reality of social studies education in elementary schools is that teachers have a great deal of flexibility in deciding what is to be taught and how it is to be taught. Some teachers may choose to abandon their school's textbooks completely in favor of different curriculum sources. In order to find out exactly how elementary school teachers disseminate information about Abraham Lincoln in practice, 37 classroom teachers were interviewed and asked to complete self-report forms. The teachers were asked to identify specifically the resources used to teach their children about Abraham Lincoln and at what time during the school year Lincoln appears in their classroom curricula, if at all.

Reflections From Primary Grade Teachers

Primary grade teachers (grades 1-3) in Colorado often use an inter-disciplinary or thematic approach when planning the social studies curriculum. According to almost every primary grade teacher interviewed, the school district's adopted social studies textbooks were not used when planning social studies lessons. Most teachers did not refer to social studies textbooks as a resource. Instead, many teachers have substituted a literature-based type of instruction, hoping to achieve a high pupil interest level.

Six first-grade teachers were interviewed, and each one reported that they share information about Abraham Lincoln in February on Presidents' Day. Every teacher recalled reading at least one picture book about Abraham Lincoln, although two teachers noted reading three or four Lincoln picture books to their students. One teacher taught her class two songs about Lincoln, and they sang them "all week." Three teachers used a filmstrip to teach about Lincoln, and two teachers asked their students to "write a fact about Abraham Lincoln." One teacher did a K-W-L activity with his class, which entailed having the class make a chart labeled "Know, Want to Know, and Learned," to which they added information as it was collected. Five of the first grade classes carried learning about Lincoln into the arts/crafts realm by making "log cabins out of milk cartons and pretzels," by cutting silhouettes and writing

K-W-L facts upon them, and by making paper hats and beards "to wear in the afternoon." Additionally, two teachers brought the Children's Mini-Page about Presidents' Day from the *Rocky Mountain News* to class.

Responses from nine second-grade teachers ranged from "I usually do not teach about the presidents because our curriculum is so full as it is" to "I spend two to three weeks teaching about Lincoln, Washington, and patriotism." One second grade class culminated its week of reading biographies about Abraham Lincoln and George Washington by making Venn diagrams of Lincoln and Washington and Venn diagrams of "self and Lincoln." Another teacher asked her students to write a mini-book "after reading a few books about Abraham Lincoln." A display of pictures of the president and books were an attention-getting device used by one teacher in her classroom book center. Additionally, her students wrote stories and considered the symbolism of Lincoln on the penny. In a related activity, another group of students wrote about what they would do if they were president.

Second-grade teachers asked their students to create several art projects that utilized a Lincoln theme. Among them, making oversized stovepipe hats upon which stories could be written, "log cabins," silhouettes of self wearing stovepipe hats, and mobiles about Abraham Lincoln were typical, if simple or stereotypical, activities.

Two second-grade teachers expressed a concern about making the study of Abraham Lincoln both historically accurate and personally meaningful for students. One teacher uses the second half of February to "focus on patriotic study." She reported that "While studying the two presidents [Lincoln and Washington], we discuss their important contributions to the freedom we have in the U. S. We also touch on some of the folklore surrounding the two men." Other activities included viewing filmstrips, writing poetry and initial introduction of family history because, as this teacher explained, "since I am related to Abraham Lincoln [a sixth cousin], I like to have a lesson when I can explain a family tree." Helping young children "to have an understanding of our history, to know the people who made history happen. . . .and to understand how these historical events affect us today" is a primary concern for another teacher. To accomplish her goals, she regularly teaches a two to three week unit in February with content that includes "both presidents, the pledge [of allegiance], patriotism, and what it means to be an American." More specifically, content about Lincoln encompasses viewing filmstrips, reading books, writing books telling about Lincoln's life, and comparing and contrasting the lives of Abraham Lincoln and George Washington.

Two of five third-grade teachers revealed that they spent very little time teaching about Abraham Lincoln. For one, this meant "briefly discussing what the children already know about him and reading a poem." When questioned, she admitted that her class study of Martin Luther King, Jr. was so comprehensive that she simply did not "have the extra time" to teach about Lincoln.

Many of the curriculum ideas or materials used in first and second-grade classes to teach about Lincoln appeared again in third grade. For example, writing stories about Abraham Lincoln, using the Lincoln silhouette, viewing filmstrips, and "writing three facts about Lincoln" were cited. Some teachers tried different approaches to the traditional Presidents' Day observance, including "having a birthday party for Lincoln," having a math lesson about ratio and proportion "because of Abe Lincoln's disproportionate hands, feet, and ears," and "having my students write a couple of opinion paragraphs as to why they felt Lincoln was important enough to be honored with a national holiday." Another teacher used comparison/contrast activities in her class study of Abraham Lincoln and Martin Luther King, Jr. Several teachers included brainstorming activities in their studies. One teacher includes both presidents Washington and Lincoln in her class biography study. While the biographies were read independently, students were asked to culminate their reading by "dressing as their character and orally presenting a time-line of their character from their character's point of view."

Reflections from Intermediate Grade Teachers

A commonly-used method of study about Abraham Lincoln at the fourth grade level is the biography study, cited by three of six teachers. One teacher revealed that her biography study lasted three weeks and encompassed the lives of several historical figures and included activities such as evaluation of one's belief system, creation of time lines and illustrations about a selected biography, and discussion of living conditions during the selected historical figure's life. Sadly, three fourth-grade teachers did not bring Abraham Lincoln into their social studies curriculum in any way. One claimed that "in fourth grade we did not do much [to teach about Lincoln] because the curriculum has demanded our time." Another noted that "for Presidents' Day nothing was done" but that she "did have to put a February bulletin board in the hall on which I highlighted February's high points—Chinese New Year, Black History Month, and Presidents' Day." The third teacher admitted that she did not teach about Lincoln because of her year-round school schedule—her school was not in session for most of February, the traditional time to study about Abraham Lincoln.

Fifth-grade teachers, like their fourth-grade predecessors, occasionally engaged in biography studies that included Abraham Lincoln. When questioned further about specific attention to Lincoln or to Presidents' Day, however, one teacher noted that she used duplicated worksheets as "fun or filler activities," another listed "word searches, crosswords, and coloring or reading sheets," and another said that "all I do is discuss why we have the [Presidents'] day off and why it's important." This teacher cited two student responses to the question "Why do we celebrate President's Day?": "Because they saved our country" and "Because they're on money." Still, she noted a commitment to "discuss the deeper issues and events of the particular era of a president." A major writing assignment about Abraham Lincoln was the culminating activity to one teacher's biography study. She noted, too, that her students also viewed a filmstrip and read two picture books about Lincoln and "did some worksheets and crafts." Another teacher noted that she taught her students several songs about Lincoln "so that they would know what the holiday [Presidents' Day] was all about." Only one teacher reported that she spent time teaching about Lincoln in a broad, reflective way. She began her Lincoln unit with a study of the symbolic element that Abraham Lincoln has become. Her students studied money, stamps, Mount Rushmore, and the Lincoln Memorial. Additionally, she taught her students the poem "The Lincoln Penny" by Alfred Kreymborg, and the class read D'Aulaires Caldecott Award-winning book, *Abraham Lincoln*. A made-for-television movie, *The Perfect Tribute,* was also viewed, and related literature was studied. The students culminated their unit with a reading of the Gettysburg Address. One teacher noted that she included Abraham Lincoln in an extensive Civil War unit that utilized activities such as writing projects, simulations, enactment of dramas, time lines, mapping, and comparison/contrast of life during the Revolutionary War and the Civil War.

Four sixth-grade teachers were interviewed. Two did not include study about Abraham Lincoln, noting that "my school devotes February to Black Awareness month" and "While we acknowledged the holiday [Presidents' Day], I need to think about how I might make this holiday more interesting for older students."

Two sixth-grade teachers incorporated a study of Abraham Lincoln in a larger unit about all presidents. Each student in one class researched the life of a president and wrote a report, prepared a timeline and taught a five-minute mini-lesson to a primary grade class in their school. These students reportedly took a great interest in an aspect of history that had "previously been unexplored." Another sixth-grade teacher used study of the presidents as a springboard for an in-depth study of Lincoln. For example, his students were required to write a report, make trivia questions, put on a play, teach younger children, watch a Lincoln video, draw a portrait, and add Lincoln-related words to their spelling lists. This teacher dressed up as Lincoln and delivered the Gettysburg Address to bring closure to the unit of study.

The attention to Abraham Lincoln in elementary classrooms seems to vary a great deal from teacher to teacher. As these interviews reveal, some teachers include no lessons about Abraham Lincoln in their curriculum, some teachers attempt to teach their students about Abraham Lincoln in a relatively stereotypical or offhanded fashion, and some teachers try to help their students understand why Lincoln is held in such high esteem.

Conclusion and Suggestions for Improvement

What are we to make of these classroom vignettes and this analysis of a popular elementary social studies textbook series? First, the interviews with classroom teachers allow one to understand typical classroom practice. A glimpse into elementary school social studies classes has shown that Abraham Lincoln is remembered, for the most part, neither wisely nor well. Only two elementary teachers mentioned that they introduced the Gettysburg Address in teaching about Lincoln, and none made a connection in their teaching about Civil Rights or Dr. Martin Luther King, Jr. with the Emancipation Proclamation. No teaching about Lincoln's character traits, such as humor, tenacity, or equanimity appeared to make its way into classrooms. The point should also be made that in elementary school social studies, critical thinking and problem-solving skills are almost always listed on several grade level scope and sequence plans. Abraham Lincoln's critical thinking skills have favorably stood the test of time and could serve as a model for young Americans; yet, apparently in these elementary school classes, neither the serious problems facing Lincoln nor how he decided to deal with them are discussed. One must assume that the rationale behind this disheartening exclusion is that teachers seem to think that young children are too young to deal with such matters in a historically accurate manner. Second, analysis of the Houghton-Mifflin elementary social studies series revealed that, in these textbooks, many historical figures are represented, and perhaps a de-emphasis of some, such as Abraham Lincoln, has, in fact, occurred. Almost every teacher interviewed stressed a multicultural emphasis in his or her social studies instruction.

Perhaps these teachers are not aware that, in their attempt to teach about issues that they perceive to be "current," the strand of history in their social studies instruction has been tragically underrepresented. Finally, an awareness of the current status of teaching about Abraham Lincoln in elementary schools reveals a need to shore up, protect, and nurture the tenets of history instruction. The events surrounding and making up the life of Abraham Lincoln and the contributions he made should not be forgotten. Instead, teaching about this American hero should be utilized in elementary classrooms to help bring understanding to contemporary issues.

Brenda J. Cox

Brenda Cox is a native of Shreveport, Louisiana. A librarian, she received her undergraduate degree from Louisiana State University in Shreveport and her M.L.I.S. from Louisiana State University in Baton Rouge in 1991. Her work has appeared in the *North Louisiana Historical Association Journal, Great Justices of the U.S. Supreme Court* (Lang, 1993), and *Abraham Lincoln: Sources and Style of Leadership* (Greenwood Press, 1994).

Select Bibliography

Anderson, Dwight G., *Abraham Lincoln, the Quest for Immortality*. New York: Knopf, 1982.

Beveridge, Albert J., *Abraham Lincoln, 1809-1858*. Boston: Houghton-Mifflin, 1928.

Boritt, Gabor S., *Lincoln and the Economics of the American Dream*. Memphis, TN: Memphis State University Press, 1978.

Borritt, Gabor S. and N.O. Forness, *The Historians' Lincoln: Pseudohistory, Psychohistory, and History*. Urbana: University of Illinois Press, 1988.

Braden, Waldo W., *Abraham Lincoln, Public Speaker*. Baton Rouge: Louisiana State University Press, 1991.

Bradford, Melvin E., *Remembering Who We Are*. Athens: University of Georgia Press, 1985.

Brooks, Noah, *Washington, D.C. in Lincoln's Time*. Athens: University of Georgia Press, 1989.

Bursey, L. Gerald, *Abraham Lincoln. Popular Images of American Presidents*. Westport, CT: Greenwood Press, 1988.

Cashman, Sean D., *America in the Gilded Age: From Abraham Lincoln to Theodore Roosevelt*. New York: New York University Press, 1988.

Charnwood, Godfrey Rathbone Benson, *Abraham Lincoln*. 3rd ed. New York: Henry Holt, 1917.

Cunliffe, Marcus, *In Search of America: Transatlantic Essays*. Westport, CT: Greenwood Press, 1991.

Current, Richard N., *Arguing with Historians: Essays on the Historical and the Unhistorical.* Middletown, CT: Wesleyan University Press, 1987.

——————— *Speaking of Abraham Lincoln: The Man and His Meaning for Our Times.* Urbana: University of Illinois Press, 1983.

——————— *The Lincoln Nobody Knows.* New York: Hill and Wang, 1967.

——————— *What is an American? Abraham Lincoln and Multiculturalism.* Milwaukee, WI: Marquette University Press, 1993.

Davies, James C., "Lincoln: The Saint and the Man," William D. Pederson and Ann M. McLaurin, *Rating Game in American Politics.* New York: Irvington Publishers, 1987, pp. 297-335.

Donald, David, *Lincoln Reconsidered: Essays on the Civil War.* New York: Vintage Books, 1989.

Fehrenbacher, Don E., *Lincoln in Text and Context: Collected Essays.* Stanford, CA: Stanford University Press, 1987.

——————— *Prelude to Greatness: Lincoln in the 1850s.* Stanford, CA: Stanford University Press, 1962.

Ferguson, Robert A., *Law & Letters in American Culture.* Harvard University Press, 1984.

Findley, Paul A., *Lincoln: The Crucible of Congress.* New York: Norton, 1990.

Greenstone, J. David, *The Lincoln Persuasion: Remaking American Liberalism.* Princeton: Princeton University Press, 1993.

Grossman, A. R., "The Poetics of Union in Whitman and Lincoln: An Inquiry Toward the Relationship of Art and Policy," *The American Renaissance Reconsidered.* Walter B. Michaels and Donald E. Pease, eds. Johns Hopkins University Press, 1982.

Hanchett, William, *Out of the Wilderness. The Life of Abraham Lincoln.* Urbana and Chicago: University of Illinois Press, 1994.

Hill, Frederick T., *Abraham Lincoln as a Lawyer,* 2 vols. Albuquerque, New Mexico: American Classical College Press, 1985.

Hofstadter, Richard, *The American Political Tradition: And the Men Who Made It.* New York: Alfred Knopf, 1948.

Jennison, Keith W., *The Humorous Mr. Lincoln: A Profile in Wit, Courage, and Compassion.* Woodstock, VT: Countryman Press, 1988.

Johannsen, Robert W., *Lincoln, the South, and Slavery: The Political Dimension.* Baton Rouge: Louisiana State University Press, 1991.

Kunhardt, Phillip B., Jr., Phillip B. Kunhardt, III and Peter W. Kunhardt, *Lincoln, an Illustrated Biography.* New York: Knopf, 1992.

Leuchtenburg, William E., "Most Americans Don't Know What Lincoln Really Represents," [Interview with Mario Cuomo] *American Heritage*, pp. 41:59-62, December, 1990.

Lincoln, Abraham, *The Collected Works of Abraham Lincoln,* 9 vols. Edited by Roy P. Basler. New Brunswick, NJ: Rutgers University Press, in association with the Abraham Lincoln Association, 1953-1955. Supplement. Westport, CT: Greenwood Press, 1974 and Supplement 2. New Brunswick, NJ: Rutgers University Press, 1987.

———— *Lincoln on Democracy.* Edited and introduced by Mario M. Cuomo and Harold Holzer. New York: HarperCollins, 1990.

———— *Speeches and Writings.* 2 vols. New York: Viking Press, Library of American, 1989.

———— *Lincoln Day by Day: A Chronology—1809-1865.* Compiled by Earl S. Miers, William Barringer, and C. Perry Powell. Dayton: Morningside Bookshop, 1992.

———— *The Lincoln-Douglas Debates, What They Really Said, The First Unexpurgated Edition.* Edited by Harold Holzer. New York: HarperCollins, 1993.

Long, David E., *The Jewel of Liberty: Abraham Lincoln's Re-Election and the End of Slavery.* Harrisburg, PA: Stackpole Books, 1994.

McPherson, James M., *Abraham Lincoln and the Second American Revolution.* New York: Oxford University Press, 1990.

———— *Battle Cry of Freedom: The Civil War Era.* New York: Ballentine Books, 1988.

Mitgang, Herbert, *Abraham Lincoln, A Press Portrait.* Athens: University of Georgia Press, 1989.

Neely, Mark E., *The Fate of Liberty: Abraham Lincoln and Civil Liberties.* New York: Oxford University Press, 1991.

———— *Abraham Lincoln and the Promise of America: The Last Best Hope of Earth.* Cambridge: Harvard University Press, 1993.

Oates, Stephen E., *Abraham Lincoln, the Man Behind the Myths.* New York: New American Library, 1985.

———— *With Malice Toward None: The Life of Abraham Lincoln.* New York: Harper & Row, 1977.

Paludan, Phillip S., *The Presidency of Abraham Lincoln.* Lawrence: University Press of Kansas, 1994.

Peterson, Merrill D., *Lincoln in Memory.* New York: Oxford University Press, 1994.

Randall, James G. and Current, Richard N., *Lincoln the President: Last Full Measure,* 4 vols. Urbana: University of Illinois Press, 1992.

Rietveld, Ronald D., *Lincoln's Views of the Founding Fathers*. Redlands, CA: Lincoln Memorial Shrine, 1992.

Simon, Paul, *Lincoln's Preparation for Greatness: The Illinois Legislative Years*. Urbana: University of Illinois Press, 1989.

Stevenson, James A., "American Voyages of Lincoln and Huck Finn," *Lincoln Herald,* Vol. 90 No. 4, Winter 1988, pp. 130-133.

Strout, Cushing, *Making American Tradition: Visions and Revisions from Ben Franklin to Alice Walker* New Brunswick: Rutgers University Press, 1990.

Strozier, Charles B., *Lincoln's Quest for Union: Public and Private Meanings*. New York: Basic Books, 1982.

————— *God, Lincoln, and the Civil War.* Redlands, CA: Lincoln Memorial Shrine, 1994.

Thomas, Benjamin P., *Abraham Lincoln: A Biography*. New York: Random House, 1965.

Thomas, J. L., ed., *Abraham Lincoln and the American Political Tradition*. Amherst: University of Massachusetts Press, 1986.

Tice, George, *Lincoln*. New Brunswick, NJ: Rutgers University Press, 1984.

Wills, Garry, *Lincoln at Gettysburg: The Words That Remade America*. New York: Simon and Schuster, 1992.

INDEX

Other Civil War titles available from
Savas Woodbury Publishers

The Campaign for Atlanta & Sherman's March to the Sea, vols. 1-2, edited by Theodore P. Savas and David A. Woodbury. Fifteen essays in a landmark series covering a broad range of topics on the pivotal 1864 campaigns. Three fold-out maps in text and two over-size, 3-color campaign maps folded into front pocket. 6x9, hardcover, photos, index. 496pp ISBN 1-882810-26-0 Price: $42.50.

"...a refreshing must for those who dare to reassess these epic campaigns, the leaders, and the challenges posed in the Empire State of the Confederacy more than 130 years ago."
— Blue & Gray Magazine

Leadership and Command in the American Civil War, edited by Steven E. Woodworth. A collection of five penetrating essays exploring myriad leadership issues during the epic events of 1861-1865. Topics include J. E. Johnston in Virginia, Bragg & Longstreet in the West, Sumner at Antietam, Pickett after Gettysburg, and Beauregard at Petersburg. 6x9, hardcover, index, 243pp. ISBN 1-882810-00-7. Price: $29.95.

Abraham Lincoln, Contemporary: An American Legacy, edited by Frank J. Williams and William D. Pederson. Papers delivered at the 1993 Louisiana State University Lincoln Symposium by some of the nation's leading Lincoln scholars. 6x9, hardcover, d.j., photos, index, 236pp. Price: $24.95. Softcover: $16.95.

Last Stand in the Carolinas: the Battle of Bentonville, March 19-21, 1865, by Mark L. Bradley. A definitive examination of the military events that culminated in the bloody fighting at Bentonville, North Carolina, between the veteran campaigners of William T. Sherman and Gen. Joseph E. Johnston's motley Confederate army. 6x9, hardcover, d.j., photos, maps, index, 458pp. Price: $29.95.

"...Bradley has researched and written a *tour de force*....there has long been a need for a quality history focusing on the Battle of Bentonville." —Edwin C. Bearss, former Chief Historian of the National Park Service

The Red River Campaign, edited by Theodore P. Savas and David A. Woodbury. This special, stand-alone issue of *Civil War Regiments* journal contains four in-depth essays on aspects of the critical, but overlooked 1864 campaign in Louisiana. Introduction by Edwin C. Bearss, Assistant to the Director, Military Sites, National Park Service. 6x9, softcover, photos, maps, index, 157pp. Price: $12.00 ppd.

The Confederate Navy on the James River, by John Coski. This major new study by a staff historian at the Museum of the Confederacy in Richmond is the first book-length account examining the critical role played by the makeshift Southern navy on the James River. Hardcover, d.j., photos, maps, index, 253pp. 6x9. Price: $29.95 plus $3.00 s&h.

Civil War Regiments: A Journal of the American Civil War, edited by Theodore P. Savas and David A. Woodbury. Published quarterly by Regimental Studies, Inc., *CWR* is the only fully-footnoted, non-partisan Civil War periodical available which showcases in-depth articles on military events in all theaters of the war. Each 120+ page softbound book contains meticulously researched articles by leading scholars in the field, original maps tailored for each essay, and comprehensive book reviews of current Civil War titles. 6x9, 120+ pages, photos, maps, index. Subscriptions: $27.00/year (4 books) ppd.

Coming in 1995/1996

"The Last Rays of Departing Hope": The Wilmington Campaign, by Chris Fonvielle. A compelling account of the complicated series of Federal combined operations designed to capture one of the most important cities in the Confederacy. Inquire as to availability.

Cleburne's Guard: Granbury's Texas Brigade, by Danny Sessums. The first comprehensive study of Confederate Brig. Gen. Hiram Bronson Granbury and his famous Texas Brigade, with appendices, rosters, and detailed tactical maps. Inquire as to availability.

The Battle of Carthage, July 5, 1861, by David C. Hinze. The only full-length study of this early war engagement in Missouri. Includes modern "guided tour" of sites associated with the battle.

The Campaign for Atlanta & Sherman's March to the Sea, vol. 3: The Atlanta Death Roster, compiled by William E. Erquitt. A unique military and genealogical reference work containing the names and original burial locations of over 3,000 Federal soldiers who died during the Atlanta Campaign. Includes essays placing the casualties within the context of the fighting.

Savas Woodbury Publishers

1475 S. Bascom Avenue, Suite 204
Campbell, CA 95008 • (800) 848-6585

Call or write for a free catalog
Please add $3.00 shipping and handling for the first book, and $1.50 for each additional book